The Cultural
Geography of
Health Care

The Cultural Geography of Health Care

Wilbert M. Gesler

University of Pittsburgh Press

Published by the University of Pittsburgh Press,
Pittsburgh Pa. 15260

Copyright © 1991, University of Pittsburgh Press

Baker & Taylor International, London

Manufactured in the United States of America

Library of Congress Cataloging-in-Publication Data

Gesler, Wilbert M., 1941–
    The cultural geography of health care delivery /
Wilbert M. Gesler.
        p.   cm.
    Includes bibliographical references and index.
    ISBN 0-8229-3664-X (cloth)
    1. Social medicine.   2. Medical anthropology.
    I. Title.
RA418.G45 1991
362.1—dc20   90-44299
                                                         CIP

For Joyce

Contents

viii   Contents

The Cultural
Geography of
Health Care

1. Introduction

A story is told about an illness-prevention campaign that highlights the importance of the cultural perspective in matters pertaining to health. It seems that a medical education team was touring in a rural area of a developing country where malaria was endemic. As part of their state-of-the-art audio-visual presentation, a slide of a mosquito was projected onto a large screen. Everything about the mosquito—its role as a disease vector, its habitat, its habits, its control—was carefully explained. After the presentation, a wise-looking old villager was asked what he thought about the whole thing. "Thank goodness that malaria isn't a problem around here," he exclaimed.

The educational team was taken aback. Mosquitoes could be heard buzzing around the audience constantly. Had he missed the point of the lecture entirely? "What do you mean?" someone asked the villager. "Well," the old man replied, "No one has ever seen such gigantic creatures around here!"

The lesson of this cautionary tale is clear: the best-constructed theories and most carefully planned explanations may fall flat in the face of cross-cultural misunderstandings. In this case, the visitors' ability to alter the scale of an object through mechanical projection was simply out of the villager's ken. There are doubtless many other anecdotes that could be related in order to illustrate the gap between a health care provider's intentions and the perceptions of the intended beneficiary. This book seeks, in the broadest terms, to reduce that gap by encouraging those involved in health care delivery to pay more attention to cultural-geographic factors. This is not to say, of course, that such factors are ignored by social scientists, public health professionals, health care planners, and medical personnel. Medical anthropologists by definition focus on cultural themes. Others must also be aware of the importance of these themes. As time goes on, more and more social science research is conducted with cultural variables in mind. And yet it is my feeling that at a time when health care delivery is dominated by technical solutions and when health care research is governed by quantitative analysis, some basic ideas about cultural behavior are often overlooked.

If one message of this book is that culture matters, then the other is that geography—the spatial aspects of health care delivery—matters as well. The anecdote related above, although fictional, we can imagine happening in a particular place. What factors came together in this imaginary village to cause the cultural misunderstanding? Did isolation or distance from sources of Western technology influence what the old man thought? These spatial factors, of course, are just two of many such elements that I, as a geographer, see as playing a very important role in health care delivery. They, in interaction with cultural factors, are the focus of this book.

The broad purpose of demonstrating the importance of spatial and cultural factors in health care delivery can not be achieved in one book or by one person. Thus, the task here will be narrowed to one that is based on my own background in both cultural and medical geography. The impetus for this book grew out of the experience of teaching courses in cultural geography and the spatial aspects of health care delivery. It seemed to me that the horizons of both topics might be extended by a synthesis of important ideas drawn from each subdiscipline. I will show how several of the recurring themes found in the literature on cultural geography can be usefully applied to the study of spatial aspects of health care delivery. This book necessarily has a limited perspective; however, I believe that this perspective is both unique and useful.

Culture and Cultural Geography

Before proceeding further, let us define culture as the concept is actually used by cultural geographers. The word "culture" has been given many meanings.[1] It has been used, for example, to indicate a certain taste for or appreciation of the fine arts (e.g., music, literature, and painting). Here, though, I will define culture broadly as the total way of life of a community of people. Many elements may be included in this definition: activities associated with providing food, shelter, and clothing; ideas, ideologies, beliefs, and values; languages, religions, economic systems, types of government, technologies, and works of art; customs, rituals, and institutions; and so on. In chapter 2, for purposes of illustration, I will separate the elements of culture into artifacts, sociofacts, and mentifacts. For culture encompasses the thoughts, feelings, and actions of a group of people as they go about their daily lives, behaving both as individuals and in interaction with others of their social group. It should be emphasized that culture is transmitted through learning from generation to generation. Some scholars stress the symbolic nature of culture, the ability of humans to bestow meaning on things and events, meanings that are shared by others who adhere to the same culture (as when a country's flag symbolizes patriotic feeling).

Cultural geography traces its roots to several German geographers in the nineteenth century (among them Karl Ritter, 1779–1859; Alexander von Humboldt, 1769–1859; and Friedrich Ratzel, 1844–1904), to a few French geographers (primarily Paul Vidal de la Blache, 1845–1918) around the turn of the century, and to the American geographer Carl Sauer (1889–1975) and the 'Berkeley School" he led in the 1920s.[2] Anthropologists also influenced the early cultural geographers, principal among them Franz Boas (1858–1942), Alfred Kroeber (1876–1960), and Robert Lowie (1883–1957). Over the next few decades, several major themes were developed, including human interaction with the environment, cultural landscapes, sequent occupance, culture regions, cultural innovation and diffusion, the distribution of culture traits such as language and religion, and cultural evolution and adaptation. Cultural geography tended to be overshadowed in the 1960s and 1970s by the quantitative revolution and the positivist approach to social science; the nomothetic idiom was favored by most geographers over the idiographic. Although many cultural geographers continued their work without incorporating quantitative techniques, some did make limited use of quantitative methods. During this period, cultural geographers were criticized for ignoring the "inner workings" of culture (people communicating and interacting with one another); for failing to seek ideas from other social sciences; for failure to incorporate social theory; and for overemphasis on rural areas, material culture, and folk themes.[3]

In recent years, there has been a renewed interest in cultural geography throughout North America and Great Britain. In part, this stems from a general reaction by many geographers, cultural or not, against what they feel is wrong with the positivist approach: namely, that it is overly objective, narrow in focus, mechanistic, and deterministic; that it fails to deal adequately with society's problems; and that it has social engineering as its chief end.[4] The "new" cultural geography attempts to deal with the criticisms leveled against the "old" cultural geography.[5] It emphasizes human interaction; borrows ideas from social, anthropological, political, and economic theory; and focuses more on urban areas, nonmaterial culture, and popular culture. The new cultural geography is strongly influenced by two perspectives that have emerged or reemerged in recent years among geographers and social scientists: structuralism and humanism. From structuralism we derive such concepts as underlying forces in society, class conflict, hegemony by elite groups, the social context of human actions, and the role of ideology. Humanism offers other concepts: the lifeworld, the importance of place, meaning in everyday life, and symbolic landscapes.

Some cultural geographers have attempted to blend the two perspectives. Much of this new thinking is captured in the following statement: "If we were to define this 'new' cultural geography it would be contemporary as well as historical (but always contextual and theoretically informed); social as well as spatial (but not confined exclusively to narrowly-defined landscape issues); urban as well as rural; and interested in the contingent nature of culture, in dominant ideologies and in forms of resistance to them. It would, moreover, assert the centrality of culture in human affairs."[6]

Medical Geography

Although medical geographers trace their roots all the way back to the time of Hippocrates, around four centuries before Christ, the concentrated study of the geography of disease began only a few decades ago, and the tradition of investigating the spatial aspects of health care delivery began even more recently, in the 1960s.[7] Medical geography is now flourishing and has active interest groups in the Association of American Geographers, the Canadian Association of Geographers, and the Institute of British Geographers. Four international symposia, in Great Britian, the United States, and Canada, have been held recently.

Geographic studies of disease had a strong cultural component from the very beginning. Specific diseases were typically studied using a tripartite approach: population, environment, and behavior (and the interactions among these factors). Concepts such as cultural systems, cultural ecology, the importance of place (natural nidus), and landscape epidemiology are often integral to these studies. Perhaps because it coincided with the quantitative revolution in geography, the geography of health care delivery was heavily quantitative from the start and did not pursue cultural themes to the same extent that the geography of disease did. Two major research foci emerged. The first analyzed the spatial distribution of medical manpower (principally physicians) and of medical facilities (principally hospitals). Concepts such as central place theory and techniques such as location/allocation modeling were used to examine existing patterns and to set up norms for ideal medical systems. The second focus of research was on the accessibility and utilization of medical personnel and facilities. Involved here were such concepts as distance decay and the relative location of providers and clients.

The positivist tradition remains strong in the geographic study of health care delivery, and there is no doubt that progress has been made within the positivist framework. Location/allocation models have become far more sophisticated. A variety of multivariate statistical models have been applied in order to assess accessibility and utilization. Geographic information systems (GIS) are beginning to be employed in assessments of manpower and facility distribution. Medical geographers, like other social scientists, are trying to keep up with new computer programs that will help them model their theories and findings. Still, something seems to be missing in these increasingly complex investigations: they begin to look like "technological fixes." Like biomedicine, they often place undue emphasis on technique rather than on the human element in health care.

A review of recent work by medical geographers and other social scientists reveals that the gap between what cultural geographers have been doing and what medical geographers might be doing (or doing more of) has been partially bridged.[8] This sort of work includes a specific focus on cultural variables such as ethnicity, the examination of ethnomedical systems, an emphasis on the importance of viewing health care delivery within its entire societal context, and the advocacy of political economy approaches. While such writing and research has deemphasized quantitative techniques, it pursues many of the themes (e.g., cultural ecology) that cultural geographers have been familiar with for decades. In addition, much recent work uses quantitative and qualitative approaches in complementary ways.

One result of my reading and thinking about how themes in cultural geography might be applied to health care delivery was an article directed at teachers and students interested in both cultural and medical geography.[9] The present book is essentially an expansion of that article. Two types of health care delivery research having cultural content were distinguished. In one type, cultural-geographic themes were not made explicit but had to be teased out for purposes of illustration. Other work pursued cultural themes more consciously. Many examples have been drawn from the work of medical geographers, but studies carried out by other geographers and other social scientists have been used so long as they satisfy the principal criterion of illustrating the interface of cultural geography and health care delivery. In some cases, when a particular theme from cultural geography needed further elaboration and appropriate examples could not be found, hypothetical situations were developed. There is always a danger that such examples might seem "forced"; however, care has been taken to make them realistic and meaningful.

An Overview

Each chapter treats a single theme in cultural geography in the following way. First, several concepts related to the theme are developed. Second, each theme and its accompanying concepts are applied to several specific studies of health care delivery. Third, the significance of the applications is discussed. No attempt has been made to review the entire literature on any one topic or subtopic. Rather, good examples are selected and discussed in detail. In many cases, additional studies are referenced in the notes. Some chapters emphasize cultural themes over geographic themes; the reverse is true in other chapters. My intent throughout is to illustrate the interaction of spatial and cultural concepts.

For each theme, the selected materials represent a variety of theoretical and methodological perspectives, reflecting the emphases of scholarly work. The earlier chapters, 2 through 7, tend to emphasize traditional themes, whereas chapters 8 through 11 stress more recent ideas, but all chapters incorporate both old and new thinking. Thus, the overall approach is eclectic, in the spirit of Peter Jackson and Susan Smith, who state that "geographers may justifiably and profitably indulge in eclecticism, provided that within any one philosophical framework their subject matter and analytical techniques are logically and consistently articulated."[10] Whenever possible, cross-references are made to similar ideas or examples from other chapters. The principal notion I wish to convey is that cultural geography offers a multivalent, interactive perspective on health care delivery.

The foundation for chapter 2, "Culture Systems," derives from systems theory, work on medical systems around the world, and research on the cultural context of medical systems. My approach is basically reductionist—breaking down a health care delivery system into its component parts—but strives to be holistic by examining interactions among components, feedback loops, and medical systems as open systems within a societal setting. The principal intent of chapter 2 is to expand our thinking about what factors influence health care.

The principal way in which geographers categorize space is by regionalizing. Thus, my particular purpose in chapter 3, "Culture Regions," is to differentiate groups of people spatially according to culture traits. Several concepts related to regions are discussed: boundaries, overlap and conflict, and cultural pluralism. Recent work in the field of social geography (e.g., on regional inequalities) and in political economy (e.g., on core-periphery relationships) informs some of the thinking in chapter 3. A variety of research is used to illustrate how such concepts have been applied to health care delivery situations—including work on medical pluralism in India, health care inequalities among small areas in the United States and between two regions of Nigeria, and the distribution of traditional medical practitioners in Bangkok, Thailand.

Chapter 4, "Cultural Ecology," has to do with the interaction of culture (expressed as technology and organization) with the environment (natural and man-made). This perspective has a long history in geography. I will focus on two themes: (1) the contrast between environmental determinism and possibilism in health care delivery and (2) the biological and nonbiological adaptation of medical systems to changing circumstances. Supporting material for the concepts developed around the first theme comes from medical thinking in ancient Greek, medieval European, and modern times. Adaptation and its attendant notions of ecological balance and carrying capacity are illustrated with examples that include cancer treatment in developed as well as developing countries and AIDS treatment in the United States.

Another well-developed theme in cultural geography, the evolution of culture, will be the focus of Chapter 5. I begin by setting out several concepts—time scales, incremental and revolutionary change, cultural lag, and conflict and stress in culture change—and apply them, for purposes of illustration, to stages in human cultural evolution. Then these ideas are elucidated through discussion of the history of biomedicine, changing patient-doctor relationships in urban North America, recent innovations in U.S. health care delivery (e.g., health maintenance organizations and alternative healers), and the causes and treatment of esophageal cancer in China.

Cultural diffusion, the subject of chapter 6, is a major concept in most branches of human geography. Ideas about types of diffusion, carriers of and barriers to diffusion, and the societal context of diffusion processes have generated a substantial literature both within geography itself and in other disciplines such as public health, sociology, economics, and anthropology. In chapter 6, I tease out some of the most important ideas on the diffusion of health care delivery by discussing in detail a few representative studies, carried out over the past three decades, that make use of quantitative as well as qualitative methodologies. Included are investigations of an innovative health care plan sponsored by the United Automobile Workers in Detroit, the spread of computed tomography scanners in the United States during the 1970s, the diffusion of birth control information along social networks in South Korea, the utilization of a maternal and child health clinic in Ethiopia, and the societal context and pathways involved in the diffusion of oral rehydration therapy in Bolivia.

A topic that is covered in some cultural geography texts is the distinction between folk and popular culture. In chapter 7, this theme is examined in the context of regions, innovation and diffusion, and cultural ecology. Although care must be taken when applying these concepts to health care delivery, several interesting health care studies exist that are suggestive for potentially productive research by geographers. These studies include work on popular medicine in developed countries, on the tradition of collecting medicinal plants in the Appalachians, on geophagy in Africa and Mississippi, on the mixture of folk and popular medicine in folk societies, on the use of chiropractors in North Carolina, and on various issues of disease and health in Kenya.

Most cultural geography texts include thorough discussion of a fundamental culture trait, language. Usually, the texts relate language to such concepts as regions, evolution and diffusion, the environment, and integration with other culture traits. In chapter 8, however, I will focus on some themes that reflect rather recent thinking about the role language plays in culture. Included are discussions, with examples, of language as it is used for communication between providers and patients; of the ways in which people classify disease and health terms; of health care language used as metaphor, myth, and model; and of semantic networks. Chapter 8 serves as a bridge between themes of the "old" and the "new" cultural geography. Few geographers who have studied health care delivery have explicitly incorporated the trait of languages, so I will necessarily draw heavily on the work of nongeographers, especially anthropologists, in order to suggest how geographers might include this sort of material in their own work.

Over the past few years, a substantial geographic literature has investigated what might be characterized as "social space." Rooted in structuralist and political economic theory, this literature emphasizes such themes as spatial and social inequalities, hegemony and resistance, territoriality, underdevelopment, and the privatization of health care. In the 1980s, this strand of thought was beginning to be applied to the geographic study of health care delivery. Chapter 9 highlights important aspects of social space by discussing a few selected studies, which include contrasts of health care policies in different countries, conflicts over establishing a hospital in New York State, the history of biomedical services in Nigeria, the impact of a capitalist economy on nutritional status in Kenya, the restructuring of Britain's National Health Service, the effects of privatization on the distribution of urban hospitals in the United States, and the role of multinational pharmaceutical firms in the production and distribution of drugs to developing countries.

Influential recent work, often associated with the humanistic movement in geography, has revived interest in "place and landscape," the subject of chapter 10. Very little research in health care delivery has been done that is explicitly based on the importance of place or the idea of symbolic landscapes. Chapter 10 suggests that concepts such as sense of place, lifeworlds, fields of care, negotiated realities, rootedness, symbolic systems, ideology, and therapeutic landscapes could usefully be applied to studies of health care delivery. Ideas of place are illustrated by the example of an urban hospital and by the life experiences of a group of alcoholics. After a brief discussion of symbolic systems and symbolic landscapes, three more examples provide further illustration of healing landscapes and places: treating the mad in Renaissance and classical Europe; protecting colonial officers in Freetown, Sierra Leone; and seeking water cures in the United States.

In recent years, geographers and other social scientists have tried to explain human behavior by blending many of the concepts that I discuss in chapters 9 and 10. Chapter 11, "Cultural Materialism," attempts to open up new ground by suggesting that health care research might be guided by one such attempt, structuration theory, which deals with the dynamic interplay of human agency and societal structures. This interplay is illustrated by doctor-patient relationships in the United States, by disease ecology, and by the deinstitutionalization of the mentally ill. Then I introduce the notion of "time geography" as a possible means for working out the agency-structure interactions of structuration; a study of health-care-seeking behavior in Savannah, Georgia, serves as an example. Finally, a detailed analysis of the everyday lives and health-related attitudes and activities of twenty-four people in Inner London encapsulates the main themes of cultural materialism. The concluding chapter summarizes the central themes of this book and shows how they interact with one another.

Specific Aims

This introductory chapter can be summed up by stating several aims or goals that have been set. The first is to exploit the interface between cultural geography and medical geography. As noted earlier, this means (for the most part) selecting basic concepts from the older of the two subfields, cultural geography, and applying them to situations in health care delivery. A second goal is to highlight research by geographers and other social scientists who employ cultural-geographic themes in their investigations of health care delivery. Following naturally from this goal is the next one: to suggest ways in which further investigations can fill some of the gaps left in the cultural geography/ medical geography interface. Finally, my fourth goal, to change people's perceptions, is perhaps the most important. Most teachers and authors wish to inform the perspectives of their students and readers. They want people to look at the world in different ways; they want to expand people's horizons, to show them how things might be done differently and, ultimately, how the world (in their view) might be improved.

2. Culture Systems

For many health care consumers and, indeed, for many who do research on health care delivery, the provision of medical care is primarily a matter of a few conspicuous elements such as physicians and hospitals. This extremely narrow point of view constitutes a barrier both to understanding and to improving health care; that is, the prevention and treatment of illness. The principal aim of this chapter is to broaden our field of view with respect to what a medical system comprises. The approach taken is to describe a medical system as one would describe a culture system, in all its complexity. Key concepts are taken from systems theory as it has been applied in the natural and social sciences.

I will begin by defining systems in general as well as culture systems and medical systems. To illustrate that there are many different medical systems in use throughout the world today, not only biomedicine (clinical medicine based on the principles of the natural sciences) but several traditional professional and nonprofessional systems will be briefly described. Then some important systems concepts will be introduced and discussed: elements, links, feedback loops, open and closed systems, and context. In the remainder of the chapter, I will use these concepts as a framework for analysis of medical care systems.

Systems Concepts

A *system* may be defined as a set of *components* (or *elements*) plus the *links, interactions,* or *relationships* among those components.[1] To use an example that will be familiar to most readers, an ecosystem is a system composed of plant and animal organisms plus various solid, liquid, and gaseous components of the physical environment, all tied together in an intricate web of interdependencies. A *culture system* is an assemblage of *culture traits,* or elements—for example, toolmaking, language, child-rearing practices, and philosophical ideas—that interact with one another. (See chapter 1 for a detailed definition of culture.) Thus, we might speak of an "Arab culture system," including such elements as the Arabic language, the Muslim religion, and certain special dietary patterns.

A *medical system,* by one definition, is "the pattern of social institutions and cultural traditions that evolves from *deliberate behavior* to enhance health, whether or not the outcome of particular items of behavior is ill health."[2] There are several different ways in which we could classify the world's principal medical systems. Here we shall use three categories: (1) traditional professional medicine; (2) traditional nonprofessional medicine; and (3) biomedicine (also called modern, Western, or cosmopolitan medicine). All these systems have bodies of medical knowledge and pharmacopoeia that are passed from healer to healer and generation to generation. What distinguishes professional from nonprofessional medical systems is that the former tend to codify knowledge in a more formal way and also have formal schools for medical training. An important point to grasp here is that biomedicine is not the only professional system in existence.

Four traditional professional medical systems—Ayurvedic, Chinese, Galenic, and unanic—predate biomedicine and are very important among a large proportion of the world's population (see figure 1). Ayurvedic medicine, whose origins lie on the Indian subcontinent, can be traced back some four thousand years. Its core area today is North India, but it is also found in other parts of India, Pakistan, Bangladesh, Sri Lanka, and throughout the Arab world. Within South Asia, it competes with *unani,* biomedicine, and homeopathy. Chinese medicine began around 1,500 B.C. When Western influence began to be felt in China in the nineteenth century, Chinese medicine was stagnating and in

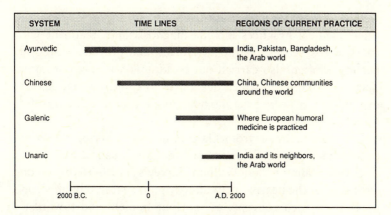

SYSTEM	TIME LINES	REGIONS OF CURRENT PRACTICE
Ayurvedic		India, Pakistan, Bangladesh, the Arab world
Chinese		China, Chinese communities around the world
Galenic		Where European humoral medicine is practiced
Unanic		India and its neighbors, the Arab world

2000 B.C.   0   A.D. 2000

FIGURE 1. *Traditional Professional Medical Systems*
SOURCE: W. Gesler, *Health Care in Developing Countries* (Washington, D.C.: Association of American Geographers, 1984), p. 19. Reproduced by permission.

danger of being pushed aside by biomedicine. Under the Communist regime, though, it has enjoyed a revival and has been partially integrated with biomedicine. The core area remains China, but it is practiced in Chinese communities throughout the world. What is today called Galenic medicine emerged in ancient Greece from the Hippocratic school of Cos (ca. 400 B.C.) but did not become a fully formed medical system until the Greek physician Galen (ca. A.D. 130–200). It was dominant in Europe until the development of germ theory late in the nineteenth century and thus was diffused, along with many other aspects of European culture, as Europeans colonized or otherwise dominated large areas of the globe. Unani was derived from Galenic medicine by Arabs in the seventh and eighth centuries A.D., shortly after the founding of the Muslim religion. Dominating the Arab world until it encountered strong competition from biomedicine in the nineteenth century, unani followed the spread of Islam to South and Southeast Asia, where it now competes with other systems.

Traditional nonprofessional medicine is practiced both in the developed world—among such groups as Native Americans—and in most developing countries—by the bulk of the population. Practitioners are called native doctors, shamans, or traditional healers. They often play other roles in their societies as well—as priests or judges of social misdemeanors, for example. Their medical practices include diagnosis and treatment with roots, herbs, leaves, charms, sacrifices, and prayers. Moreover, healing is often also carried out by kinfolk who are not native doctors. (Chapter 7, which deals with folk and popular culture, expands on this very brief introduction to traditional nonprofessional medicine.)

Biomedicine arose from Galenic medicine during the European Middle Ages. Beginning in the Renaissance, a series of discoveries, among them William Harvey's (1578–1657) demonstration that the heart is a circulatory pump, steered biomedicine away from such concepts as the four humors and toward its current ideas. A turning point for biomedicine came in the late nineteenth century when discoveries by Louis Pasteur (1822–95), Robert Koch (1842–1910), and others led to the development of *germ theory,* the idea that many diseases are caused by microorganisms and parasites. More recent scientific discoveries have greatly enhanced the prestige of biomedicine, and today it is the medical system that is most widespread, having made its way to some degree into every country in the world. (Chapter 5 provides more details about the evolution of biomedicine.)

At the beginning of this section, I said that a system is made up of components. The components of a culture system are its culture traits. These can be divided, using a scheme devised by Aldous Huxley, into artifacts, sociofacts, and mentifacts. Artifacts are the materials that humans produce for use in their daily lives—tools, food, shelter and clothing, books, sports equipment, and so on. Institutions such as kinship structures, educational systems, and government bureaucracies are classified as sociofacts. Mentifacts are ideas, including such diverse notions as systems of political thought, food preferences, and polytheism. In many cases, culture traits are difficult to place in a single category. For example, a school system consists of artifacts (chalk, computers, buildings); sociofacts (teacher-pupil relationships, hierarchies of degrees that can be obtained); and mentifacts (ideas about the importance of a "basic education," equal educational opportunity for all).

Medical systems contain a wide range of artifacts, sociofacts, and mentifacts as well. Yet, most people probably have a very limited view of how wide this range actually is, and we can name only a few components here. Artifacts would include everything from a native doctor's herbs and a Band-Aid to a CAT scanner and a kidney dialysis machine. Under sociofacts, we could list the various ways in which health care is organized (free enterprise, welfare state, socialism), the relationships between patients and doctors, and how the different members of a family typically react to illness. Concepts concerning health care—that is, mentifacts—encompass not only modern scientific medicine, but also the idea in Galenic medicine that good health requires the proper balance of the bodily humors and the folk medical idea that illness is the result of the displeasure of the gods. As with the elements of a culture system, the components of a medical system are often difficult to classify. Consider a hospital. As a structure, it is an artifact and contains within it many medically useful objects; its organization, which includes patients, medical personnel, administrators, financial officers, and others, exemplifies a sociofact; and the hospital as an idea, as a way of trying to cure the sick, is a mentifact.

Once we have an idea of the elements of a system, we can begin to examine the multitude of links or relationships among them. Consider the Arab culture system mentioned above, along with its three traits of language, religion, and dietary patterns. The Muslim religion is literally given voice from the minarets of mosques, in Arabic cadences from the Koran, five times each day. The Koran sets out rules for human dietary behavior, such as forbidding the use of alcohol. So what are some examples of links within a medical system? Consider the following. A patient (person) with a cancerous growth (disease) consults a physician (person and medical practitioner) trained in chemotherapy (medical technique) at a particular medical school (training facility). Whether the patient is willing to be treated by the doctor depends on the doctor-patient relationship. Whether or not the doctor will use a particular chemotherapy treatment depends on his or her medical training.

An important aspect of system linkage is the potential to form *positive* and *negative feedback* loops. Suppose element A affects element B in some way. If B in turn reinforces A, then there is positive feedback and both elements tend to be strengthened; if B depresses A in some way, then feedback is negative and both elements tend to be weakened. Let us consider a simple illustration from a medical system involving patients and a hospital. If patients feel that they are being treated well at the hospital, they will tend to return (positive feedback) and the hospital may expand its services. If people do not feel they are treated well, they will go less often to the hospital; as a result, the hospital will lose prestige and, ultimately, may even close.

A system can be either *open* or *closed*. If it is closed—that is, if it is not influenced by external factors—then it is relatively easy to analyze and change. Cultural systems, however, are always open. It is impossible to draw a boundary around a system such as a health care system. Which elements would we include, and which would we exclude? Is, for example, the basic economic policy of a country (free enterprise, socialism, mixed economy) a part of the medical system, strictly speaking? Perhaps not, but government policy clearly influences how health care is delivered. Thus, we must always think beyond those system elements which are clearly medical to those which influence them, however indirectly.

This leads us to the important idea that medical systems must be seen in the *context* of larger cultural and environmental systems. The context consists of many subsystems—social relationships, political and economic systems, attitudes and beliefs, topography and climate—all of which influence how health care is delivered. Changes in the context produce changes in the medical system. For example, medical systems that operate in a free enterprise economy will be quite different from those based on socialist principles. (Chapter 9, which discusses the political economy of health care, reemphasizes the notion of the importance of societal context.)

The remainder of this chapter will be devoted to the application of the foregoing ideas to medical systems. Throughout the discussion, a contrast will be made between the developed and the developing countries, for health care in these two very broadly delineated worlds differs fundamentally. In the developed world, biomedicine dominates, whereas in the developing world, biomedicine is usually present but faces strong competition from traditional systems, both professional and nonprofessional. Of course, medical practice and access to medicine vary greatly *within* countries; this issue will be dealt with as well. In the following sections, various medical systems will be more fully described and compared in terms of their elements, links, and context.

Medical System Elements

In the preceding section, we saw that the elements of a medical system could be classified as artifacts, sociofacts, and mentifacts, and also as processes. Here another categorization will be introduced for purposes of illustration: illness, people, environment, resources, and beliefs.[3] Each of these components has numerous characteristics that vary from one medical system to another (see table 1).

Medical systems exist to prevent or cure illness. But the types of illnesses that beset people differ greatly from region to region. This is not the place to discuss the geography of disease occurrence in detail; rather, I will merely point out a pattern in the types of diseases that predominate in the more-developed versus the less-developed areas. In developing countries, the leading causes of sickness and death are infectious and parasitic diseases such as dysentery, pneumonia, measles, schistosomiasis, cholera, and malaria. A century ago, many of these infirmities were important in what are now developed countries, but today the dominant health problems in these same countries are degenerative diseases such as heart disease and a variety of cancers. The developed countries, we may say, have made the *epidemiologic transition*. As developing countries modernize, they too can expect to experience a higher incidence of degenerative disease.

TABLE I.

ELEMENTS OF HEALTH CARE DELIVERY SYSTEMS AND EXAMPLES OF THEIR CHARACTERISTICS	
Elements	**Characteristics**
Illness	type severity duration
People	age ocupation ethnicity
Environment	house type water source lavatory type
Resources	practitioner/facility type distributional equality hierarchies
Cultural system	illness beliefs medical system mix practitioner preferences
Economic system	capitalist/socialist expenditure priorities level of development
System of government	ideology sector priorities degree of local autonomy
Barriers to care	distance costs waiting time

SOURCE: W. Gesler, *Health Care in Developing Countries* (Washington, D.C.: Association of American Geographers, 1984), p. 7. Reproduced by permission.

A second element to consider is people and their characteristics. There are a variety of population traits that interact with other medical system elements. These include age, sex, ethnicity, income status, occupation, marriage status, lifestyle (e.g., smoking, drinking, eating, and exercise habits), stress (from work and family relationships), plus many others. Populations in developed and developing countries differ with respect to these characteristics. For example, developing country populations tend to be younger, to have lower average incomes, to have much higher proportions in agricultural occupations, and to experience different stresses. Populations within countries may also differ greatly, of course; think of the contrast between inner-city and suburban people in any large metropolitan area of the United States.

The environment must also be considered as a contributor to medical systems. Under this component one can list climate, topography, type of housing construction, source of drinking water, toilet facilities, and many others. It can be seen from these examples that "environment" includes the natural or physical environment as well as man-made environments. Most countries, at whatever stage of development, contain a range of physical environments—tropical rain forests, grasslands, deciduous forests, prairies, hot and cold deserts, and so on. Populations also differ with respect to the quality of their man-made environments. Compare the African villager who lives in a hut infested with disease agents, who uses the "bush" for a toilet, and who draws water from a polluted well to an apartment dweller in a Western city who lives in a far more sanitized environment (but one, of course, that is not without its environmental contaminants).

Further, medical systems differ with respect to available resources. Three important resources are personnel, facilities, and equipment. It is easier to distinguish resources among medical systems than among countries. All biomedical personnel directly involved in health care are trained in modern science, although the extent and type of training are not the same for different medical specialists, nurses, paramedics, and technical assistants. Other types of personnel are also involved, including administrators, accountants, receptionists, and service workers. Most of these workers are quite highly specialized. The principal medical personnel in the ancient professional systems (Chinese doctors, vaidyas in Ayurvedic medicine, hakims in unani, and doctors who practice Galenic medicine) also have different levels of training, and may specialize to some degree, but tend to be more generalist than is now the case in biomedicine. Most receive their training either through apprenticeship to a master healer or at a school. Most have a good understanding of their system's ideas about disease causation, prevention, and cure; a wide-ranging treatment pharmacopoeia consisting of preparations made from leaves, roots, and herbs; established techniques for diagnosis and treatment; and some understanding about the importance of the doctor-patient relationship.

In folk societies, it may be more difficult to decide who is a doctor and who is not, because many people who heal also play other roles such as priest or community guardian of morals. Important people within one's kinship network often make important decisions concerning health care, whether or not they give treatment directly (this is of course true, albeit to a lesser extent, in developed societies). Nevertheless, folk medicine has practitioners who may be generalists or who may specialize in such things as infectious disease, bonesetting, cures by witchcraft, problems of pregnancy and childbirth, and mental problems. Most have a fund of herbal preparations. They also make use of charms, sacrifices, and exorcism in order to effect cures. They are noted for having a knowledge of their patients, their patients' family and kin, and the problems of the patients' community. Many are believed by their clients to have special powers or relationships with the supernatural.

Biomedical health care in developed countries takes place in a wide variety of facilities: general and special hospitals of many kinds, clinics, doctors' offices, group homes, and even within the patient's home (though much less than in the past). Many of the same kinds of facilities will often be found in developing areas, but they exist in far fewer numbers. The facilities used by practitioners of traditional professional and nonprofessional medicine are much more humble. Some healing takes place in clinics and hospitals, but much of it is carried out in the doctor's office or in the patient's home. There is also a vast difference between medical systems with respect to the equipment that is available for health care. At one end of the spectrum is the native doctor with his or her herbs and charms; at the other is the increasingly complex array of high-tech equipment that physicians in developing countries have access to.

Finally, let us consider health care beliefs. Modern medicine arose out of a belief that the application of the sciences, in particular the natural sciences such as biology and chemistry, is the best way to address health care problems. Although most people in areas where biomedicine is dominant understand little of the science used by doctors, they are familiar with the terminology, talk impressively about their ailments, and tend to hold physicians in some awe (although these attitudes may well have changed in recent years).

The beliefs held by practitioners of the traditional professional systems are a blend of ideas about disease causation, prevention, and cure that go back many centuries together with more modern notions, usually assimilated from biomedicine. Chinese medicine is known for such concepts as the importance of achieving a balance between yin and yang in the human body, acupuncture, massage, and pulse diagnosis. Yet, practitioners of Chinese medicine today have been trained in many biomedical protocols and techniques. Ayurvedic, unanic, and Galenic medicine share a belief that there needs to be a proper balance between certain bodily fluids. The Galenic notion is that there are four important humors—blood, mucus, yellow bile, and black bile—that must be in equilibrium. The four traditional professional systems have all developed ideas about proper diet, climatic influences on health, and standard procedures for treating specific ailments.

Beliefs about disease and health care vary a great deal among doctors and patients in folk societies, but some ideas seem to persist across cultures. These include beliefs about the supernatural causes and cures for some problems, about the close association between religious (animist) ideas and healing, about the power of witchcraft to make people ill or well, and about the importance of kinship networks throughout an episode of illness.

Links and Feedback

There are ten possible links between the five elements discussed in the preceding section. Each link could itself be described with a multitude of examples because each element has several characteristics, so I must be selective. Illustrations will be taken from different types of systems in developing as well as developed areas of the world.

The first link is between people and disease. For a start, age has a clear connection with illness. Certain diseases, such as measles, affect children mostly, while older people are more likely to contract, for example, cancer. The age factor creates a difference in the illnesses experienced by developed and developing areas because developing populations are usually younger. Another population characteristic that is connected with differential levels of disease is socioeconomic status. Where incomes are low, diseases that can be traced to poor nutrition, sanitation, and housing quality often predominate. High-income areas might be associated with illnesses, such as heart disease, brought on in part by overnutrition and lack of exercise.

Natural and man-made environments also obviously affect the types and levels of illness. In developing countries, the natural environment is largely responsible for the prevailing infectious and parasitic diseases, but humans there can help or hinder the spread of those diseases by altering the environment. For example, the snail that is essential to the life cycle of the schistosomiasis worm agent is found naturally in areas of still water where certain grasses grow. Thus, people create additional snail habitats when they build dams and irrigation ditches; they have also tried to destroy such habitats. The diseases that are most important in developed countries often stem from the man-made environment. The noise created by traffic and construction in urban areas can contribute significantly to stress; many cancers can be traced, at least in part, to air, water, and ground pollution created by industry and various modes of transportation; damp houses may contribute to bronchitis, and children may ingest poisonous lead from peeling paint.

In an ideal medical system, the appropriate resources would always be brought to bear on specific illnesses. For example, a vaccine would be developed to prevent malaria, and malaria-bearing mosquitos would be eliminated forever. Even if we knew how to prevent or cure all diseases, though, experience has shown that the resources-to-illness link is often made inappropriately. In the first place, the balance between medical manpower, facilities, and equipment used to prevent and treat illness should be tipped far more toward prevention. For some reason or reasons (greed, glamor, prestige?) the old adage that an ounce of prevention is worth a pound of cure goes largely unheeded. Often, there is also a misapplication of resources. Developing countries spend vast sums on large hospitals that can treat only a small fraction of the population and that employ Western-trained doctors who like to concentrate on rare and interesting cases while the mass of the people suffer from mostly preventable diseases. In a country such as the United States, cancers and other diseases may be "in" as far as research funding is concerned; but, in the meantime, measles immunization may become lax and an epidemic can ensue. Another facet of the resources-to-illness link is that different medical systems may be used by the same people for different ailments. The generalization has often been made, for example, that people in developing countries use biomedicine for acute problems but rely on indigenous healers for chronic ailments and mental problems.

It is important to remember that different people think about illnesses in very different ways. Ideas about disease causation, prevention, and cure vary tremendously among medical systems and societies around the world. The reasons for these differing beliefs include ignorance, superstition, the difficulty of understanding complex disease processes, and the fact that our knowledge about disease changes constantly. A person living in a folk society might think that a stomachache is caused by witches pounding on his or her insides. An uneducated person living in a Western society may believe that a certain preparation cures cancer, not knowing whether this might be chemically or physiologically impossible. Even a well-educated person has cause to be unsure about whether or not a daily alcoholic drink helps prevent heart disease, for current evidence is contradictory. Whether illness beliefs are scientifically sound or not, however, it is a fact that they affect the way illness is dealt with—to the extent that a strong belief in certain treatments or practitioners can even help bring about one's recovery. That is to say, we know that the mind and the body are linked in ways we are just beginning to explore.

The general ways in which people deal with the environment—the subject matter of cultural ecology—are reserved for discussion in chapter 4; here I will illustrate a few specific links between population characteristics and the physical and man-made environment. In developed societies, where populations are experiencing increasingly longer life spans, concern is often expressed about the unhealthy environments in which the elderly live. Many of the elderly feel stress from loneliness, suffer from a lack of adequate heat in damp, drafty buildings, and have neither the inclination nor the money to eat nutritious food. Low socioeconomic status is related to poor housing, malnutrition, and inadequate health care the world over. Workers in the asbestos or coal-mining industry may be exposed to hazardous and unhealthy environments. Because of their religious beliefs some people may refuse to take certain nutritious foods from the environment.

The link between people and resources is a vital one. It is probably the link that is most studied by medical geographers, who have investigated the accessibility and utilization of health care resources in great depth. It is useful to think of the people-resources relationship in terms of barriers or lack of barriers. Other things being equal, the wealthy usually have better access than the poor to physicians and other medical personnel, health care facilities, and state-of-the-art medical equipment. In many societies, men have higher social status than women and will expect and receive better medical treatment. For most people in developing countries, the traditional professional and nonprofessional systems are more accessible than biomedicine. Distance is a well-known barrier between people and health care practitioners or facilities; however, we also know that the importance of distance (however measured) will vary according to such factors as income (e.g., with respect to available transport) or lifestyle (e.g., with respect to a person's daily round of activity).

What are some links between the characteristics of people and their illness beliefs? Education clearly plays a role. One hopes that people can be educated to overcome their superstitions and ignorance about health matters. Unfortunately, education can also lead to poor health practices. In many countries, educated women have been induced by advertising to feed their babies formula from bottles rather than milk from the breast. People who come from different ethnic backgrounds may have different attitudes toward disease. Thus, some groups tend to be stoic and attempt to ignore their pain, whereas others may be much more indulgent of complaining.

The environment acts both to constrain the availability of medical resources and to provide opportunities for resource development. Constraints in the physical environment might take the form of topographic or climatic conditions that make it difficult for health practitioners to carry out their jobs. A poorly designed transportation system or hospital complex is an example of the constraining effects of the man-made environment on the efficiency of medical resources. On the other hand, the physical environment produces the materials necessary for everything from herbal medicines to X-ray machines, and well-designed laboratories can help to find medicines that prevent or cure disease.

To say that the environment, the physical environment in particular, affects beliefs may run the risk of environmental determinism. Nevertheless, one can certainly speculate about possible links between these two components of all medical systems. An environment in which disease agents abound might lead to a rather fatalistic attitude toward disease, especially if high morbidity and mortality rates result. A relatively germ-free environment, on the other hand, might lull people into thinking that they will never become ill. When a new disease agent such as the AIDS virus enters such an environment, many people might not be inclined to take precautions against it. Illness beliefs can also be linked to the man-made environment. Our belief in germ theory and scientific medicine in general leads us to drain swamps, spray mosquitos, build sewage systems, establish pharmaceutical firms, and construct hospitals full of sophisticated equipment.

The final link to be considered is that between medical resources and beliefs. It is well known that if health care personnel and patients share the same ideas, then healing becomes easier. This is one reason why folk healers may have a curative advantage over biomedical personnel when they are treating their own people. The quality of medical resources also affects beliefs. Clean facilities and equipment and caring doctors and nurses help people to believe that they will get better.

Most of the links discussed above seem to go in one direction: one of the components affects the other. Thus, we normally think of the environment as affecting disease rather than the other way around. Disease, of course, can also affect the environment. Think of the changes brought about by the Black Death on the human and even the physical landscape in Europe during the Middle Ages (e.g., the abandonment of large areas in many cities). In many situations, traits from different components affect one another and create feedback loops. I end this section with some illustrations of positive and negative feedback. Note that either type of feedback can have either positive or negative impacts on health.

Socioeconomic status and disease often become involved in a vicious cycle: poverty breeds illness, people weakened by illness have trouble finding work or staying on the job, they remain poor and the cycle continues. This is an example of positive feedback, even though the effect on health is negative. A health education program can be another example of positive feedback. Suppose a mother in a developing country enters an education program believing many superstitious and false ideas having to do with childhood diseases and their treatment; for example, she thinks that a child with diarrhea should never be given liquids. She learns how to perform oral rehydration therapy, treats her baby, and the child recovers. Her thinking changes and she is eager to learn other things about caring for her baby.

Negative feedback can be illustrated by the example of a doctor who is asked by the government of a tropical country to serve a population in an area where most roads are impassable during the rainy season. The enthusiastic young doctor sets out by car or jeep to cover this uncongenial territory, but he or she becomes frustrated again and again by the environment and a vehicle that constantly breaks down. The doctor's links to most of his or her clients are gradually weakened and further frustration sets in. Yearning for a job in a city, the doctor then loses all effectiveness. Breaking into disease cycles might also be thought of as a form of negative feedback. Take the case of malaria-bearing mosquitoes that breed in certain habitats. If these habitats are systematically destroyed, the vector's link to its environment is weakened and may even be broken.

Systems Context

Earlier in this chapter, I emphasized the related ideas that medical systems are open and that it is important to look at a medical system in the context of wider societal systems. It is hard to know where a medical system ends and its context begins, however. Thus, we might have considered illness beliefs as context rather than calling them a medical system component. In this section, I provide a few brief indications of how three interdependent contextual systems—social systems, cultural systems, and political-economic systems—might affect elements and the links between elements within medical systems.[4] Some of these ideas will be taken up again in more detail below (see especially chapters 9, 10, and 11).

Social systems influence the health care received by populations having different characteristics. I mentioned before that males are often given preferential treatment over females because of status differentials. In a few societies, old people may be left alone to die, but most try to care for the elderly. Yet, how this care is provided varies: some families put their elderly relatives out of the way in institutions, while others keep them in their own homes. Prestige may affect the degree of trust people place in physicians. Medical personnel have been given various degrees of status in different social systems. The comparison is often made between the high social and economic status enjoyed by physicians in the United States and the relatively low status that physicians (who are mostly women) have in the Soviet Union.

Some very general types of cultural beliefs held by a society could influence attitudes toward health care. If people tend to be fatalistic about what happens to them, they may not try to do much about their illnesses. People who believe that it is God's will that they be sick or that someone has put a curse on them may have a very difficult time getting well. The general way in which people interact with the environment also has a bearing on health. Those who try to alter the environment (say, by building solid, warm houses) may be able to live healthier lives, provided they do not go too far (say, by polluting the air).

The whole way in which an episode of illness is treated can vary tremendously among people in different places (see chapter 7 for more details on how people deal with illness in folk and popular cultures). When most Westerners become ill, depending on the type and severity of the illness, they do one or more of the following: take a medicine kept at home or bought at the drug store, consult a few friends or relatives, consult a doctor, or go to a hospital or clinic. In folk societies, a much wider range of people are usually involved at different stages of an illness. Certain important people (not only traditional healers) decide who is really sick, what the illness is, and what should be done about it. There may be a great deal of discussion about a serious illness. Treatment will include not only medicine (both traditional and Western), but also prayers, sacrifices, and purification rites.

We are coming to realize more and more that a country's political and economic systems play a crucial role in health care delivery. Consider the simple fact that the funds which national governments are willing to spend per capita on health care may range from around fifty cents to a thousand dollars per year. The proportion of the health budget spent on basic care for the entire population, as opposed to high-quality care for elites, is also important. Moreover, it is important *where* the money is spent. Is the government's policy one of trying to achieve regional equity, or will some areas (e.g., cities and towns or places where people are engaged in cash-crop agriculture or manufacturing) receive preferential treatment?

Another important political and economic question is who

controls health care resources and their accessibility. A strong central government may either try to provide equitable health care for all or pander to the elites that helped bring it to power. In a more decentralized political system, several different kinds of organizations may wield influence over health care matters. In many countries, professional associations such as the American Medical Association or herbalist associations put a great deal of pressure on the government to further their position and prestige. Consumer groups may try to generate grass-roots support for or against government legislation that is related to health (e.g., laws on drug abuse or abortion clinics).

Thinking in Systems Terms

How can an emphasis on health care delivery as part of a medical system be of value? Suppose one wishes to improve an existing system. The first response of many people would be to concentrate on the only element they perceive to be important: medical personnel, notably doctors. They would increase the number of physicians and/or improve their technical competence and then feel confident that the entire system would improve. When one considers the other elements just discussed, however, one might well begin to question whether such confidence is well founded. Has any attention been paid to the kinds of illnesses *most* people are going to have *most* of the time? Could most of these illnesses be prevented by nonphysicians? What are the characteristics of the people being served? Can they afford specialist care, for example? Why not focus on changing people's lifestyles, which are responsible for as much as 70 percent of all health problems? Which illnesses are linked to the man-made environment and which to the natural environment? Can any features of these environments be altered in some way in order to improve health? Would an educational campaign, aimed at dispelling a wide range of false ideas about illness, be more useful than the purchase of additional high-tech equipment for physicians? What political, economic, and social pressures might be brought to bear from outside the medical system in order to improve health? Of course, people do think about these questions. Perhaps if they thought more about the importance of all components and also about the myriad component interactions, they would begin to see that the focus needs to be shifted away from isolated components such as physicians.

To date, medical geographers who specialize in disease ecology have directed most of their research at illness, people, the environment, and the links between these components. In other words, they operate on a system basis, although they tend to neglect beliefs and context. Medical geographers who specialize in health care delivery appear to have used the systems approach less (or in a more restricted manner) in their work. Traditionally they have focused on resources and the resources-to-people link. It must be admitted that it is difficult to decide on the relative importance of different systems elements and links. It is also impossible to analyze more than a few elements and links in any one study. Still, it would seem that researchers interested in health care delivery would gain a much greater understanding of their area of concern if they expanded their thinking to include illness, the environment, beliefs, and all the links between these elements and people and resources.

In this chapter I may appear to have used a reductionist approach to describing medical systems. That is, I broke down these systems into component parts, each part having several characteristics, and then described those components and their links in some detail. This was done in order to expand our thinking about what really constitutes a medical system. The intent of the chapter, however, was actually to counter reductionist tendencies. The point is that the *interrelationships* among elements and the *context* of health care delivery are most important. We need to know something about the parts before we can see how the whole works, but the manner in which the whole works is of paramount interest.[5] There is an interesting analogy here with the two approaches to the workings of the universe that are currently being debated by physicists.[6] One group of physicists wants to build equipment such as the multibillion-dollar superconducting supercollider in order to break down matter into smaller and smaller particles. Others say that much more useful and elegant theories will come out of investigations into how the parts of the universe interact. They point out that the great advances in physics over the past century, by such geniuses as Werner Heisenberg and Albert Einstein, were of this type (and often were worked out on the backs of envelopes). Complex phenomena, they argue, obey laws of their own, which can not be discovered by examining individual elements.

3. Culture Regions

One of the earliest traditions in cultural geography was *areal differentiation,* or the division of geographic space into *regions* based on certain culture traits. Regionalization is the way in which geographers create spatial categories that divide up their subject matter, just as historians use time periods, sociologists discuss social classes, and political economists deal with different types of government. Cultural geographers have tried to differentiate culture traits on a variety of geographic levels. At the global level, for example, a textbook in introductory human or regional geography might identify a dozen culture realms, such as the Arab realm, which is concentrated in the Middle East and North Africa. There is a close connection between areal differentiation and systems analysis (chapter 2) because one often tries to place boundaries around a particular system or to regionalize one or more elements in a system. For example, one might try to map out the areas where Chinese medicine is predominant throughout the world, or one might try to regionalize the United States using physician-to-population ratios as a criterion.

During the 1960s and 1970s, the use of the regional concept of areal differentiation came under attack from some geographers who felt that it took too simplistic a view of cultural complexity and was not very informative.[1] It is true that simply dividing up space on the basis of one or two culture traits (say, religion or language) tells us very little about how that division came into being. Some regional studies did describe areas in great depth and synthesized the influence of several culture traits. However, it would be useful to know what forms of social organization, human behavior, or beliefs led to a particular spatial configuration of culture traits or complexes; this type of analysis has often been absent from regional studies.

Over the past several years, a "new" regional geography has begun to take root that attempts to answer the criticisms directed against areal differentiation.[2] The new regional geography is based on recent ideas in social geography (e.g., the importance of social relations, the interaction between human agency and societal structures) and cultural geography (e.g., the importance of place for individual or group identity, symbolic landscapes). It emphasizes the specificity of regions—the mosaic of cultural, social, political, economic, and historical factors that come together in unique patterns in particular places.

In this chapter, I will focus on the earlier, simpler ideas of regionalization; however, I will also emphasize the complexities and the difficulties associated with areal differentiation and will discuss some of the external factors that lead to regional patterns. The new regional geography will be taken into account in the last few chapters of the book, particularly in chapter 9 (on social space) and chapter 10 (on the importance of place and symbolic landscapes). The present chapter commences with a brief description of several major region-building concepts, including boundaries, criteria, overlap and conflict, pluralism, inequalities, and core and periphery. These ideas are then illustrated with several examples: medical pluralism in India, the delineation of hospital service areas, inequalities among health service regions, and traditional healers in Bangkok, Thailand.

Geographic Regions

A region should be a cohesive unit, with a number of more or less coinciding *boundaries* around it that are based on certain *criteria* such as natural features or cultural traits.[3] What sorts of criteria might be employed in order to regionalize health care? We might base our answer on the ideas generated in chapter 2. Thus, regional boundaries could be formed according to the various components of health care systems. A few examples will serve to illustrate this point. If one is trying to differentiate among population subgroups on the basis of their need for health care, one might use mortality or morbidity rates for certain diseases such as malaria or lung cancer as criteria. One might want to classify countries according to whether the predominant medical system is free enterprise, welfare state, or traditional. If one were interested in carrying out an educational campaign in a developing country, one might want to find out what people in different areas believe about disease etiology or about the relative efficacy of traditional medicine and biomedicine.

On reflection, one will see that regions based on culture traits usually have fuzzy boundaries, especially if those regions are based on more than one culture trait. It would be very difficult, for example, to draw boundaries around the "Spanish-speaking population" of the southwestern United States. In states such as Texas, Spanish- and English-speaking people are intermixed, many people are bilingual, and various words from each language are commonly used by people who speak mostly the other language. In the zones where *overlap* occurs, people will be exposed to more than one culture trait: this is termed *cultural pluralism*. Southern Texas clearly experiences linguistic pluralism. Overlapping culture zones have the potential to become areas of *conflict*. Again, southern Texas is an area where Anglos and Hispanics have experienced racial strife at times. To take another example, developing countries often have overlaps of indigenous cultures and one or more European cultures, imposed at the time of colonization. Friction is inevitable under such conditions. Medical pluralism of many types also exists. People in most countries of the world can choose from overlapping professional and traditional systems (see chapter 2). Practitioners in these systems often vie for patients and power; witness the struggle today between physicians and chiropractors in the United States.

Often, when one divides up an area into regions based on culture traits, one discovers that certain *inequalities* exist among regions. Some regions might have more services than others, or the people of one region might be pursuing activities that attract more wealth than the activities pursued in other regions. Inequalities among regions abound within health care systems. Resource-to-population ratios, funds available for prevention and treatment, and accessibility to care vary tremendously across space.

Another important feature of regions, related to inequality, is that often they can be divided (again, in a rather fuzzy way) into *core* and *periphery* areas. The culture traits used as criteria are often concentrated in one or more core areas (not necessarily near the region's center) and are diluted as one moves away from the core. To take one example, French speakers in Canada are concentrated in a core area of the Province of Quebec; other parts of Canada are peripheral in that they have smaller proportions of French speakers. One could cite numerous examples of core-periphery situations in health care. Studies of the use of health facilities, notably hospitals, often show that people who live close to them use them more often than those who live farther away. In developing countries, health services are typically concentrated very heavily in primate cities and other urban areas, while the countryside is generally underserved. It is obvious that intraregional inequalities will often exist between core and peripheral areas.

Medical Pluralism in India

When India is studied in world geography courses, emphasis is placed on the enormous variety of cultures that are intermingled there today.[4] Throughout its history, India has seen the birth of world religions (Hinduism and Buddhism), the development of elaborate social structures (the caste system), the building of architectural marvels (the Taj Mahal), and many other cultural phenomena. Some culture traits (e.g., the Muslim religion and the English language) have been brought to India over the centuries by invaders. India has absorbed or integrated most of these traits. The result is a crazy-quilt patchwork made up of local artifacts, mentifacts, and sociofacts. In *Midnight's Children* (1981), Salman Rushdie likens India to a disintegrating human body, torn by factions that often are cultural in origin.[5] But cultural pluralism can also be a sign of vibrant life.

Given India's cultural diversity, it comes as no surprise that a variety of medical systems have existed there in the past and overlap one another today. Three major traditional professional systems, Ayurveda, unani, and biomedicine, were described in the preceding chapter. Ayurvedic medicine originated in India around 2000 B.C. In recent decades it has enjoyed a revival, aided by the establishment of Ayurvedic colleges in several states. Unani, an offshoot of Greek medicine, was brought to India by Moslem conquerors several centuries ago. Europeans introduced biomedicine. Another system, homeopathy, has also had singular success in India. Homeopathy was developed in Germany at the end of the eighteenth century by a physician, Samuel Hahnemann. In contrast to biomedicine, which uses allopathic therapy (i.e., treats symptoms with "opposites"), homeopathy attempts to cure diseases with "likes" in extremely minute concentrations.

These four medical systems are mixed together in varying proportions throughout India, reflecting the cultural milieus that exist in different areas (see figure 2). Unani is relatively successful in the far north in Jammu and Kashmir, where the majority of the population is Muslim. Homeopathy is the choice of a good portion of the people in several northeastern states and in Tamil Nadu to the south. Ayurvedic medicine is prominent in Rajasthan (northwest) and Andhra Pradesh and Kerala (south). The proportion of biomedical practitioners varies greatly from state to state. In some areas, nonprofessional healers are relatively important. There is no doubt that it would be extremely difficult to delimit boundaries for these four medical systems; in fact, all of India is an overlap area for at least two major systems. Each system has core and peripheral zones. Homeopathy's core lies along the Indo-Gangetic plain in the northeast, for example. In local areas, various subcultural mixes are found. To take one example, Ayurvedic pratitioners in some places tend to

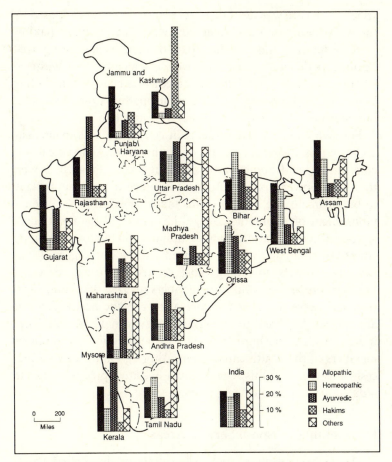

FIGURE 2. *Types of Medical Practitioners in Rural India, by State, 1963–64.*

SOURCE: S. M. Bhardwaj, "Medical Pluralism and Homeopathy: A Geographic Perspective," *Social Science and Medicine* 14, B (1980): 213. Reprinted by permission of Pergamon Press PLC.

follow their ancient traditions very strictly, whereas in other places they are eager to learn many biomedical practices.

When these medical systems came into contact with one another in India, conflict often resulted. The Westerners who brought biomedicine to India believed that their system was superior to the long-established indigenous systems. Western-style health care was just one of several culture traits imposed by the colonialists on India. Ayurvedic vaidyas and unanic hakims were denigrated and were not part of the officially recognized health care delivery system. It is well to remember that Westerners intruded with several different medical subcultures, including biomedicine, homeopathy, and naturopathy; practitioners of biomedicine attempted to suppress the latter two.

Following India's independence in 1947, there was an interesting change in the relative status of biomedicine, Ayurvedic medicine, unani, and homeopathy. Although the ruling elites who took over power from the British continued to grant supremacy to biomedicine, the other systems made some progress. The establishment of Ayurvedic colleges has already been mentioned. A resurgence of nationalism in India, as in many developing countries, brought with it a renewed interest in indigenous values and symbols, including those related to medical practice. Furthermore, some health care planners realized that biomedical resources were not nearly sufficient to provide health care for all, and so they tried to encourage vaidyas, hakims, and other indigenous and traditional healers to become more prominent members of the health care system. Although not nearly so successful as China in this regard, India has attempted to integrate indigenous and biomedical practice.

Determining Hospital Service Areas

Health care resources such as hospitals are distributed across space. Each hospital serves a population that lives in what is often called its service area.[6] It is useful to think of a service area as a culture region. Recall from chapter 2 that hospitals can be characterized as artifacts (they consist of buildings and equipment), sociofacts (they are important institutions), and mentifacts (they fit into systems of thought concerning how health care should be delivered). The character of a hospital's service area or culture region depends a great deal on the character of the hospital. The following hospital traits will serve as illustration: the quality of care provided (however measured), the equipment and physician specialties available, how active the hospital staff are in the community (e.g., in educating people about AIDS, drug abuse, or teenage pregnancy), where the hospital is in the service hierarchy, how payments are made for services, and whether minorities are welcome or not. In this section I will show how several of the ideas generated in the introductory section above can be used both to describe existing hospital regions and to show how plans for delineating new hospital service areas might be made.

Hospital regions can be set apart from one another by means of boundaries based on certain criteria; that is, one can regionalize this component of a health care system. How can one characterize hospital regions that already exist? One might, first of all, try to draw boundaries around them. But what criteria should one choose? Definitions for hospital service areas contain phrases such as "where most of the patient population resides." This seems reasonable since, conceivably, a patient might find it necessary to come to a hospital from halfway around the world. But what does "most" mean? Where does one draw the line? One could say, for example, that 90 percent is "most." This still would not enable us to draw a precise boundary. One could include all spatial units (census tracts, counties) in which at least 20 percent of the population visited the hospital over the past year, or one could determine that 90 percent of the hospital patients came from thirty miles or less and draw a circle with a thirty-mile radius around the hospital. These ways of drawing boundaries tell us very little about the service area as a culture region, however. One could learn much more, for example, if one could draw separate boundaries for blacks and whites or for people from low- and high-income areas.

There are many ways to characterize hospital service areas besides drawing geographic boundaries. Compare, for example, the "culture regions" that exist around three hypothetical urban hospitals (figure 3). One of these (A) is a prestigious private hospital in the central business district. It provides very high quality care and attracts relatively wealthy clients from revitalized or gentrified downtown residential areas, from the suburbs,

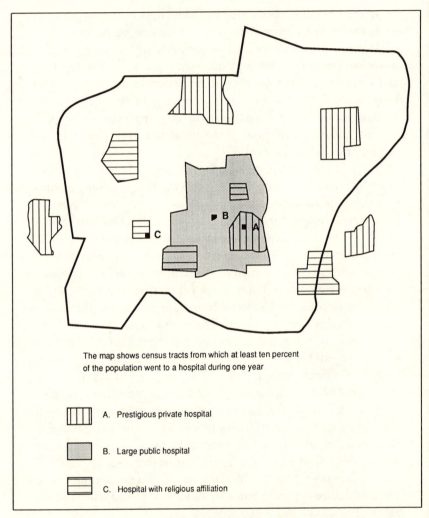

The map shows census tracts from which at least ten percent
of the population went to a hospital during one year

A. Prestigious private hospital

B. Large public hospital

C. Hospital with religious affiliation

FIGURE 3. *Hypothetical Map of Three Hospital Service Areas*

and from newly settled, rural nonfarm areas beyond the city
boundaries. The bulk of the poorer people living in the zone of
transition just outside the central business district cannot afford
hospital A's services, although some Medicare and Medicaid
patients are treated there. A large public hospital (*B*) is located
nearby. The poor flock to it, and the wealthier sort shun it

almost completely. The third hospital (C) is run by a charitable religious group. It treats people of all incomes, most of whom come from the immediate area, but it also tends to attract people of the same religious persuasion from other areas of the city who often bypass intervening hospitals to travel to this one. The extent of the service areas, their physical and man-made environments, and the composition of the client populations differ markedly for these three hospitals. The three hospitals and their patients, in other words, constitute very different culture regions.

If one were to draw boundaries around several hospitals in an area, one would expect to find overlap. This would be the case more often in urban than in rural areas. In fact, in rural areas, there could easily be gaps between hospital service areas; people living in these "gap zones" might very rarely go to any hospital. In urban areas, hospitals often compete for patients in zones of overlap.

The core-periphery concept clearly applies to hospital regions. Many studies show that "distance decay" operates in hospital utilization. That is to say, there is high use in a core area close to the hospital, but people living farther away travel to the hospital less often. The core area based on distance varies with several other factors, however, such as disease severity or the type of hospital facility being used (e.g., outpatient clinic versus emergency room). There are also factors that may override distance in determining core areas. Think of the private hospital described above: its "core" areas may be multiple and quite diffuse, stretching from the CBD through sections of the suburbs and out to clusters in the countryside.

Thus far, I have described hospital service areas as they usually are. But what if one could plan new areas from scratch? How might one proceed? What problems in existing regions might be solved? How might the different components of health care systems be used to regionalize?

One possible criterion is based on an attempt to provide various levels of hospital service to specific ranges of population size. In this scheme, practiced in countries such as Sweden, the largest hospitals with the greatest variety of services are set up to serve approximately one million people, the next largest to serve a quarter of a million people, and so on. Hospital boundaries are drawn around the appropriate populations. This approach to health care delivery is hierarchical and has been termed a spatial-functional system. Another type of criterion might be based on illness need. If data on morbidity levels throughout an area were available, a map showing core areas of need could be drawn and hospitals could be constructed in or near those areas. The boundary criterion could also be disease-categorical; that is, hospital zones could be set up to cover populations having specified health problems. This brings to mind the regional medical programs (RMPs) begun in the United States in 1965 to combat cancer, heart disease, and stroke. The program included schools and research units as well as hospitals, and the federal law which established RMPs stated that "appropriate" geographic areas be set up. Boundaries, however, were not clearly established. Some RMPs overlapped with other programs, which competed with the RMPs. Most had a large urban center at the core, and many rural areas were either peripheral or not covered at all.

Inequalities Among Health Service Regions

So far in this chapter, we have seen that practitioners from several competing medical systems are available in different proportions in different parts of India. Likewise, hospital zones differ in the quantity and quality of care they provide, in levels of need, in population characteristics, and in accessibility for various groups of patients. In this section, two specific health care systems are described, with an emphasis on unequal inter-regional components of health care.

There has been a great deal of interest in recent years in how various components of the U.S. biomedical system vary across small areas such as counties, townships, census tracts, or minor civil divisions. Often, service provision in these small areas does not correspond to the need for services. Vermont is one place in which this was found to be the case (1975).[7]

The population of Vermont was grouped into thirteen nonoverlapping hospital service areas, based on the state's 251 towns (its smallest administrative units). Towns were grouped according to which hospital was most frequently used. The kinds and levels of illness experienced by the population did not vary greatly throughout the state. Several aspects of medical care, however, did vary considerably across the thirteen hospital service areas. The number of beds per ten thousand people ranged from thirty-four to fifty-nine. Hospital expenditures per capita varied by a factor of two. Hospital discharge rates for all types of treatment (adjusted for age structure) ranged from 122 per thousand to 197 per thousand. The total surgery rate varied from 360 per ten thousand to 689 per ten thousand. Money spent on hospitals and doctors did not correspond to mortality levels across the thirteen hospital service areas.

What lies behind these inequalities in service provision across the state of Vermont? Although several small area studies have demonstrated that a wide variety of factors are important, results from the Vermont study suggested that the most significant is how physicians in different places practice medicine. Each hospital area has a distinct medical culture that is defined largely in terms of what MDs think and do about various illnesses. Physicians provided more services in areas with larger populations and higher incomes and fewer services among populations with large proportions of people over age sixty-five. In other words, physicians distributed themselves unequally. Doctors in some areas recommended or performed surgery for certain conditions far more often than doctors in other areas. Whether because of their medical training, or because of medical customs that have evolved over time in local areas, or for some other reason, physicians seem to develop local-practice cultures. Consumer behavior also varied considerably. Guided by their own attitudes or income levels, or influenced by doctors, consumers spent varying amounts of money on health care. Nonnatives used physician services twice as often as natives of similar age and income. The evidence from Vermont indicates that the health care system appears to be driven by demand for services rather than need.

Developing countries around the world are trying to solve their health care problems by providing primary health care to all their people. Primary health care is largely a response to the World Health Organization's call for "Health for All by the Year 2000." One goal of primary health care is to initiate programs for prevention and cure at the local, grass-roots level. The idea is that communities should assess their own needs and be instrumental in meeting them. Health problems, the resources to attack them, and many other components of health care systems will vary throughout developing countries. Inequalities, that is, will be evident. The following example demonstrates health care differences between two regions of Sierra Leone.[8]

One region consists of three chiefdoms centered around Makeni, the capital of the Northern Province (see figure 4). Kenema, the capital of the Eastern Province, is the focus of the two chiefdoms that are found in the second region. These areas represent two distinct subcultures within Sierra Leone. The people of Kenema are mostly Mende, and the people of Makeni are mostly Temne, although members of several other ethnic groups live in both areas. The Makeni area's chief agricultural products are groundnuts, tobacco, and cattle, whereas in the Kenema area palm kernels, coffee, and cocoa are most important. The people around Kenema came into contact with Europeans earlier; as a result, they modernized more quickly, have a stronger economy, and have more highly developed Western institutions such as schools.

A systems approach (see chapter 2) was used in the Sierra Leone study. Table 2 contrasts the two regions in terms of several important health system elements. The data are derived from a household survey of children younger than five and their parents in eight villages selected from each region. According to parental reports, children in the Makeni area had a higher incidence of illness. Kenema-area mothers were better educated. Yet, the Makeni parents seemed to have more modern beliefs about disease causation, even though their European contact came later. Kenema-area people had better houses, took their sick children to practitioners more often, and had better transportation available.

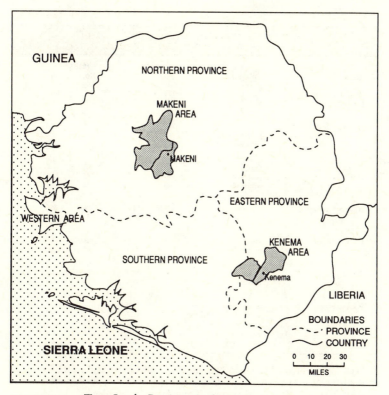

FIGURE 4. *Two Study Regions in Sierra Leone*
SOURCE: W. Gesler and G. Gage, "Health Care Delivery for Under Five Children in Rural Sierra Leone," in R. Akhtar, ed., *Health and Disease in Tropical Africa: Geographical and Medical Viewpoints* (Chur: Harwood Academic Publishers, 1987), p. 428. Reproduced by permission.

Although government and mission facilities were present at about the same levels in both areas, Makeni-area people used mission facilities more than Kenema-area people did.

Interactions among health system elements also differed between the two regions. In the Makeni region, for example, parents living in better houses (a sign of higher socioeconomic status) took their ill children to practitioners more often; this association was not found in the Kenema region. Kenema-area parents with more education traveled farther to visit practitioners; in Makeni, Temne as opposed to Loko parents traveled farther to care.

TABLE 2.

		Kenema		Makeni	
Element	Categories	No.	%	No.	%
Childhood illness	yes	178	52.4	224	61.4
(last two weeks)	no	162	47.6	141	38.6
Mother's education	none	265	77.9	335	91.8
	some primary	48	14.1	19	5.2
	some secondary	27	7.9	11	3.0
Beliefs about causes	God	72	23.2	65	20.8
of childhood diseases	poor health care	199	64.0	245	78.5
	witchcraft	40	12.9	2	0.6
House construction	wood/sticks/metal	234	68.8	293	80.5
	concrete	106	31.2	71	19.5
Use a health practitioner	yes	106	59.6	84	37.5
	no	72	40.4	140	62.5
Travel mode to	walking	61	53.0	73	79.4
health care	motorized	54	47.0	19	20.6
Practitioner type	native doctor	8	7.0	4	4.4
	government hospital	13	11.3	1	1.1
	government clinic	36	31.3	27	29.4
	mission facility	27	23.5	45	48.9
	other western	31	27.0	15	16.3

ELEMENTS OF HEALTH CARE DELIVERY SYSTEMS
IN TWO REGIONS OF SIERRA LEONE

SOURCE: W. Gesler and G. Gage, "Health Care Delivery for Under Five Children in Rural Sierra Leone," in R. Akhtar, ed., *Health and Disease in Tropical Africa: Geographical and Medical Viewpoints* (Chur: Harwood Academic Publishers, 1987), pp. 427–68. Reproduced by permission.

So, here again, within one country we have an example of very different medical cultures, as defined by frequency of illness, population characteristics, beliefs, physical environment, practitioner use, and barriers to care such as travel distance and treatment cost. Local communities face different problems and require different levels of resources to solve them. Health care planners should take such apparent inequalities into account.

Traditional Healers in Bangkok, Thailand

Thailand is located in Southeast Asia, a region that has been influenced throughout history by Chinese as well as Indian culture and, in modern times, by European culture. These three cultures lie behind the medical pluralism found in Bangkok, the capital city. Thai and Chinese traditional medicine and biomedicine overlap. Although the official medical system is dominated by biomedicine, traditional practitioners are an important part of the health care system. Most people use practitioners from different medical systems, depending on such things as the nature of their illnesses and their socioeconomic status. I will discuss Thai and Chinese medical practice in Bangkok in terms of culture regions and describe their principal components and spatial characteristics within the city.[9]

Traditional Thai medicine is an offshoot of Ayurvedic medicine and is thought to have been brought from India along with Buddhism. It is well integrated into Thai culture. Healers learn their medicine from elders in their family, become disciples of famous practitioners, or join traditional medical schools for training. Thai medicine has ties to religion: older practitioners often first studied to be monks, and some training schools are located on temple grounds. Most practitioners are generalists who use herbs to cure people; some may be classified as masseurs, magic doctors, spirit mediums, astrologers, or monk doctors.

Chinese traditional medicine was brought from China by migrants to Thailand many centuries ago. It is usually found in places where groups of Chinese have congregated. Like Thai medical practitioners, Chinese healers have an extensive pharmacopoeia. Some of them are specialists, such as bonesetters, eye doctors, acupuncturists, and hemorrhoid experts. Others are spirit mediums or astrologists, and some treat mental illness. Whereas Thai traditional healers can receive formal training in Thailand, Chinese practitioners must either learn by apprenticeship or study in China, Hong Kong, or Taiwan.

Thai as well as Chinese traditional healers are required to pass licensing exams to practice legally. It is known, however, that many of them have practices without being licensed. The Chinese are at a disadvantage because, in order to pass the exams, they need to acquire a considerable knowledge of the Thai language and Thai medicine. Neither traditional system comes into cultural conflict with modern medicine. At the same time, traditional medicine receives little government support, and very little effort has been made to integrate it with biomedicine (in contrast to the situation in China today). Thus, in their practices, Thai, Chinese, and biomedical practitioners maintain rather distinct culture regions. Spatially, they overlap a great deal and, as noted above, people use all three systems interchangeably.

Where are traditional healers to be found within Bangkok? Most are located near the center of the city in the commercial, densely populated, built-up areas. Forty percent have their clinics along major roads, 39 percent are located on side streets or smaller roads with through traffic, and the rest are in less accessible places. Compared with Thai healers, Chinese practitioners are more likely to be located along major roads. Very few practitioners have their clinics in the residential zones away from the city center. As one might expect, Chinese healers usually cluster in areas that are predominantly Chinese, whereas Thai practitioners are more dispersed but are rarely found in Chinese areas.

The geographical distributions of the four different types of traditional healers (Thai and Chinese herbalists and semi- or nonherbalists) can be distinguished by their locations and spatial extent. Thai herbalists are the most spread out across the city; they are found both in the inner city and in intermediate zones. Chinese herbalists are far more concentrated in the inner city area. Thai semi- or nonherbalists have a distribution similar to that of Thai herbalists but are more clustered downtown. Finally, the Chinese semi- or nonherbalists are also clustered downtown. Almost no practitioners had their clinics on the outer edges of the city. The city center is the core area of practitioner clinics; the intermediate and outer zones are peripheral.

The individual locations and group extent of practitioners provide a rough idea of their regions of potential influence within Bangkok. Note, however, that the actual influence of an individual practitioner might be quite extensive. The regions over which three practitioners actually had an influence, based on the addresses of their patients, have been investigated. Figure 5 shows the clinic locations of these healers (square, circle, and

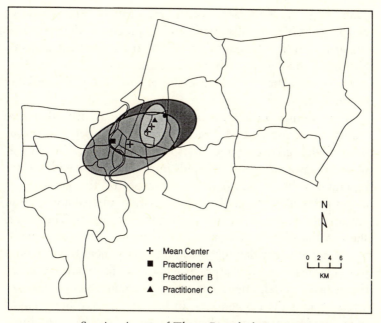

FIGURE 5. *Service Areas of Three Bangkok Practitioners*
SOURCE: B. Techatraisak and Wilbert M. Gesler, "Traditional Medicine in Bangkok, Thailand," *Geographical Review* 79 (1989): 180. Reprinted by permission of the American Geographical Society.

triangle); the ellipses indicate the main area of concentration of those patients who come from Bangkok itself (around 30 percent of each practitioner's patients come from outside the city). Practitioner A is a Thai semiherbalist who is sixty years old. Although he works full-time as a technician in a factory, he practices Thai medicine on Sundays, offers massages through hired masseurs on weekdays, and gives a daily radio broadcast on health that is beamed to the eastern region of Thailand. He clearly has the largest patient-origin region of the three healers, reflecting, perhaps, his use of mass communications. The mean center of his Bangkok patients is about two and a half miles (four kilometers) to the east of his clinic. Practitioner B, a middle-aged woman, is a Chinese semiherbalist who specializes in acupuncture. She was trained in a Chinese university and runs a full-time clinic. Her practice is also rather extensive, but, like practitioner A, she is not located very near the mean center of her patients. The most spatially limited practice is that of practitioner C, but her clinic is the closest to the bulk of her patients. She is a middle-aged Thai herbalist who runs a modern pharmacy. Her practice of Thai medicine is limited to three weekday afternoons.

If one thinks of the areas of patient origin as medical culture regions surrounding each practitioner, one can begin to speculate on what gives each region its unique character. The reputation of the practitioner is probably important; those with greater reputations (A, perhaps) might be expected to operate over larger areas. Practitioner B had successfully treated a marathon hiccup case and was written up in the newspapers. Thereafter, she was consulted for hiccups more frequently, her average number of patients per day increased, and her patient-origin region was enlarged. The type of practice may also be important; other things being equal, one might expect specialists to operate over larger regions than generalists. In our examples, other occupations besides health care clearly played a role. Also, the three healers treated different proportions of common illnesses such as influenza or pain in the limbs. Other factors that differentiate regions might include cultural congruence between the practitioner and his or her patients, ease of access to clinics by public transportation, and where people went as they carried out their daily activities.

The Regional Perspective

In this chapter, I have taken a rather unusual approach. Ordinarily, one thinks of medical systems or patient-origin zones as rather vague entities that occupy vaguely defined geographic spaces. When one begins to think of such spaces as culture regions, however, one can breathe new life and meaning into them. To start with, we are forced to consider which medical system components are important in which regions. How do the patient populations of two inner city hospitals differ? What sorts of diseases are treated by a Thai herbalist as opposed to a Chinese healer who specializes in acupuncture? What does treatment cost in two different parts of Sierra Leone?

Describing health care regions leads us to think of the criteria that might help to classify these regions in ways that would help us to understand them better. Several such criteria were discussed here: professional medical systems such as Ayurveda and biomedicine, individual healing practices, patient flows to hospitals, illness frequencies, and population size. Once useful regionalization criteria have been developed, one can attempt to establish boundaries between regions that are based on them. The examples given above show how difficult this is in practice. Where, for example, does a patient-origin region really end? Should administrative units or actual patient flows be used to delineate hospital regions?

No matter what criteria are employed, various types of overlap between regions are inevitable. In many cases, overlap causes few problems and in fact can often be viewed as beneficial in that it implies choices for the users of health care. As has been shown, multiple use of the resources offered in a pluralistic setting is widespread. People everywhere appear to be pragmatic; they choose the medical system, facility, or practitioner that they feel or have been told will suit their particular problem best. Furthermore, the choice of practitioner is usually not a question of "either/or" but, rather, one of "as well as." That is to say, people go to more than one healer within the same system and also patronize practitioners from different systems. Health care regions with different characteristics can also come into conflict in areas of overlap. If medical systems overlap, one of them often becomes dominant—as, for example, biomedicine is officially dominant in Bangkok today. When hospital service areas overlap, there may be competition for patients as well as wasteful duplication of services.

By rethinking health care regions as culture regions, one also finds it easier to discern inter- and intraregional inequalities. The case study of variation in physician practice styles in Vermont demonstrated inequalities between hospital service areas in a relatively small area. The example of India showed how the proportions of practitioners from several professional and traditional medical systems varied across an entire country. Intraregional inequalities were examined in terms of the core-periphery concept. We saw how traditional healers in Bangkok tended to cluster in the downtown area and to shun the intermediate and outer zones of the city. Most medical facilities have zones from which the majority of their patients come, depending on such factors as distance or socioeconomic status.

4. Cultural Ecology

C ultural geographers have defined cultural ecology in various ways, depending on which aspects of the subject they wish to emphasize.[1] In its simplest terms, cultural ecology studies the *interaction* between *human culture* and the *physical environment*. Medical geographers who have studied the spatial aspects of disease are very familiar with the basic ideas of cultural ecology. Often they study disease using a tripartite approach which includes population characteristics, characteristics of the physical environment, and human behavior. Medical geographers who have been most interested in health care delivery have been slower to take on the cultural ecology approach. In this chapter, I seek to help remedy that situation by pointing out how some concepts of cultural ecology are relevant to the study of health services. The first section describes aspects of culture and the environment that are pertinent to the study of health care and then goes on to a historical account of how environmental as well as cultural aspects of medicine have assumed various degrees of importance relative to one another in different societies. In another section, I will then discuss the process of medical adaptation to changes in culture and environment.

Culture and Environment

Culture, of course, has many aspects, which can be categorized in many different ways (see chapter 2 on culture systems). Here I will emphasize two principal characteristics of culture: *technol-*

ogy and *organization*. Technology refers to the techniques that humans employ to extract resources from the environment and to pursue cultural objectives. Organization refers to the ways in which humans form groups in order to carry out resource extraction and pursue cultural goals. Much of cultural ecology concerns itself with how human groups having different levels of technology and organization extract resources from the physical environment. Some cultural geographers think that the environment considered in culture-environment relationships should be extended to include the *built,* or *man-made, environment.* After all, people respond both to physical and built environments. I will emphasize the built over the physical environment, though, because it is often more germane to health care delivery. Inclusion of the built environment emphasizes the importance of interaction in the definition of cultural ecology, for technology and organization are employed to create that environment.

It is useful at this point to recall the systems approach used to analyze health care delivery in chapter 2. There I said that medical systems were composed of five important elements—illness, people, resources, environment, and beliefs—and that medical systems should also be seen in their societal context. In this chapter, as in chapter 2, the environment consists of the physical and the built environment. Note, however, that in this chapter the environment will also encompass illness. This is important because we need to discuss the application of technology and organization to health problems. Humans, interacting with the environment, act either to increase or to decrease health or disease. "Culture" (technology and organization), as the term is used here, is composed of the resources (especially the ways in which these resources are used), beliefs, and context (e.g., political and economic systems) noted in chapter 2. Thus, chapter 2 overlaps to some extent with the present chapter, but the approaches they take to health care delivery are quite different. Chapter 2 focuses on the usefulness of thinking in systems terms; it tends to give all elements and all links between them equal weight. In this chapter, I emphasize the interaction between the environment (including illness) and several system elements taken together as culture.

Determinism and Possibilism

The emphasis that various human groups throughout history have placed on either the environment or on culture in the culture-environment interaction has shifted back and forth to a remarkable degree. An almost total stress on the role of the environment is called *environmental determinism,* whereas an emphasis on the ability of people to control the environment through their culture (by way of technology and organization) is called *possibilism.*[2] Determinism dominated geography from the late eighteenth to the early twentieth century; it was promoted (in varying degrees) by such prominent geographers as Karl Ritter (1779–1859), Ellen Churchill Semple (1863–1932), and Ellsworth Huntingdon (1876–1947). Deterministic ideas, however, eventually gave way to a greater emphasis on possibilism. As science and technology advanced, people began to be more optimistic about the opportunities for altering the environment to their advantage. The geographers Paul Vidal de la Blache (1845–1918), Isaiah Bowman (1878–1950), and Carl Sauer (1889–1975) are counted among this new generation of possibilists. The tendency in the literature on cultural ecology has been to say that, as culture evolves (see chapter 5), there is a movement from a more deterministic to a more possibilistic perspective. Still, so-called primitive societies are recognized to have very sophisticated strategies for dealing with their environments, and modern societies often have little understanding of their physical (and man-made) environments, even though they feel that they can be controlled. One can find possibilist as well as determinist attitudes among people in most societies. Furthermore, over time, emphases on possibilism and determinism shift within socieites. Here I will provide a few examples of the two perspectives in the history of medicine.

Determinism in medicine can be traced back to the ancient Greeks. In fact, the body of medical knowledge that grew after the time of Hippocrates (460?–377? B.C.) was the main stimulus for early determinist theories. These theories can be divided into those based on physiology and those based on place (see chapter 10 for more on the importance of "place" in health matters).

The principal physiological idea was that health and disease depended on a proper balance of the four bodily "humors"— blood, phlegm, yellow bile, and black bile. The dominance of one or another of the humors was believed to depend on climatic influences. The theories based on place derive mainly from a book ascribed to Hippocrates entitled *On Airs, Waters, and Places,* which describes, among many other things, the good and bad qualities of air and water, the seasonal distribution of disease, how the cold-climate Scythians were often sterile but also strong and energetic, and how people who lived in rich, well-watered lands tended to be fleshy, lazy, and cowardly.

Despite their emphasis on determinism, however, the Hippocratic writings also point out many examples of the influence of culture on health. Sterility among the Scythians, for example, was said to be caused by riding horses as well as by the cold climate. Nor were the Greeks unaware of the health implications of other cultural elements: people domesticated plants and animals and cooked their food; and social institutions were at least partly responsible for their activities. The description in chapter 5 of the conflict between those in ancient Greece who favored either curative or preventive medicine also indicates that Greek medicine was not strictly deterministic.

The idea that the environment had a strong effect on health and disease persisted in the minds of laymen and physicians alike well into the nineteenth century. Many examples can be cited. Sir Thomas Elyot's book *Castel of Health* (1536) likened the body to a castle (see chapter 8 below for a discussion of how metaphors influence perceptions of health) besieged by external, environmental forces; and it advocated such health measures as access to clean water, fresh food, pure air, and the proper disposal of waste. Charles Ticknor, in *Philosophy of Living* (1836), praised the salubrious climate of North America and recommended it for invalids. Many diseases were linked (often with justification) to specific environmental conditions. It was commonly thought, for example, that malaria was caused by a "miasma," or bad air, that arose from swamps. In the late eighteenth and early nineteenth centuries, the Hippocratic ideal of living in harmony with nature was revived and the virtues of the noble savage were extolled. The public health movement of the nineteenth century, which lowered European death rates so dramatically, focused on cleaning up the environment.

Later in the nineteenth century, medical possibilism was given a tremendous boost by the discoveries collectively called germ theory. Now that the specific causes of infectious and contagious disease could be identified and their ecology described, hopes were raised for the control and perhaps total elimination of all disease. It was the mosquitoes that arose from the swamps, not a miasma, which carried the malarial agent; and mosquitoes or swamps could be eliminated (see chapter 10 for the effect of this discovery on colonial housing policy in West Africa). Instead of trying to live in harmony with the environment, people began to rely on scientific technology. Over the past century, biomedicine has made many successful attacks on disease. Indeed, one disease, smallpox, was eliminated from the earth by the World Health Organization.

It is not correct to say that biomedicine is entirely possibilistic, however. Although its proponents may feel that they are conquering the disease environment through undisputably advanced technology and organization, biomedicine nonetheless has a very strong deterministic side in that it focuses narrowly on biochemical and molecular data. It has often been accused of being reductionist, neglecting the broader medical systems and the sociocultural contexts whose comprehension is essential to the prevention and treatment of illness (see chapter 2).[3]

The two ideas about environment-culture interactions sometimes come into conflict and sometimes are blended together. Let us consider a study of physician beliefs about disease causation in North Carolina during the late nineteenth century.[4] Older physicians, who had absorbed deterministic ideas throughout long years of practice tended, naturally enough, to resist new ideas about germs. They raised such questions as why germs would discriminate among people. Younger doctors were more likely to embrace the new possibilist ideas about etiology and treatment. They wondered why people who lived in different environments sometimes had the same diseases. The annual meeting of the North Carolina State Medical Society in 1889 brought this conflict into the open. Quarrels broke out. Many older physicians, however, attempted to mix their determinist theories with the new ideas from germ theory. They accepted germs as disease agents, but they also continued to believe that miasmas, fermentations, and exhalations were causes of disease. Some physicians tried to demonstrate that components of local environments (e.g., soils, air, and forests) influenced the presence of germs. One physician thought, for example, that sandy soil and pine trees afforded protection against malarial and other disease agents.

What is the current assessment of the relative worth of possibilist and determinist ideas? Let us attempt to answer this question by setting out the principal advantages and disadvantages of each approach. Clearly there is a lot of truth in the claim that the environment affects health. Although Hippocrates and many others understood little about specific sources of disease, these early physicians were essentially correct in associating poor environmental quality with certain diseases and good environments with health. Today we still think that the physical environment can produce either disease or health, but we also place far more emphasis on the built environment. Over the past few decades, there has been a reaction against the "magic bullets" (drugs, vaccines, high-tech equipment) of biomedicine and a new awareness that the environment is strongly implicated in those diseases, such as cancers and heart problems, which are the principal killers in Western societies today. The disadvantage of the environmental approach is that it may fail to credit humans with the ability to modify their environments in order to make them more or less healthy. Determinism may lead to a kind of fatalism, to giving up in the face of what may seem to be odds that too heavily favor the environment. Determinism may also blind us to the fact that we are creating unhealthy environments. In contrast, possibilism provides hope that we can alter our surroundings and thereby live healthier lives. It focuses our attention on the social context of health and disease.

There are at least three noteworthy dangers in using an exclusively possibilistic paradigm, however. The first is that the environment may be ignored, and it clearly must not be; hence, the recent reaction to the magic bullets of biomedicine referred to above. Second, technology and organization may be focused too narrowly or in the wrong direction. Recognition of this disadvantage lies behind the current questioning of biomedicine's reductionist concern with narrowly biological factors, rather than with humans as social beings, and with treatment as opposed to prevention. A third problem associated with possibilism is that organization and technology often alter the environment in unforseen ways which are detrimental to health. Thus we have become familiar with the notion of *iatrogenic disease,* health problems that are caused by the medical providers and facilities themselves.[5] The environment of a hospital, for example, may be conducive to the spread of certain infectious diseases.

Given that possibilism and determinism both have good and bad implications for human health, our strategy obviously should be to formulate a workable blend of the two. One way to do this might be to invoke the notions of thesis, antithesis, and synthesis. The thesis of determinism inevitably, and in different periods of history, gave rise to its antithesis, possibilism, and vice versa. The synthesis of possibilism and determinism has been called *probabilism,* which states that the environment does influence human actions, that technology and organization can be applied to alter environments, and that knowledge of both the environment and culture is essential to understanding the interaction between them. In the following section, I will discuss these ideas in more detail.

Adaptation

Perhaps the most important aspect of cultural ecology is its examination of how culture-environment interactions lead to changes in physical as well as in built environments, in social institutions, and in human behavior. Both culture and the environment change constantly over space and time, and so both are constantly involved in processes of adaptation.[6] To cite just one example, humans have made great progress in adapting to life in large cities. Cities have become places where a tremendous variety of political-economic, artistic, and leisure activities are carried out. Sanitation, food supplies, pollution control, and health care delivery have vastly improved in many cities over the past few centuries. Yet, humans have also created many problems in cities (indeed, parts of some cities have become almost unlivable), so there is a continuing need for readjustment.

It is important to make a distinction between *biological* and *nonbiological* adaptation. Humans make successful biological adaptations to environments if they are able to occupy them, use their resources, and multiply their own numbers there. Biomedicine has been developed primarily to aid in biological adaptation. Thus, environments are cleared of the habitats of disease agents and vectors, the health of workers who extract resources from the environment is provided for, death rates are lowered, and infertility is treated. As I have emphasized throughout this book, however, humans are much more than biological entities, and their adaptive responses go far beyond the biological ones. Nonbiological responses arise from the ways in which humans organize themselves, their technology, their values, and their attitudes. Improved health owes more to such nonbiological adaptations as better diet, sanitation, and changes in lifestyle than it does to biomedical advances. Sometimes biological responses will lead to problems such as overpopulation or a society that is overburdened medically and economically by people whose lives have been prolonged. These problems require nonbiological solutions such as changes in attitude about having large families and difficult political decisions about which segments of the population should be given what sort of medical care.

One way to think of adaptation is as an attempt by humans to strike a *balance* between themselves and their environment by means of their culture. In terms of the systems discussion in chapter 2, this requires a manipulation of positive and negative feedback loops until a new position of equilibrium is reached. Suppose that we think of the balance of humans and environment in terms of the *carrying capacity* of a given environment—that is to say, what population density that environment will support without causing undue stress either to the population or to the environment. Carrying capacity will depend partly on the environment itself, but also on the technological and organizational skills possessed by the population. Hunting-and-gathering societies, which have relatively low levels of technology and organization, require a great deal of space to strike a successful balance. Societies that are more advanced in technology and organization can have very dense populations and yet maintain a balance with the environment.

In this chapter, we are concerned with how a balance of humans and environment can be achieved that will result in a healthy population. The kinds of adaptations people make in order to meet the challenges of their environment and improve their health depend to a large extent on their technological and organizational resources. One important implication of this statement is that each society must have an appropriate system of health care delivery that is suited to its own peculiar environmental challenge and cultural response. In this regard, simple societies can, in general, do less in the way of technology and organization than more advanced societies. Such peoples often survive because they have learned how to live in harmony with their environment. They have developed immunities to infectious agents and have acquired a knowledge of how to extract many curative agents from the environment. When people from less technologically advanced cultures are suddenly thrust into environments created by more modern peoples, their balance is upset, often with devastating effect. More technologically advanced societies have developed more sophisticated techniques and institutions for dealing with health problems. At the same time, modern societies are continually altering their environments (often to a more complex level), which, again, requires an adaptive response, an adjustment of various systems to new states of equilibrium. An extreme example of this is the prolonged period of weightless existence that is required for travel in outer space. Astronauts are trained to adapt biologically, socially, and psychologically to this extraterrestrial environment. Although many people still strive to live in harmony with nature, this utopian ideal is very difficult to achieve today because we are constantly tinkering with nature. Unfortunately, we can rely less and less on natural defense mechanisms against disease agents in the environment, and culture is called to the rescue more and more. The danger lies in the fact that cultural applications will almost certainly create further health problems.

With the help of several examples, let us now explore these ideas about cultural-environmental balance and the application of technology and organization to medical problems. As we shall see, human adaptations have had varying degrees of effectiveness.

Suppose, for purposes of illustration, that we compare technological and organizational responses to two different environments, those typically found in less-developed countries (LDCs) and those found in more-developed countries (MDCs). To be more specific, consider the treatment of cancer in Western and non-Western settings. Cancer environments will be quite different in terms of the proportion of the population at risk, perhaps the body sites involved, and the funds available for treatment (see chapter 2 on MDC and LDC differences in disease experience). Given the kinds of problems that predominate among MDC populations and given their level of wealth, it might be appropriate for them to spend a considerable portion of their health budget on expensive cancer treatments. One possible response to the cancer problem in an LDC would be to apply exactly the same kinds of technology and organization used in MDCs. A large hospital, equipped with very expensive radiation-therapy machinery, might be established in the capital city. This choice would benefit only a few people; it would be a poor response with respect to alleviating the cancer problem among the general population. It would also channel funds away from other health programs that could help far more people. A better response might involve adapting rather than adopting the MDC technology and organization. Perhaps far more could be done for more people and for less money if chemotherapy were emphasized rather than radiation therapy. Perhaps cancer treatment could then be provided in several small, more accessible hospitals scattered throughout the country.

The designation of diagnostic-related groups (DRGs) in the United States is an example of an organizational innovation that is an attempt to adapt to rising medical costs (part of the "context" environment). Under the DRG scheme, Medicare payments to hospitals are based on predetermined rates for each of 468 diagnosis-related categories of illness. The use of DRGs has been the subject of a great amount of controversy, and their effectiveness is continually being assessed.[7]

The AIDS epidemic clearly calls for organizational changes, but it is sometimes difficult to know what these changes should be. Here we would have to include value-laden judgments under "organization" or "context." For example, should intravenous drug users be supplied with clean needles in an attempt to stop the spread of AIDS? Should the Food and Drug Administration (FDA) relax its usual thorough, controlled clinical trials and approve the use of a drug that might alleviate the suffering of AIDS patients or that might inhibit the spread of the AIDS virus?

The recent history of biomedicine has proved over and over again the efficacy of technological solutions for enabling people to improve their health. Western antibiotics, anesthetics, and other pharmaceutical products, not to mention sophisticated surgical procedures, are examples. Cultural ecologists, however, are aware of the dangers of such technological fixes. Health care innovations often carry with them hidden problems. Chemotherapy, for example, almost inevitably has side effects and may sometimes prolong suffering unnecessarily.

Technological and organizational responses to health care situations often interact with one another. Thus, the development of drugs that alleviate many mental illnesses has enabled many patients to be deinstitutionalized (see chapter 11 on the difficulties brought about by deinstitutionalization). Modern life, which involves industrial pollution (evidence of technological as well as organizational change) has led to new laws such as (in the United States) the Clean Air Act (1970), which in turn forced industries to make technological changes (pollution controls) and organizational changes (e.g., ways of passing control costs on to consumers).

It would be interesting to document how the different types of systems discussed in chapter 2 (traditional professional, traditional nonprofessional, and biomedical) have adapted to various environments in different places at different times. I have already given an example (cancer treatment) of the sort of difficulty biomedicine may have in adapting to non-Western environments. Nonetheless, people in many developing areas who have been exposed to Western medicine have come to place their faith in biomedical cures. In addition, governments often encourage the development of biomedical health care delivery. Some practitioners in traditional professional systems are trying to adapt to this situation by adopting some biomedical techniques and by organizing themselves into groups for greater political influence. They appear to be more successful than many traditional nonprofessional healers, who may not be as adept at adapting to the changing perceptions of their patients and to changing political realities.

The preceding discussion of different environments, technologies, and ways of organizing suggests that the cultural-environmental health interaction is a *dynamic* process. That is to say, it is not enough simply to achieve a healthy balance between people and their environment and then expect this equilibrium to remain for very long. For technological and organizational solutions to changes in the environment lead to further changes. Thus, the cultural-environmental interaction becomes an endless, circular process of alternating challenge and response. Medical systems, like cultural and social systems, change over time; they evolve (see chapter 5). Environmental changes are often very rapid, especially in modern societies. We often have the helpless feeling that we are losing control of the environment. Health care delivery systems must be flexible enough to respond quickly; disease is often a result of adaptations that did not take place rapidly enough.

Complete adaptation is impossible, a utopia that will never be reached. Indeed, if a society should somehow lull itself into thinking that it has, through its organization and technology, made an adaptation that will be the final solution to a health problem, that society will almost inevitably suffer a devastating blow at some time in the future. When the new changes in the environment are felt, the adaptive capability of the society may well have been lost. For humans survive only when challenged. A person who is constantly shielded from environmental insults never builds up the resistance to counteract environmental challenges.

Ecology and the Distribution of Physicians

When medical geographers and other social scientists attempt to explain the distribution of doctors, which varies considerably across space, they usually focus on macro models in which large areas such as states or provinces are the units of analysis and in which explanatory variables are regressed on physician-to-population ratios.[8] An approach that is more in line with the themes of this chapter was taken in a study of the distribution of physicians across the counties of New York State.[9] In that investigation, populations of physicians were taken as the units of analysis, and their environments were examined in order to determine the effect of environment on either the growth or decline of physician populations.

The model used in this study had its origins in the well-known work of Charles Darwin and Alfred Russel Wallace and is termed *environmental selection*. It proceeds in three stages. First, there is variation in organisms. In the case of physicians, new specialties or different forms of health care (e.g., nurse practitioners) are created. Next, the environment "selects" some variations over others. Some physicians are better suited for specific localities than others. In order to survive, physicians may move, retire early, or change specialties. Third, there is a retention mechanism which acts to maintain a positively selected organism in the environment. Physicians who fit certain environments remain there or are replaced (reproduced) with people who possess similar qualifications.

Again, the environmental selection process involves continual movement from equilibrium to equilibrium as environmental factors change over time. The equilibrium concept used in the New York State study was carrying capacity, defined as "the size of the population of physicians that a region would eventually support, given enough time with no changes in the environment."[10] Since the environment does change, however, the *rate of response* to disequilibrium was also measured.

At the heart of the study was the identification of environmental factors that might be related to the second stage of the environmental selection process. These factors included (1) the quantity of resources (primarily paying patients, but also office space and hospital facilities); (2) environmental stability, or the turnover of elements in the environment (e.g., patient mobility, change in the socioeconomic status of an area); (3) environmental homogeneity, or the amount of similarity between elements (e.g., a community of elderly persons versus a more typical residential area); (4) environmental concentration, or the geographic concentration of various resources such as patients; (5) domain consensus, or the amount of cooperation among health care providers; (6) environmental turbulence, or the amount of interaction among elements in the environment; (7) environmental growth/decline, or the change in resources such as patients; (8) environmental density, or the average concentration of resources in an area as compared with other areas; and (9) system development, or the improvement of such things as facilities, laboratory services, and referral systems.

Physician distribution studies often distinguish between specialists and general practitioners. For example, it has been shown that specialist-to-population ratios tend to increase as a region becomes more metropolitan (and as population density increases), whereas the opposite is true for general-practitioner-to-population ratios. The environmental selection model states that general practitioners and specialists will tend to be successful, or prove their "fitness," in certain environments. In general, specialists should thrive in environments with many resources, high growth, or high density, whereas general practitioners should survive better in environments that are not so well endowed. Specialists cannot respond to changes in carrying capacity as well as general practitioners can and are less able to move successfully out of a formerly nourishing environment.

The foregoing ideas led researchers to a set of hypotheses (e.g., that carrying capacity increases with population size; that the response rate of specialists to deviations from carrying capacity is slower than that for general practitioners) which they examined using pooled cross-sectional and time-series data for New York State counties. The statistical procedures used need not concern us here. What is important to note is that the study tested empirically some primary ecological notions. Only a limited number of factors associated with physician populations and environments (quantity of resources, population growth and density, and system development) were actually tested, however, having been chosen because the data (annual estimates of the numbers of physicians in office-based patient-care practice by specialty, size of county, and annual census estimates of population) were easily available and because these factors had been thoroughly discussed in the literature. Similar models, it is hoped, will be tested using other aspects of the environment, especially those which involve cultural elements such as attitudes toward physicians. Obviously, the data for these types of studies are more difficult to obtain; perhaps they should be carried out in smaller areas. Also, some models that take more aspects of the environment into account might not lend themselves to sophisticated statistical treatment. On the other hand, they might yield very valuable information about physician distributions.

Using Cultural Ecology

In this chapter, I have tried to demonstrate how the concept of interaction between human culture (measured by technology and organization) and the physical and man-made environments can be applied to the study of health care delivery systems. Different aspects of this interaction have been emphasized or studied in the past. Biomedical practitioners often stress improvements in technology. Social scientists, including medical geographers,

have made significant contributions to the study of the organization (e.g., spatial, functional) of delivery systems. What is often
lacking, though, is an appreciation of the role the environment
plays and of the dynamic link between cultural and environmental factors. Part of the problem lies in the difficulty of studying
more than one or two aspects of a dynamic relationship. But if
one does not keep the entire relationship in mind, one fails to
understand fully the significance of one's findings about any part
of that relationship.

This chapter has suggested two ways in which the concept of an
cultural-environmental relationship might be used to understand
the ways in which health care delivery systems operate. The first
way was to ascertain the relative influence of culture and environment in any particular system. Emphasis on environment (determinism) or on culture (possibilism) has shifted back and forth
among different societies at different times throughout history.
Each emphasis has its advantages and disadvantages. Thus, a
balance—one that reflects local cultures and environments—
should be struck between these emphases. Local situations, then,
can be assessed within the cultural ecology framework and adjustments made accordingly.

The second approach was to examine how well the system is
adapting over time to new environments. Here again it is necessary to strike a proper balance between culture and environment, but one also has to think about how a system responds
culturally to changes within the environment in order to reach a
new balance. One must remember that there are both biological
and nonbiological adaptations to consider. I also discussed how
changes in environment, technology, or organization can affect
the adaptations that should be made. All these ideas can usefully
be applied to a wide range of health care delivery systems
throughout the world.

5. Cultural Evolution

Most studies of culture examine various culture traits at one point in time. Yet, even though culture is essentially conservative, it does change over the years. The study of such change, or cultural evolution, is closely allied to the subject of the preceding chapter, cultural ecology. As medical systems and their contexts evolve, environmental and cultural interactions undergo change, and adaptations are continually required. Cultural-environmental interactions and adaptations, in turn, are fundamental reasons for medical evolution. Let us begin our study of cultural evolution with some basic definitions, illustrated by a brief survey of stages in human evolution. Medical examples of evolution include the history of biomedicine, changing doctor-patient relationships in the United States, recent changes in U.S. health care delivery, and a study of the tracing and treatment of cancer in China.

Basic Concepts

There are many approaches that one can take in the study of cultural evolution.[1] To begin with, one can deal with change over vastly different *time scales*. Contrast, for example, the thousands of years it took to develop rotary-motion technology (from the invention of the wheel to the complex gear systems of modern lathes) with the short time—just one human generation—it took to produce several "generations" of computers.

One can also distinguish between changes that occur in *small increments* (modifications in pottery design might be an example) and changes that are *revolutionary* (say, twentieth-century changes in the U.S. family system). This distinction is a rather fuzzy one, however, because it depends a great deal on one's perspective in time. From today's perspective, changes in rotary-motion technology appear to be very slow and incremental, but there were "revolutionary" discoveries along the way (e.g., the shift from the solid to the spoked wheel used for transportation). Another good example is the first agricultural revolution, also known as the Neolithic revolution. The move for some societies from a hunting-and-gathering existence to settled agriculture is certainly a landmark "event" in human history, one with tremendous consequences, but it took place over hundreds of years.

When many people talk about evolutionary change, there seems to be an implication that change brings *advancement* of some sort—a better way of life, more sophisticated ways of doing things. If a society fails to adopt an innovation (especially when we feel that it would benefit them to do so), we call this a *cultural lag,* implying some sort of failure. What is often forgotten, however, is that new technologies and ways of organizing ourselves usually carry with them a new set of problems. The potential hazards of the toxic wastes generated by modern industry is a salient example. Furthermore, change is usually accompanied by, and often caused by, *conflict* and *stress.* Old ways do not give way to new ones easily; at least some members of any society undergoing change will suffer. Thus, wealthy, educated elites in developing countries might well benefit from rapid industrialization, but the move toward a more modern economy might also be extremely disruptive to the majority of the population. Chapter 9, on social space, further explores the idea of conflict.

Akin to the notion of cultural advancement or progress is the idea that culture *accumulates*—that artifacts, sociofacts, and mentifacts (see chapter 2) build upon one another. This was the basic idea behind James Burke's intellectually stimulating television series *Connections,* in which he showed, for example, how the motion-picture projector was built on inventions as disparate as the theater limelight (leading to the very bright light required), billiard balls (leading eventually to Celluloid film), and "magic lantern" shows (a step on the way to simulated motion). We might perceive cultural accumulation as providing more choices and (perhaps) better ideas as a result; the downside may be the accumulation of unnecessary cultural baggage. We certainly welcome, for example, the wide variety of foods available in the supermarket; we benefit from the worldwide exchange of food plants and recipes for delicious dishes from many lands. On the other hand, many of us are tempted by the variety of food choices and current fads to overindulge in meals that have relatively little nutritional value. In some societies, overnutrition and improper nutrition can be as serious as undernutrition.

Let us fix some of the preceding ideas with an example that relates to long-term cultural changes during human evolution.[2] This progression can be outlined in five stages: (1) *primitive* hunter-gatherer societies; (2) *archaic* societies which practice subsistence agriculture; (3) *historic* societies arising out of the world's great religions; (4) *early-modern* societies whose origins lie in Europe's rise to power; and (5) *modern* societies, which are characterized as secular, industrialized, and bureaucratic. In very general terms, there has been an evolution from one stage to the other over thousands of years. Note, however, that no value judgments are made about which stage is "better." Each stage still finds living representatives somewhere in the world today. Some of these societies are making revolutionary changes from one stage to the next and might even be jumping over intermediate stages. A group of Amazonian Indians, for example, may reluctantly be dragged into modern Brazil. The conflicts and stresses of that situation are obvious.

We can trace various culture traits from stage to stage and make some generalizations. Social mobility tends to increase, as does specialization of tasks. Societal organization tends to proceed from an emphasis on kinship (stage 1) to kingship (stage 2), from status hierarchies such as the Hindu caste system (stage 3) to nation-states with all their institutions (stage 4), and thence to all the complex arrangements of modern times (stage 5). Are these changes for the better or for the worse? Sound judgments are difficult to make as situations vary markedly among groups in different places.

Most people would automatically see progress in this chain of stages. Surely one would prefer to live with modern conveniences rather than face nature in the raw in the Kalahari Desert. This is a matter of cultural perspective, of course; we prefer what we are used to. There is no doubt that the African who practices slash-and-burn agriculture could benefit from better cropping methods and fertilizers, especially if the carrying capacity of the land has been exceeded. On the other hand, an intimate knowledge of local climate and soils is often beyond the grasp of agricultural "experts" from developed countries. In other words, as culture changes, there are gains as well as losses. In addition, it is not strictly correct to claim that complexity always increases for all culture traits as one moves from stage to stage. The complexity of many technologies obviously increases, but people living at the "primitive" stage have been shown, for example, to have very complex religious systems and beliefs.

The History of Biomedicine

The history of the world's major professional medical systems—Chinese, Ayurvedic, Galenic, unanic, and biomedical (see chapter 2 for brief descriptions)—contains numerous instances of the foregoing ideas concerning cultural evolution. I will discuss biomedicine here, as it is the one most familiar to Western, English-speaking readers.[3]

Like many other sciences, biomedicine traces its roots back to the time when there was a flowering of culture among the Greeks, several centuries before the birth of Christ. Hippocrates (460?–377? B.C.), a physician and scholar, is considered to be the founder of modern medicine, although Greeks before him (and, we may assume, members of all societies throughout human history) attempted to heal. One of the books attributed to Hippocrates, *On Airs, Waters, and Places,* emphasized the effects of climate on various cities and countries of Europe and

Asia, but it also made clear that the effects of climate could be changed by social institutions (see chapter 4 for more on the roles of environment and culture in Greek medical thought). Many environmental determinists in later times ignored this latter notion. One of the foundations of Hippocratic thought was that the body had four humors—blood, phlegm, yellow bile, and black bile. A healthy person maintained a proper balance of these humors, which originated from four parts of the body and were associated with the four basic elements (see figure 6).

For several hundred years after the time of Hippocrates, various schools of medical thought vied for dominance among the Greeks and Romans. The followers of Hippocrates, the Dogma-

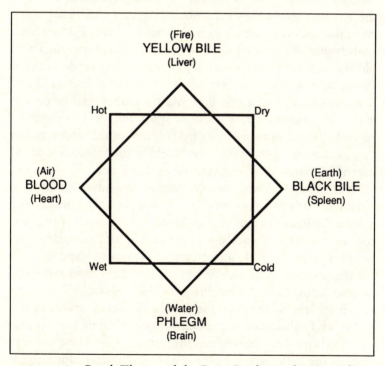

FIGURE 6. *Greek Theory of the Four Qualities, the Four Elements, and the Four Humors*

SOURCE: E. H. Ackerknecht, *A Short History of Medicine*, rev. ed. (Baltimore: The Johns Hopkins University Press, 1982), p. 53. Reproduced by permission.

tists, and the school of Herophilus were all humoralists, whereas the followers of Erasistratus and the Methodists, Empiricists, and Pneumatists were nonhumoralists. This is an early instance of conflict within the evolution of medical concepts. It was not until Galen of Pergamon (A.D. 130–201) that the humoral theory regained undisputed sway, a dominance that was kept alive in Galenic medicine for another fifteen hundred years. During this relatively long period within the history of medicine, rather little progress was made. Much of the medical work by the monks and Scholastics of the Middle Ages consisted of compilations and interpretations of the classical texts.

Although even during the Middle Ages there were incremental changes in such fields as anatomy and surgery, it was not until the Renaissance, which marked the beginning of modern science, that medicine began to make rapid strides. The sixteenth century was again a time of conflict as new discoveries vied with old stagnant ideas. For example, Pierre Brissot (1478–1522) of Paris criticized the Arab methods of bloodletting; for this he was considered a worse heretic than Martin Luther, and he died in exile. Nevertheless, a new scientific spirit, nurtured by discoveries and changes in many other fields (think of the discoveries of new medicinal plants in the New World or the anatomical drawings of Leonardo da Vinci) spurred medicine on.

Over the next few centuries, biomedicine advanced rapidly, although many errors remained and new ones were made. The Belgian Andreas Vesalius (1514–64) and others made great progress in anatomy. Paracelsus (1493–1541) of Switzerland revolted against bookish medicine and advocated experience as the true teacher. Although he practiced alchemy and astrology, he also made advances in chemistry that initiated the modern search for specific remedies for disease. William Harvey (1578–1657), an Englishman, is credited with establishing the fact that the blood circulates throughout the human body. These are only three of the better-known people who made significant medical contributions; hundreds of others were involved as well. Advances came through observations drawn from numerous experiments combined with insightful discoveries. Thus the Frenchman Antoine-Laurent Lavoisier (1743–94), who first explained the workings of respiration, built on the work of several men who experimented with various gases: Joseph Black of Scotland (1757, carbon dioxide); Henry Cavendish of England (1766, hydrogen); David Rutherford of Britain (1772, nitrogen); and Joseph Priestly of England (1774, oxygen).

The culmination of medical progress since the Renaissance came toward the end of the nineteenth century, when several important discoveries were made in bacteriology. It is interesting to learn that a theory that epidemic diseases were transmitted by contagion and were caused by microorganisms had been put forward in the sixteenth century by Fracastorius of Verona. Support for the idea waxed and waned and, in fact, was thought by most medical people in the mid-nineteenth century to be erroneous. The anticontagionists of the period felt that they had the upper hand because quarantines had proved to be ineffective against such diseases as yellow fever, typhus, and cholera. The contagion-anticontagion conflict is another fascinating chapter in the evolution of medicine.

The late-nineteenth-century discoveries that collectively led to germ theory are very well known. Experiments by Louis Pasteur (1822–95) of France showed that the theory that bacteria originated directly from lifeless matter ("spontaneous generation") was false. He discovered what caused anthrax and chicken cholera, and he developed preventive vaccinations for these diseases as well as for rabies. In Germany, Robert Koch (1842–1910) identified the organisms involved in tuberculosis and wound infections. Between 1875 and 1905, several more agents of contagious disease were found. During this same period, disease ecology made great strides when it became known that vectors (e.g., mosquitoes and tsetse flies) carried specific disease agents (e.g., malarial protozoa and the protozoa that cause trypanosomiasis, or sleeping sickness).

Advances in all the various branches of medicine (surgery, gynecology, and mental health, to name only a few) continued into the twentieth century. The discovery of the antibiotic penicillin is just one of many interesting new finds. Before 1929, it had seemed impossible to produce an effective antibacterial drug. The ability of certain molds to kill bacteria, however, had been known since the 1870s. Many attempts had been made to derive drugs from molds, but were given up for lack of funds or sufficiently promising results. In 1929 Sir Alexander Fleming (1881–1955) made a chance discovery. He was experimenting with a culture plate of staphylococcus bacteria that somehow became contaminated with spores of *Penicillium notatum,* a mold. The bacteria colonies began to undergo dissolution, and the mold was found to be destructive of bacteria but nontoxic to human cells. Although Fleming usually receives credit for penicillin's discovery, it was the work of Howard Florey, Ernst Chain, and others at Oxford University, starting in 1939, that revived the old attempts to manufacture antibiotics.

Thus far, mention has been made of several medical conflicts that took place in history: humoral versus nonhumoral medicine, contagion versus anticontagion, and post-Renaissance versus pre-Renaissance ideas. Another conflict of great importance predates Hippocrates. René Dubos characterizes this conflict as a debate between the followers of Hygeia and Asclepius. Hygeia, a Greek goddess, was the guardian of the health of Athens.[4] She was not involved in the treatment of illness; rather, she symbolized the idea that people could live well by using their reason. Living wisely, though, is not easy for humans, and after the fifth century B.C. Hygeia's importance gradually gave way to that of Asclepius, the god of healing, whose origins are earlier than those of Hygeia. Followers of Asclepius emphasized the use of the scalpel and medicinal plants to treat illness.

It is probably obvious what these mythical Greek deities symbolize today. Asclepius is the patron of curative medicine, the main concern of the modern physician. Hygeia is associated with prevention and the modern public health movement. Down through the ages, she has competed with Asclepius for the attention of medical practitioners and of the population at large. Which deity should assume the greater importance is still a matter of contention throughout the world.

Changing Doctor-Patient Relationships in Urban North America

When I lived in a medium-size town in the late 1940s, my bouts with flu, scarlet fever, and other childhood diseases were seen to by "old Dr. Blackburn," who lived just two blocks down the street. The ubiquitous family doctor whose office (often home, too) was within walking distance was a common feature of the urban landscape in the earlier part of this century. That sort of relationship between patient and practitioner has changed radically over the past several decades, of course. A more familiar sight today is a group practice consisting of various specialists, located in an office complex within a suburban mall. What prompted this evolution in the relative spatial location of people and their doctors? Is the relationship better or worse now than it was in the "good old days"?[5]

There are no simple answers to these questions, because, as I emphasized in chapter 2, medicine must be seen in its broad societal context. In particular, several economic, social, political, and spatial factors have interacted to produce changes in the spatial structure of U.S. cities. Researchers have traced the origins of some of these changes to around 1870.[6] In the economic sphere, U.S. society experienced a heightened division of labor. People, including doctors, tended to become more specialized. Over time, the proportion of general practitioners declined and the proportion of specialists increased in a wide variety of medical fields. This trend was closely tied to the proliferation of hospitals; naturally, specialists often located their offices either in or close to the hospitals where they spent so much of their time. Large hospitals were often located in downtown areas, near the commercial centers, although smaller units were also constructed in the suburbs. Medical costs rose sharply as the price of new technologies increased and as consumer demand rose.

U.S. social structure has also changed considerably over the past century. During this time, the middle class expanded, there was increased social stratification into economic and ethnic groups, and personal social interaction became less frequent. The poor, at least until the advent of Medicare in the 1960s, were grossly disadvantaged in terms of access to care. Even though they often lived near large hospitals, they might be denied entry because of the expense involved or because of prejudice; the number of "charity cases" a hospital would accept was limited. Free dispensaries, once a resource for the indigent, were eliminated, partly—it was claimed—because they were "demoralizing." There was also a change in family structure, with the extended family being replaced by the nuclear family as the basic unit. But the nuclear family was less able to cope with the health problems of its members. In addition, the tertiary or service sector, which includes health care, expanded.

Several important developments also occurred in the realm of political and social policy. Around the turn of the century, medical diploma mills were turning out many doctors with dubious qualifications, and the laissez-faire atmosphere of the day allowed many unorthodox, alternative practitioners such as chiropractors and naturopaths to flourish. The medical profession reacted by raising its standards and became both more professional in outlook and more politicized. Unorthodox practitioners were eliminated whenever possible by such measures as strict state-licensing laws. As physicians organized, they enjoyed collective upward social mobility and a consequent rise in prestige. To maintain their new standing, they acquired well-furnished offices, usually separate from their homes. They also began to accumulate expensive equipment and to hire secretaries and attendants. All these changes raised fees-for-service significantly. At the same time, the output of doctors was controlled during a time of increasing demand for services, so that certain segments of the urban population—notably, those living in the poorer sections of the city—were underserved. Furthermore, paramedical personnel such as nurses and midwives and public health professionals were making many of the skills of the general practitioner obsolete.

Important changes also took place with respect to how people moved about the cities to carry out their daily activities. Home and workplace became separated for more and more people as production shifted from home manufacture to large-scale factory manufacture. There was increasing residential mobility; as cities expanded, people at the middle- and upper-income levels moved to the suburbs and beyond. They were followed by a segment of the physician population. All this increased mobility was made much easier by a series of transportation innovations. Walking gave way, in succession, to riding the streetcar, traveling by automobile, and using rapid-transit subway and bus systems. Despite traffic congestion, millions of city dwellers were transported across cities to work, shopping, leisure activities, and health care.

It now becomes clear why the old family doctor no longer lives just down the street. The settings for health care have changed, and the relative locations of patients and practitioners have changed. Is this a good or a bad thing? On the negative side, we feel the loss of the knowledge that the general practitioner had about the entire family and community situation. We miss the intimacy of the doctor's house calls or walking those few blocks to wait in a simply furnished but cosy office. We deplore the high costs of medical care and worry about how accessible health care is to those with no health insurance or the necessary information about what public services are available.

Change also had a positive impact on the patient-practitioner relationship. Although most people became more separated spatially from health care resources, temporal separation did not change so much (and may even have decreased for many), given the increased mobility of urban populations and the fact that a health care visit can often be made part of a multipurpose outing. Seen in this light, the location of physician office complexes in such places as shopping malls seems to make sense. There is no doubt that we benefit from specialist care, provided we can afford it or have appropriate health insurance. We also have reason to be more confident in modern cures than in the remedies the family doctor of old could provide.

Recent Changes in U.S. Health Care Delivery

Compared with the history of biomedicine, and even to the urban transition covered in the preceding section, this discussion will deal with a rather short time span: the past three or four decades.[7] Our society seems to have a predilection for thinking in crisis terms; and when talk turns to the health care situation in the United States, one often hears of a need for "revolutionary" change in the system. It does seem that there has been a revolution of sorts in recent years which has brought about several important changes in the way people receive health care—and those changes have been set in motion, in large part, because of criticisms made of the biomedical system. Since the development of germ theory at the end of the nineteenth century, biomedicine (as noted above) has made tremendous progress in many areas. Sophisticated diagnostic equipment, better surgical techniques, and improved methods of physical therapy are just three of the rapidly accumulating medical tools and practices. Many people have felt, however, that biomedicine has also been picking up some undesirable traits. I will discuss three of these, together with some of the attempts made to correct contemporary health care problems.

One of the oft-repeated criticisms of the medical system in the United States from the 1940s through the 1960s was that too many citizens had very poor access to health care. Studies showed that resources such as physicians and hospital beds were very unevenly distributed across geographic areas and among groups of people with different income levels or from different ethnic backgrounds. Part of the official reaction to poor accessibility was the passage of several laws at the federal level. The Hill-Burton Act of 1946 attempted to distribute hospital beds more equitably. In the mid-1960s, Medicare for the elderly and Medicaid for the indigent represented a massive federal intervention into health affairs. These and other laws did not solve the accessibility problem, but they often helped. During the past several years, access seems to have been eclipsed as an issue by other concerns.

Biomedicine has also been attacked because of the high costs it incurs. Not only is it expensive to receive treatment in the United States, the proportion of public money spent on health care has escalated dramatically. In 1950, the United States spent 12.7 billion dollars, or 4.4 percent of the gross national product, on health care; by 1981, these figures had increased to 286.6 billion dollars and 9.8 percent. Among the reasons for this rise in cost are an aging population that requires more care, better treatment for minorities, more expensive treatments, and better access to health facilities for a large portion of the population. What makes this expense seem inexcusable is the fact that several European countries spend far less proportionally on health care and yet compare favorably with the United States on such vital statistics as infant mortality.

The response of the federal government to the issue of cost has been interesting because it includes regulatory as well as antiregulatory measures. The most notable federal regulatory move was the creation of diagnostic-related groups (DRGs; also mentioned briefly in chapter 4). The federal government now makes uniform Medicare payments to hospitals (40 percent of all hospital revenues) based on predetermined rates for each of 468 groups of illness. Previously, payments had been made according to hospital cost reports.

For what appear to be antiregulatory motives, however, the government has also encouraged competition among providers of health care. One result has been the growth of hospital corporations that compete for market share in the health care business. Also, there has been a marked increase in such alternative modes of health care provision as health maintenance organizations (HMOs) and preferred provider organizations (PPOs). Both of these systems are prepaid group practices; the PPOs offer more choice of physicians and hospitals. Those hospitals which lost out in the marketplace competition have had to close down or consolidate with other hospitals, and one result (again) has been a loss of accessibility in rural areas and in the poorer sections of large cities. There is no doubt that these changes have provided more consumer choice, but many people fear that medical care is becoming more and more a two-tier system in which a rich elite will be able to afford very high quality care whereas the majority will have to settle for far lower standards.

A third major criticism leveled against biomedicine is that it has become less caring of the individual patient. An overemphasis on high-tech equipment and specialized training, the argument goes, obscures the personal attention a patient requires in order to rally against illness. This, of course, is a general criticism that may do an injustice to the many medical personnel who have not lost the ability to care. As with the first two issues discussed, response to this problem has been varied. One important reaction has been a resurgence of interest in alternative healers, especially those considered to be holistic in their approach (see chapters 3 and 7 for more on these practitioners and on medical pluralism). Since the 1950s, holistic health centers have increased exponentially and have diffused across the United States. Well over twenty thousand chiropractors treat approximately 7.5 million citizens each year. They have been legitimized and given more status because they receive Medicare and Medicaid and workmen's compensation payments. The mass media often carry articles and television news stories about New Age healers, psychic healers, acupuncturists, and many others outside the medical mainstream. Some of these alternative groups have come into conflict with practitioners of biomedicine over questions of legitimacy and treatment modalities. At the same time, other physicians have made use of some alternative health care practices (e.g., acupuncture), and there have been successful attempts to establish health care centers where both biomedicine and alternative techniques are employed. Some people think that systems such as HMOs and PPOs will tend to force alternative practitioners out of business; whether that is so is not yet clear.

The Cancer Detectives of Lin Xian

One of the television programs from the "Nova" series provides an excellent illustration of how several lines of scientific inquiry that have evolved independently over many years can be pulled together in order to address a specific health problem.[8] In the 1960s, the approximately seventy thousand inhabitants of one end of the Lin Xian Valley in China had the highest rates of esophageal cancer in the world. About one in four people in this area died from the disease. Carefully constructed cancer maps showed a core region of high rates in this area and a concentric ring pattern of decreasing rates as distance from the area increased (see chapter 3 on distance decay within regions). How could this phenomenon be explained? How could further occurrences be prevented?

A team of scientists set out to work on the cancer problem. They included virologists, epidemiologists, chemists, pathologists, soil scientists, pharmacologists, and surgeons, so the approach was clearly an interdisciplinary one. The team had a strong suspicion that diet was a key factor. The scientists knew from reading the literature on known carcinogens that chemical compounds known as nitrosamines had been associated in animal experiments with cancer of the esophagus. But nitrosamines could not be found in the local environment; artificial fertilizers and pesticides, the usual source of these compounds, were not used in the valley. Perhaps people manufactured nitrosamines within their own bodies from some combination of foods. Experiments on pigs showed that when they were given food containing both nitrites and amines, nitrosamines showed up in their stomachs. But where did the nitrites and amines come from? Soil scientists showed that because local soils lacked the trace element molybdenum, plants had high concentrations of nitrites. Furthermore, there was little vitamin C in local vegetables, and vitamin C protects the body against nitrites. Scientists knowledgeable about molds discovered that when the people made steamed maize bread, a mold containing amine fragments formed on the bread.

Once the scientists were sure that they had isolated the probable cause of esophageal cancer in Lin Xian Valley, they initiated efforts to prevent further occurrences. Barefoot doctors (paramedics on the lowest level of the Chinese health care hierarchy) educated people about proper diet. Food was stored in special barns that prevented it from becoming moldy. Molybdenum was added to grain seeds prior to planting. People were tested for hyperplasia of the esophagus—a precancerous, nonsymptomatic growth that often led to irreversible cancer. Pharmacologists discovered that both a traditional Chinese medicine made from local herbs as well as an imported drug attacked the hyperplastic cells. Surgery was performed for those who had developed cancer. As time went on, more and more lives were saved as surgical techniques improved.

The point of the Lin Xian story is that the scientific knowledge brought to bear on a baffling medical problem came from a wide variety of scientific fields. Each of these fields has its own history of accumulated knowledge that stretches far back in time. It took a dedicated, cooperative group of people to bring all this knowledge together and focus it on a single problem. Thus, the prevention and treatment of esophageal cancer in Lin Xian, China, is an excellent example of the benefits of comprehensive health care.

The Lessons of History

It is important to review history from time to time. Often we become so wrapped up in the present that we can fall into the error of believing there is nothing to be learned from what has gone on before. But what can we learn from the past? For a start, the study of evolutionary change in medicine (or any field of endeavor) helps prepare us for further change. It motivates us to think ahead to where present trends may be leading us. For example, we can begin to ask what impact such innovations as DRGs and HMOs will have on accessibility to health care. Will alternative medical practices increase in importance? Will compromises be made between practitioners of biomedicine and alternative healers, or will the split between them widen?

The study of change should stimulate us to overcome historical inertia at moments when change might produce better health care. It is fortunate for all of us that the pioneers in the discovery and production of antibiotics persevered. At the same time, history should warn us that not everything changes for the betterment of society or for the benefit of every member of society. Thus, the persistence of humoral theories for so many centuries after Galen reinstated them blocked other thinking that might have been more scientifically sound. In other words, it does not make sense to maintain the status quo when change promises to produce useful choices and improvements; we must be ready to discard potentially harmful accretions.

Another lesson from history is that we have to be prepared for both incremental and revolutionary change. Incremental change may be hard to detect, simply because it is relatively slow. Its impact creeps up on us, and we may rather suddenly realize what has been happening for some time. Very few people thought about how family doctors were fading out and group specialist practices were being phased in. It is also difficult to deal with revolutionary change. Germ theory made the knowledge and practice of generations of physicians obsolete. Some doctors resisted the change, ridiculed the new findings, and continued, with varying success, to treat their patients by the older methods. In the end, of course, medical practice changed for most physicians.

One of the fascinating aspects of evolutionary change is the sort of surprises that come about when accumulating inventions and ideas combine to produce a revolutionary piece of equipment or an innovation in health care treatment. To illustrate this point, I described the diverse ideas that lay behind the prevention and treatment of esophageal cancer in Lin Xian, China. Other examples are the computed tomography scanner, whose development depended on a series of technical advances, and heart transplant surgery, which brings together the fields of surgery, anesthesia, and immunology, among others.

6. Cultural Diffusion

Although culture is essentially conservative (that is to say, cultural information is passed on from generation to generation and thus resists change), it is continually being modified by the adoption of new ideas, products, and techniques. In fact, every culture is the result of the adoption of countless innovations, some of which were taken up far in the past and some more recently. A society's acceptance and use of innovations tells us how well that society adapts to its changing physical and man-made environments (see chapter 4) and in what directions that society is evolving (chapter 5). In this chapter the processes of cultural innovation and diffusion will be explored. After introducing some basic definitions and illustrating them, I will offer a series of examples of health care delivery that in themselves show an evolution toward more complex thinking about innovation and diffusion.

Diffusion Processes

In the first stage of cultural diffusion,[1] an *innovation* (e.g., stone tools, the wheel, hybrid corn, and television) comes into existence through discovery or invention. Some innovations can be traced back to a single place of origin. For example, writing was invented in the Middle East a few millennia B.C., printing was discovered in China by the end of the second century A.D., and Johannes Gutenberg, who lived in the fifteenth century, invented printing from movable type. Other innovations occurred independently within different cultures and had different effects. The dome was developed both by the Romans, who used it in magnificent buildings, and the Eskimos, who used it for their relatively humble but functional igloos.

Once an innovation is produced, it spreads across space and time. People who come into contact with the innovation either accept and use it or they do not. This process, studied by geographers and others, is known as *spatial diffusion* or *space-time diffusion*. It is the components of this process that I seek to illuminate here—why some innovations travel faster than others, why some inventions are widespread whereas others remain localized, and why some peoples accept innovations and others do not.

The diffusion process can take different general forms. A basic distinction is usually made between *expansion* diffusion and *relocation* diffusion. If individuals or groups migrate to another area and introduce an innovation there, that is known as relocation diffusion. An example would be the spread of Christianity, which was carried by European colonizers all around the world. In expansion diffusion, an innovation spreads throughout a population from group to group and place to place so that it is accepted and used by an increasingly greater number of people. In this way, for example, the Islamic religion spread throughout the Arabian Peninsula, westward across North Africa, and eastward to the Tigris-Euphrates Valley and beyond. Expansion diffusion can usefully be broken down into at least two more types of diffusion. *Contagious* diffusion, as the name implies, takes place when there is close personal contact, as when one farmer tells another about a new type of fertilizer. *Hierarchical* diffusion occurs when an innovation passes down (or up) some hierarchical structure within a society. This hierarchy may be based on such things as urban size (e.g., Christianity tended to spread from larger to smaller places throughout the Roman Empire), degree of fashion consciousness (e.g., the diffusion of new clothing styles), or willingness to take risks (e.g., the "miracle" wheat or rice developed in the "green revolution" may be accepted first by wealthier farmers). Many diffusion processes involve combinations of different types of diffusion. Thus, a new clothing style may originate in Paris, relocate to New York, travel down the urban hierarchy to smaller places, and spread contagiously in local areas. Note that in this example the type of diffusion is partly a matter of geographic scale.

The diffusion of innovations assumes that spatial interaction between people and places has taken place. This interaction occurs along *networks,* which include transportation routes (e.g., roads and airline routes) and communication links (e.g., face-to-face contact, telephones, television, newspaper advertisements) through which ideas, products, and techniques travel. We may think of these networks, and the people involved in them, as *carriers* of an innovation. It is obviously important to study the characteristics of these carriers in order to understand a diffusion process.

Whereas carriers speed the flow of innovations, *barriers* tend to stop them or slow them down. Some barriers, such as mountains, oceans, rivers, and deserts, are *physical;* others, such as taboos and political or religious ideologies are *cultural.* If a barrier completely halts a diffusion, it is an *absorbing* barrier. The Atlantic Ocean, until recently in human history, prevented the transfer of food plants between the Old and New Worlds. Most barriers, however, are *permeable;* that is, they retard an innovation to some extent, but the innovation can pass through the barrier in a diluted form. Canada attempts to lessen the impact of U.S. culture by such measures as requiring foreign-owned magazines, published in Canada, to contain material about Canada, but this barrier is very permeable.

Many scientists who have studied diffusion processes have emphasized the *context* or *environment* in which the spread of an innovation occurs (see chapter 2 on the importance of context). Thus, they have analyzed and tried to measure the physical environment, the political and economic climate of an area, the socioeconomic characteristics and attitudes of carriers and potential innovators, and many other factors that lend added meaning to the basic elements of diffusion just described. Contextual factors may either stimulate or retard innovation and diffusion.

It might be, for example, that people have the knowledge and technology to accept an innovation, but lack the financial means or "felt need."

There is a very extensive geographic literature on diffusion theories and on practical applications of those theories. Although medical geographers have used diffusion concepts extensively in order to understand the spread of disease, contagious diseases in particular, they have used these ideas in a relatively small number of studies of health care innovation. At the same time, other social scientists have investigated several kinds of health care innovations, but have paid relatively little attention to their spread over time and space. I will explore the foregoing ideas by discussing a few interesting studies that have dealt, in a variety of ways, with the origin and spread of some important elements of health care delivery.

The Community Health Association in Detroit

Our first example is a good illustration of how a particular spatial model was used to investigate a diffusion process.[2] Many studies of space-time diffusion are based on variations of a basic model developed by Torsten Hägerstrand (b. 1916), a Swedish geographer. An idealized diffusion process can be depicted as an S-shaped curve if total adoptions (vertical axis) are plotted against time (horizontal axis). Such a curve indicates that there are few accepters in the early stage of diffusion, that there is rapid growth in acceptance at a second stage, and that a tapering off of new accepters follows as the innovation saturates an area or population. Another important feature of Hägerstrand's model is that the degree or intensity of acceptance of an innovation decreases as distance from the point of origin increases. This is called *distance decay* or *time-distance decay*. Hägerstrand used his model to simulate the expected diffusion of such agricultural innovations as bovine tuberculosis control, subsidies for the improvement of grazing, and other diffusions in Sweden. He then compared his simulations to the observed diffusion pattern. The basic Hägerstrand model can be modified by factoring-in physical and cultural barriers, absorbing and permeable barriers, and various characteristics of carriers and carrier networks.

In 1961 the Community Health Association was established in Detroit under the sponsorship of the United Automobile Workers union. This was a health care plan offered to employees of Chrysler, Ford, and General Motors as an alternative to a Blue Cross–Blue Shield plan. Research was carried out to discover whether or not there was a spatial pattern to the diffusion of this health care innovation among the auto workers who lived in the Detroit area. It was assumed that the role of personal influences (as opposed to the role of the mass media) would be very strong in the spread of this innovation; in other words, diffusion would be contagious. Distance decay was also assumed. These are two basic elements of the Hägerstrand diffusion model.

A considerable amount of preliminary work must be done to operationalize the Hägerstrand model. Two diffusions have to be developed: one is empirical and the other is a simulation based on the theoretical model. The empirical diffusion developed in the Detroit study was based on the date when members of the Community Health Association joined the plan and on the place where they resided. These data were mapped to show how acceptance grew over six-month periods between 1961 and 1968. In general, growth appeared to be directly related to where potential accepters of the plan lived. Growth was very concentrated within the city limits of Detroit. The Detroit River to the east and south and Lake St. Clair to the northeast were absorbing physical barriers. Two permeable human barriers appeared to impede the spread of the innovation to the (predominantly white) suburbs lying to the west of Detroit. These barriers were the plan's requirement that hospital treatment be given at only one facility, which was located in the mostly black city center, and the fact that physician house calls were limited to an area which was mostly within the Detroit city limits.

The simulation model is based on the assumptions of personal contact and distance decay. The degree of distance decay varies from situation to situation and must be derived empirically. It requires the development of a mean information field (MIF), a grid whose cells represent the probabilities of contact being made at various distances between accepters of an innovation and their potential contacts who might become new accepters. The center cells of the grid contain relatively high probabilities; these decline toward the periphery of the grid. In this study, a five-by-five MIF was developed from data on actual contacts made by 170 members of the United Automobile Workers during their daily round of activities (going to work, visiting friends, attending meetings of voluntary associations, and so on).

Simulations of the Hägerstrand model are run in a series of rounds. The process begins with a set of initial accepters. In the first round, these accepters pass the innovation on to others. In the second round, all the accepters, old and new, spread the innovation, and so on. For each round, the MIF grid is centered over each accepter in turn and a random number is picked—hence, these are known as "Monte Carlo" simulations—in order to determine the cell in which a contact is made and a new person becomes an accepter. Several runs are made, and the average of their results is used as a final simulation model. In the Detroit investigation, the simulation was stopped when the theoretical number of accepters equaled the empirical number. Then the empirical and simulated diffusions were compared by looking at the percentage of accepters in a twelve-by-ten grid (with cells of twenty-five square miles) laid down over the Detroit area. The values in the two grids were remarkably close. The simulated model, however, reached its total number of accepters faster than the empirical diffusion. Perhaps this was because a "psychological resistance" barrier had not been factored in. Another problem (one common to Hägerstrand models) was that the diffusion process depended on the location of the initial accepters, which may or may not have been typical.

The researchers in the Detroit study concluded that their simulation mirrored reality quite closely and, therefore, was potentially a good method for investigating medical innovations such as the Community Health Association plan. The study appears to demonstrate that acceptance of the plan was basically a contagious process. It must be stressed, though, that the Hägerstrand model has its limitations. It is based on two major assumptions that might not always be true: namely, that diffusion is contagious and that distance decay is important. The model has also been criticized on the grounds that it is narrowly based and mechanical, that it does not give enough emphasis to cultural variables, that it does not account for nondiffusion (i.e., the failure of diffusion), and that it fails to *explain* diffusion.

Computed Tomography Scanners in the United States

Most diffusions cannot be modeled as neatly as that in the preceding example. Still, the spread of most ideas, products, or techniques can be examined to determine whether patterns or departures from patterns reveal important features of diffusion processes. The diffusion of the computed tomography scanner throughout the United States between 1973 and 1977 is a case in point.[3] On the surface, it might appear that this diffusion followed no clear pattern, but closer examination reveals several interesting details about the spread of high-tech equipment.

Computed tomography (CT) scanners were developed in Britain in the late 1960s and early 1970s and were introduced to radiologists in the United States in 1972. The scanners were a vast improvement over X-ray technology owing to their "noninvasive" ability to show the nature and extent of lesions and to monitor the effect of treatment. During the late 1970s, a survey was made of the directors of radiology of 333 acute-care, nonfederal U.S. hospitals having more than two hundred beds. Analysis of the data collected revealed that from 1973 to 1977 the number of CT scanners in use or on order increased from zero to around two hundred fifty. Figure 7 displays the distribution of the scanners during the 1973–77 period. The pattern of growth followed an S-shaped curve, except that growth had tapered off only slightly by 1977.

Because several competing companies sold CT scanners, there were several points of origin for the diffusion. With respect to hospital size, diffusion was hierarchical: larger hospitals tended

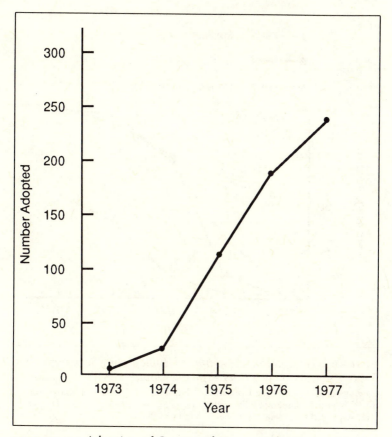

FIGURE 7. *Adoption of Computed Tomography Scanners in the United States, 1973–77*

SOURCE: S. R. Baker, "The Diffusion of High Technology Medical Innovation: The Computed Tomography Example," *Social Science and Medicine* 13D (1979): 156. Reprinted by permission of Pergamon Press PLC.

to adopt the scanners sooner. Diffusion was not so clearly hierarchical, however, with respect to hospital status, as measured by the extent of teaching responsibility (figure 8). Community hospitals (lowest status) were the last to adopt; teaching hospitals connected with medical schools (highest status) took an early lead in adoption but by 1977 were caught up by medical centers (middle status), largely because CT technology improved so rap-

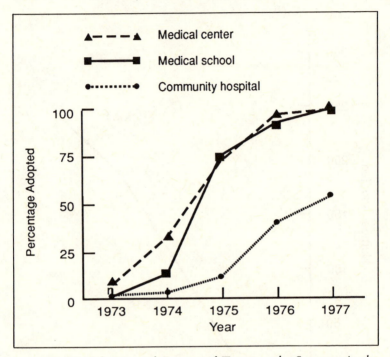

FIGURE 8. *Adoption of Computed Tomography Scanners in the United States, 1973–77, by Type of Adopter*

SOURCE: S. R. Baker, "The Diffusion of High Technology Medical Innovation: The Computed Tomography Example," *Social Science and Medicine* 13D (1979): 158. Reprinted by permission of Pergamon Press PLC.

idly that early adopters often found themselves burdened with obsolescent equipment. In 1977, moreover, the scanners were located in several clusters in and around cities, notably New York, Chicago, Los Angeles, and San Francisco; this indicates expansion diffusion at the local level.

When studying diffusion, it is advisable to pay close attention to the carriers of the innovation and their characteristics. In the Detroit study, for example, discussed in the preceding section, it was important to know that members of the United Automobile Workers were a rather homogeneous group of blue-collar workers; thus, socioeconomic status as a possible differentiating factor in diffusion of the Community Health Assocation plan was not a significant factor. Adopters of the CT innovation were mostly radiologists (who knew the most about the technical and clinical capabilities of the scanners). Radiologists, therefore, were asked why they wanted their hospitals to buy CT scanners. The reply given most often was that the scanners had been proven to be effective in diagnosing disease. The second most frequent response was that the benefits far outweighed the costs (in the early 1970s, the average cost of a CT scanner was 500,000 dollars), even though no data were then available to substantiate this claim.

Information about the innovation was passed along both by long-distance and fact-to-face communication. In order of importance, the means of communication were as follows: medical conventions; journal articles; colleagues; sales pitches; and advertisements in medical journals.

There were several barriers to the spread of CT scanners. High cost was mentioned by many radiologists, but the investigator felt that cost was not a major factor inhibiting purchase. Of clear importance in some states was government regulation in the form of certificate-of-need requirements; those states which had no such requirements tended to purchase more CT scanners earlier. Two other barriers were long lead time (i.e., the time between an order and installation, which was about one year) and rapid obsolescence.

Analysis of CT scanner diffusion raises several interesting and interrelated questions about the diffusion of medical innovations in general. One issue concerns whether the spread of innovations should be regulated. If there is no regulation, hospitals may purchase technology such as the CT scanner with little regard to the cost or to genuine patient demand. Some equipment may be used unnecessarily in order to justify its expense. Some people have argued that high-tech medical innovations should be tested before they are allowed to be used. The certificate-of-need concept came into being in order to ensure that patient demand justifies a given acquisition of high-tech equipment. Regulation, however, has its downside: it stifles innovation and reduces the potential of new equipment in the treatment of disease.

Closely related to the regulation issue is the speed-of-diffusion issue. How fast should an innovation travel in order to achieve the maximum benefit for a health care delivery system (measured by, say, the cost-benefit ratio)? This is an especially difficult question when high-tech equipment is involved, for there are strong pressures—from buyers and sellers alike—to adopt, and critical review of effectiveness often falls by the wayside. There is very little time to measure effectiveness, and new designs appear while the effectiveness of older models is still being tested.

Inevitably, the question of equality arises—with respect both to the adoption and the benefits of medical innovation (see chapters 3 and 9 for more discussion of inequality issues). Early adopters sometimes have an advantage. The characteristics of carriers, the effectiveness of barriers, and the nature of contact networks all have an effect on the degree of inequality. If an entire geographic area becomes saturated with an innovation, then equality might be approached, but inequalities are bound to occur along the way. The imbalances may be either spatial or hierarchical. In the case of CT scanners, spatial inequalities appeared among the states and between large cities and rural areas. Hierarchical imbalances were found with respect to hospital size and (to some extent) hospital teaching status. It is clear that this issue is closely tied to the issue of regulation, for one goal of regulation usually is to ensure equality.

Family Planning in South Korea

Many aspects of diffusion processes are not strictly spatial. Indeed, it would be very surprising if the spread of innovations could be explained entirely by concepts such as distance decay. We always have to be very careful that simplifying assumptions such as distance decay and person-to-person contact are not so far removed from reality as to be meaningless. This cautionary note is one of the principal lessons of a recent study of the diffusion of family planning information among women in South Korean villages.[4] The researcher argues that when individuals are used as the unit of analysis (as they were, for example, in the Detroit study, above), there is a concomitant failure to take social relationships into account. People are taken out of their social context (for more on context, see chapters 2 and 9). The Korean study is also interesting because its methodology is based on *network* or *graph* theory. Geographers have used network analysis to trace the flow of products and people along connecting links between nodes. Here networks are used as the sociologist employs them—to investigate how people relate to one another in groups. Recall that networks are described in the first section of this chapter as the pathways along which innovations are diffused.

Sociological network analysis uses interpersonal relationships, rather than individuals, as the unit of analysis (a typical unit would be a sociometric dyad, an interaction between two people). These relationships are used to build up patterns of communications and to predict how information will diffuse throughout a group of people. Typical groups and specialized communication roles emerge. *Cliques,* or small groups of closely interacting people who freely pass information among themselves, can be identified. Many groups have *opinion leaders,* who are often the first accepters of an innovation. *Liaisons* link cliques but are not members of them; *bridges* belong to one clique and communicate with people in other cliques. People who do not communicate with anyone are called *isolates.* Finally, some of the same indices that geographers use in network analysis can be calculated, including *centrality* and *connectivity.* Centrality measures how well placed a person is within a clique or communication network, and connectivity measures how well the members of a clique or network are joined together.

In the Korean study, personal interviews were conducted with 1,003 married women of childbearing age who lived in a sample of twenty-four South Korean villages. Two of these villages were compared with respect to their acceptance of a family planning program. Both villages had been exposed over a ten-year period to a standardized national family planning program. However, in village A, 57 percent of the women were currently using a family planning method; in village B, only 26 percent were. There is space here to report only a few of the results from this very thorough network analysis of all the women in both villages.

The mothers' club leader in village A was more centrally located in the communications network, and there was greater involvement of pro-family-planning opinion leaders in village A's mothers' club. Women were more likely to adopt a family planning method if a larger proportion of women in their cliques had already adopted. Close-knit groups communicated effectively among themselves, but were not very open to new ideas from the outside. Some subjects such as abortion were taboo, not usually talked about, and diffused slowly.

Sociological network analysis introduces a valuable degree of complexity into diffusion studies—valuable because it helps to explain diffusion processes. Recall that the Hägerstrand model was criticized because it did not give enough emphasis to cultural variables, did not account for failures of diffusion, and did not explain diffusion processes. Analyses such as the present one help address such problems. The challenge to geographers is to integrate spatial and sociological models into their research.

A Maternal and Child Health Clinic in Ethiopia

It is clear that innovation diffusion is so complicated that studies such as the preceding ones can emphasize only a limited number of the manifold aspects of the diffusion process. Some studies, such as the one about to be discussed, focus on the temporal component. This study also clearly distinguishes between different types of users or adopters and shows how adoption patterns differ for these types.[5]

In 1972 a maternal and child health clinic was established in Kirkos, a section of Ethiopia's capital, Addis Ababa, which had never had medical facilities. A very detailed investigation of the clinic included a study of the people who used the clinic over a period of three years, from 1972 to 1975. More than a thousand households in which there was at least one child under twelve years old were interviewed in three geographic areas. Two areas were about one kilometer from the clinic, and the third area was about half a kilometer away. Households as well as children were used as units of analysis. Four categories of potential adopters (i.e., users of the clinic) were developed, depending on (1) whether or not households or children resided in one of the areas over the entire study period or had moved in after the clinic opened and (2) whether or not a child had been born before or after the clinic opened. Since there were large variations in observation time vis-à-vis the potential adopters, the researchers made the necessary adjustments by means of a life table method. They also had to deal with problems of missing data and people moving out of the study area.

The researchers were able to estimate cumulative proportions of adopters among the four subgroups of children and households over time. The plotted curves, unlike the model S-shaped curve, rose sharply and then began to taper off after about one year. In general, the curves for those who were born after the clinic opened increased more rapidly. Curves for in-migrants rose more sharply than those for residents. (Perhaps the in-migrants had already been using medical facilities elsewhere.) The lowest-income groups adopted more quickly than higher-income groups, and caretakers of newborns adopted more quickly than those of older children. Spatial comparisons were made of clinic utilization by residents born before the clinic opened. Utilization was highest among those in the area closest to the clinic—twice as many adopters as in the other two areas after six months. Thus, an expected spatial finding appeared within a basically temporal investigation.

The designers of the Kirkos study felt that the cumulative adoption curves they developed were a good way to evaluate the success of a health care innovation. They can be used to measure differences among users with different socioeconomic and demographic backgrounds. They can also identify target groups such as children younger than six who should be coming to the clinic for vaccinations and other preventive health care. What is of special interest to geographers is the fact that the temporal adoption curves varied according to distance from the clinic. This is another opportunity to combine spatial and nonspatial models in diffusion studies.

Oral Rehydration Therapy in Bolivia

Theories about the diffusion of innovation are constantly evolving. Some of the newest ideas are currently being employed by two researchers (a geographer and an anthropologist) who are investigating the diffusion of oral rehydration therapy in South America's poorest and most politically unstable country, Bolivia.[6] Oral rehydration therapy is a good example of "appropriate technology." It consists of having children with diarrhea drink water that contains specific amounts of sugar and mineral salts. Although it does not cure diarrhea and does not solve the underlying causes of diarrhea (poverty, malnutrition, poor sanitation, etc.), it is a cheap and effective alternative to hospitalization and intravenous rehydration. It can even lower childhood mortality in an area.

The researchers attempted to bring several aspects of diffusion theory to bear on the practical question of how oral rehydration therapy is diffused to needy children in Cochabamba (one of Bolivia's nine departments, or states). They strongly emphasized that messy "real world" problems do not lend themselves to simple solutions. Besides examining the process of *adoption,* they also focused on the *introduction* of innovation by agents of change and on the *impact* of innovation on a group of people. Special attention was also paid to two of the components discussed in the introduction to this chapter: context and carriers (people as well as networks).

Context was examined by gathering data on two kinds of variables that might be associated with the knowledge and use of oral rehydration therapy: spatial characteristics (physical and social accessibility) and population characteristics (socioeconomic status, ethnicity, illness beliefs, and migration status). One spatial variable used was the accessibility (indicated by distance or some other measure) of a place, health care agency, or individual to the city of Cochabamba, capital of the study area.

The other spatial variable was the position of a place (Cocha-bamba, other towns, villages, and sites of periodic markets) within a hierarchy of places. This position was measured by such variables as the presence or absence of electricity, piped water, a sewage system, telephone service, and television reception; types of economic and health-related activities; and means of access such as paved roads. Several characteristics of potential adopters could also be of importance. Most of the (Hispanic) health care professionals spoke Spanish, whereas the majority of the population (Indians) spoke Quechua. This created language barriers as well as class antagonisms (see chapter 8 on the importance of language in practitioner-patient contacts, chapter 9 on class structures). The researchers collected data on several socioeco-nomic status variables, including age, sex, formal education, occupation, and purchasing power. One of several hypotheses to be tested with this information was that poor people would be less likely than richer people to adopt oral rehydration therapy. Another potentially important variable comprised beliefs about the causation, diagnosis, and treatment of diarrhea. Causation beliefs, for example, ranged from informed ideas about dirty water and food to traditional notions having to do with cold weather and colds. Migration is still another factor that might have led some people to become more exposed to information about oral rehydration therapy.

Network analysis was utilized in this study, for the diffusion of oral rehydration therapy was seen as a process that involved a chain of actors who passed along information either hierarchi-cally or by contagion; each actor was potentially both an adopter and an innovator. These actors included international agencies such as the World Health Organization, the Bolivian Ministry of Health, clinics run privately or by churches, physi-cians, pharmacists, independent practitioners (those with little formal training), small-scale vendors, traditional healers, and people who personally took care of children (mostly women). Each of these actors was questioned about his or her knowledge and use of oral rehydration therapy. Results showed, for exam-ple, that people working in government health facilities rated high in knowledge and use, whereas street vendors rated low. A very important aspect of the adopter chain was the nature of the interchange between various pairs of actors (recall the importance of relationships in the South Korean study discussed above). Pharmacists, for example, would be more likely to purchase oral rehydration therapy packets from trusted wholesalers. A native doctor would be more likely to adopt oral rehydration therapy in his practice if a representative of the Ministry of Health treated him with respect and spoke to him in Quechua.

The Challenge of Diffusion Ideas

The basic elements of diffusion, with which cultural geographers have been familiar for many years, are themselves diffused throughout the literature of social science. Economic geographers, social geographers, and political geographers, have used diffusion models in a variety of ways. So have sociologists, anthropologists, economists, and others who practice social science. Some recent thinking has opened up the possibilities for fruitful diffusion research considerably.[7] Researchers are urging more work on why innovations are *not* accepted, more in-depth analysis of people's beliefs and attitudes, further study of the institutions and individuals who are carriers of an innovation (the suppy side), and more emphasis on *why* diffusion works (process) as opposed to *how* it works (form). It would seem that a researcher who is thinking of applying diffusion concepts to the spread of medical innovation is faced with an embarrassment of riches. The challenge is to select the appropriate elements in an creative way that will help solve a particular diffusion problem. That selection, we have seen, is difficult. Various models, such as the Hägerstrand model, have their advantages and their disadvantages. Always present is the danger of leaving an important consideration out of a model. Sometimes one may need to focus on a single aspect of a diffusion process in great depth. It is more likely, however, that several aspects must be considered. The challenge then is to integrate the selected elements in a meaningful way.

7. Folk and Popular Culture

Cultural geographers have distinguished between two types of societies, those which practice folk culture and those which practice popular culture.[1] In this chapter, differences between the two cultures will be pointed out and illustrated, and then the popular/folk dichotomy will be modified somewhat to fit the literature on health care. Sections will cover popular medicine in Western societies, the production of folk drugs in Appalachia, the practice of geophagy in Africa and the United States, folk societies in general, and two studies that emphasize some geographic aspects of folk and popular medicine. Whenever possible, the discussion will be related to the themes of cultural geography that have already been covered in earlier chapters.

Basic Definitions and Classifications

Descriptions of folk and popular cultures incorporate several opposing traits. Folk societies are usually found in *rural* areas, *isolated* from other cultures, and have a high degree of *self-sufficiency*. These societies are relatively *small*, are *homogeneous* with respect to such characteristics as religion and lifestyle, and are marked by a strong sense of *cohesiveness* brought about by close interpersonal relationships. They tend to be culturally *conservative;* that is to say, their products, institutions, and ideas change very slowly. Economic characteristics of folk societies include *minimal division of labor,* a *subsistence* (mainly agricultural) economy, and *homemade, functional goods.* Individualism is not encouraged, and the rules of the society are strongly adhered to. In contrast, popular cultures are relatively *large,* mostly *urbanized,* a *heterogeneous* mix of ethnic groups, population characteristics, and lifestyles, and *dependent* on others for most of their needs. They are *not cohesive,* for *individualism* is encouraged and interpersonal relationships are more ephemeral. Popular culture economies, moreover, are well advanced beyond the subsistence state; each person has *specialized* tasks to perform; products are usually *manufactured,* and often those products are not very long-lasting. The artifacts, sociofacts, and mentifacts of popular culture are *constantly changing.*

In many ways, folk cultures share the characteristics of the primitive and archaic stages of cultural evolution outlined in chapter 5. Thus, one might think of groups such as the Australian aborigines or the Bushmen of the Kalahari Desert as folk societies. Yet folk culture also exists in the midst of very developed parts of the Western world. The Amish are probably the best-known example in the United States. In most areas of the United States, folk societies have disappeared as cohesive groups, but evidence of their *material* culture (e.g., houses and cooking utensils) and their *nonmaterial* culture (e.g., folktales and superstitions), remains. In places like the Appalachians or the Ozarks, some folk-cultural elements are still kept alive; however, the bulk of the population in developed countries belongs to the popular culture. As developing countries modernize, larger proportions of their populations also enter the realm of popular culture.

It is helpful to relate folk and popular cultures to some of the other themes of cultural geography. Distinct *regions* can often be identified for folk cultures, such as French Canada or the Upland South. Within these regions, specific elements of material and nonmaterial culture can be identified. Popular culture, because it is by definition so widespread, is more difficult to regionalize. Nevertheless, cultural geographers have delineated regions in countries such as the United States where certain sports predominate and also vernacular regions, such as the South or the Midwest, that are presumed to exist in the minds of many people, although their boundaries are usually fuzzy.

Since folk cultures are conservative, relatively few *innovations* (e.g., an improved agricultural tool) arise from them. *Diffusion* of folk innovations is often limited to the people within the society of origin. Occasionally, folk-cultural items do spread, however. One example is the diffusion of religious folk songs between 1750 and 1950 from New England to the lower South of the United States. Also, folk cultures as a whole may *relocate*. Thus, the Amish moved from Europe to eastern Pennsylvania, and later some of them moved to locations farther west. Within popular cultures, innovations are constantly arising and then spreading rapidly. Computers, dress designs, leisure activities, diet fads, slang: all these are examples of the bewildering number of cultural products that the popular culture disseminates around the world.

Although popular and folk cultures have been described in terms of opposites, they do interact with each other. Very few folk societies today can totally isolate themselves from the influence of popular culture. While some Amish groups shun such modern conveniences as the telephone and electricity, others have accepted these inventions. Conversely, many elements of folk culture find their way into the popular realm. Thus, members of the popular culture avidly collect early American antiques or show off their compact-disc recordings of African tribal music.

Many of the concepts that pertain to popular and folk culture can be applied to health care delivery, but in the latter case we must be careful of our definitions. The three social arenas that exist within all health care systems, described by Arthur Kleinman, suit our purposes here rather well.[2] The *popular arena* is defined to be laypersons involved in evaluating episodes of illness and health care alternatives and in making decisions about illness and health concerns. These persons include family, those in social networks, and important members of the community. This arena is responsible for 70 to 90 percent of all health care activity in the developing and the developed world. The *folk arena* pertains to the traditional, nonprofessional medical systems described in chapter 2. The *professional arena* includes the five professional systems mentioned in chapter 2:

namely, biomedicine and the four traditional systems (Chinese, Ayurvedic, Galenic, and unanic).

Two clarifications of these arenas must be made if they are to be compatible with the folk/popular dichotomy employed by cultural geographers. The first issue has to do with the natural tendency to say that people in folk cultures practice folk medicine only. This is not true for at least two reasons. One is that, unless the folk culture is almost entirely cut off from the outside world, people in that culture will seek help from the professional as well as the folk arena. Moreover, within folk societies there is a very strong element of what can only be called a popular arena, as defined above. The second issue concerns the place of professional medical systems in the folk/popular scheme. For our purposes, it seems best to say that professional medicine is a part of popular culture in folk as well as popular societies. We are then left with two categories of medicine, as follows. *Folk medicine* will be equated with the formal practice of traditional nonprofessional medicine, the core of which is the beliefs of and therapies used by its practitioners (called, among other things, native doctors and shamans). Folk medicine has many of the characteristics of folk culture outlined above: it is a practice that is usually limited to relatively isolated, small, homogeneous groups of people who live in rather distinct regions, and that changes and diffuses slowly. It is by no means a simple medical system. *Popular medicine* will be equated with *lay beliefs* about and actions related to illness and therapy in folk *and* nonfolk societies. It involves the health-seeking behavior that is part of everyday life. As we shall see, it is often difficult to distinguish between folk and popular medical practices. There are mutual borrowings, just as there are interactions between folk and popular culture in general. In the following sections of this chapter, I will discuss these two types of medicine.

Popular Medicine in Western Societies

When people are ill, even quite seriously ill, they do not always consult a doctor. In fact, studies show that doctors are contacted directly in regard to only 25 to 50 percent of all illness episodes. What, then, do most people do to get help? Even though most people would say that the proper thing to do is to see a doctor, a variety of strategies are in fact used. In line with what was said above about popular culture in general, we know that people's health-seeking behavior will be highly individualistic and subject to change because there are so many conflicting sources of health care prevention and treatment. In this section, I will discuss some of the alternative sources that make up lay or popular health care culture.[3]

Self-treatment is a very important component of popular health care. Many people feel that the simplest thing to do for a health problem, especially a minor one, is to take some easily obtained medication. They might be influenced in their choice by a previous consultation with a physician for a similar problem, by family and friends, or by advertisements in the mass media. Indeed, pharmaceutical companies and those who market "self-help" products—from Band-Aids to kits for measuring blood pressure—put a grat deal of pressure on people to treat themselves. Many over-the-counter drugs and health-care products diffuse rapidly and are passing fads, as is characteristic of popular culture.

Friends, relatives, and coworkers are often involved as laymen within the sphere of popular health care. Most people ask those around them questions such as these: Do I look ill? What do you think is wrong with me? Did you ever have this problem? What did you do about it? This lay referral system, or social health network, provides us with a great deal of information about potential treatments. Although the network is usually informal, some people belong to self-help groups that meet, sometimes quite regularly, to talk over one another's problems, including those having to do with health.

Most of us receive expert medical advice without actually consulting a physician face-to-face or over the telephone for a specific problem. Sometimes a person will ask a physican about a host of ailments while ostensibly consulting him or her about a particular problem only. Or someone might take a child to the doctor and ask him or her to comment on a problem of their own while in the doctor's office. Many people receive advice during their regular (or irregular) checkups.

Hardly any data are available on the use of nonbiomedical personnel such as chiropractors, naturopaths, root doctors (used by blacks in some places), and *espiritistas* (used by Hispanics in some places), but it is estimated that millions of people consult such practitioners. Often friends, relatives, or coworkers will recommend alternative healers. The medical establishment appears to be reluctant to investigate nonbiomedical practitioners, often preferring simply to label them as quacks and their treatments as worthless.

Any discussion of popular medicine must remain rather vague, largely because it is so difficult to document how people seek care outside the medical establishment. However, some important points can be made. Health-seeking behavior is such an ingrained part of daily life that laypeople are continually asking for or giving medical advice. The advice given is an indication of what people really know and believe about illness and health. Some people, for example, have become "medicalized" to the extent that they always accept what physicians recommend and always believe the "scientific" claims of medical advertisements. Others are suspicious or cynical about these recommendations and claims. Each group gives and receives lay advice accordingly.

Folk Drugs in Appalachia

An important part of professional as well as nonprofessional medical systems throughout the centuries has been their pharmacopoeia, the collections of drugs that healers and laypersons have used as treatments. Most medicines in use today come originally from a knowledge of plants. Early Americans made medicines both from plants brought from Europe and from native plants, which in some cases the Indians taught them how to use. Although the bulk of the drugs used in Western countries come from cultivated plants or are manufactured synthetically, there are areas, such as Appalachia, where plants are still gathered for domestic and commercial use.[4]

Appalachian folk drugs have an interesting cultural ecology, involving both a particular physical environment and a particular folk culture (see chapter 4 for a full discussion of cultural ecology). The places where one would expect to find medicinal plants being collected are places where two phenomena overlap: distributions of medicinal plants and folk societies that know about and use those plants. Most of the common medicinal plants are found in deciduous forests that provide a diversity of habitats. Such forests have been disappearing at lower altitudes in the United States but still survive in the more mountainous areas. Remnants of folk societies are also found in mountainous areas such as the southern Appalachians and the Ozarks. In East Tennessee, one researcher was told by an old collector that "the good Lord has put these yerbs for man to make hisself well with. They is a herb, could we but find it, to cure every illness."[5] This idea is related to the medieval concept of nature as God's "signature" or book (see chapter 8 on metaphors in medical thought).

In the late 1950s, there were several dealers who bought crude, plant-derived drugs from collectors and sold them to manufacturers, small distributors, and exporters (figure 9). These dealers are clearly concentrated in the Upland South and in parts of North Carolina, Tennessee, Kentucky, West Virginia, and Virginia. Collecting plants is not an easy job, for they are spread out widely across the landscape. Also, the collector does not receive much money for them. Most collectors have other jobs; many are marginal farmers. In the late 1950s, the volume of business in medicinal plants was decreasing, and prices fluctuated substantially as market demand for particular plants changed.

Geophagy

The word *pica* refers to the habitual, compulsive eating of materials (e.g., earth, chalk, and lead paint peeling off walls) that are normally not considered to be foods. Geophagy, or earth eating, is a form of pica that has been discovered around the

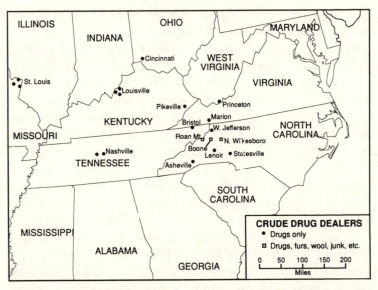

FIGURE 9. *Location of Dealers in Crude Botanical Drugs*
SOURCE: E. T. Price, "Root Digging in the Appalachians: The Geography of Botanical Drugs," *Geographical Review* 50 (1960): 11. Reprinted by permission of the American Geographical Society.

world and can be traced back at least two thousand years.[6] Deeply ingrained in certain cultures, geophagy has health implications because it may meet physiological and psychological needs and also because it can have detrimental effects. It is particularly interesting from a cultural-geographic perspective because it includes elements of regionalism, ecology, evolution, and diffusion.

Geographers have studied geophagy in two regions: Africa and the United States. Earth eating is quite widespread on the African continent (see figure 10). In some parts of Africa there are highly organized geophagic industries that include extraction from particular sites, processing, and sales through middlemen to consumers at periodic markets. In the United States, geophagy is concentrated in the South, where it is associated mainly with rural blacks. Rural whites also eat earth, however, as do people in urban areas in the West and North.

Geophagy clearly represents a close interaction between people

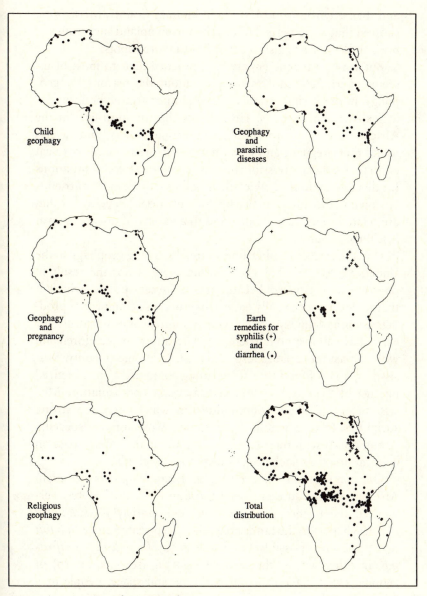

FIGURE 10. *Geophagy in Africa*

SOURCE: J. M. Hunter, "Geophagy in Africa and the United States: A Culture-Nutrition Hypothesis," *Geographical Review* 63 (1973): 172. Reprinted by permission of the American Geographical Society.

and their environment. A study in Holmes County, Mississippi, showed that earth tended to be taken from upland sites from soil horizon B. Africans also seem to have favored spots.

But why do people engage in a practice that, to most of us, seems aberrant? Scholars disagree about the reasons for geophagy. In the African context, John Hunter argues for a physiological-stress hypothesis. He believes that the nutrients in the African clays serve to supplement people's diets, and he has found that pregnant and lactating women are more likely to eat earth than others—possibly because these are stressful situations for them, situations in which their bodies require more nutrients. Geophagy, then, may make up for nutritional deficiencies that are related to inadequate diet and to a variety of diseases prevalent throughout Africa.

Donald Vermeer and Dennis Frate, discussing geophagy in the United States, feel that earth eating there is not the result of physiological disorders because it is quite sex-specific (why is it that males do not usually eat earth?); because commercial products such as laundry starch, which some people substitute for earth, have almost no nutrients; and because young children and women past menopause also eat earth. In Holmes County, Mississippi, it was found that earth eating continued to be practiced because of a cultural context that favored its perpetuation. Mississippi's rural black communities, in which there are strong social ties, behave as folk communities. Women have especially strong bonds with their children; in particular, mothers pass on cultural practices such as geophagy to their children.

One can speculate that the health dynamics of earth eating in Africa are quite different from those in the United States. Perhaps in the former area geophagy does satisfy *physiological needs*, whereas in the latter area it is a deep-seated *cultural habit* that perseveres, possibly because it is *psychologically comforting*. In other words, the medical *meaning* (see chapter 10) of geophagy may have evolved over time and space; people may have adapted it to new situations. Geophagy may represent a form of *cultural inertia*, a cultural phenomenon that persists despite its loss of physiological meaning.

Scholars do agree that geophagy diffused from Africa to the southern United States, having been brought over with the slaves. The practice diffused to whites in the South as well. Furthermore, during the twentieth century, geophagy moved with blacks as they migrated in search of employment to the cities of the North and the West. Southern blacks even sent packets of earth to their relatives and friends who had moved away, and some urbanites substituted laundry starch bought at supermarkets.

Folk Societies

Anthropologists and others have carried out a large number of fascinating ethnographic studies that address medical practices among folk societies.[7] Most of these investigations have been carried out in developing areas of the world. Here I will emphasize some of the main features of folk and popular health care within folk societies.

As noted above, folk medicine, as it is practiced by native healers, conforms to many of the characteristics of folk culture set out in the definitions-and-classification section of the present chapter. Remember, however, that practitioners of folk medicine borrow from other medical systems and that people in folk societies have their own popular systems of health care. There is a danger here that one might think of folk medicine as primitive. In fact, though, folk medicine is far more complex than most people imagine. Its beliefs, rituals, and treatments have evolved over many centuries. Although folk societies are often characterized as relatively homogeneous in their beliefs, diversity is a key concept in their health-seeking behavior. There are always many alternative folk explanations for illness and many treatments for illness within any particular cultural context. The Nyole of eastern Uganda, for example, recognize three healing functions: curing, protection with medicine, and divination. There is also great variation in beliefs and practices among different societies that reside within relatively small areas. Whereas Westerners tend to categorize all practitioners of folk medicine as "witch doctors," "medicine men," or "native healers," one must remember that a great many different specialties and combinations of specialties are performed by these various practitioners. There are herbalists, diviners, midwives, priests and priestesses, spiritists, surgeons, faith healers, and bonesetters, among others.

It is very important to view folk medicine and folk healers within their social and cultural context. Illness and its treatment are integrated with other aspects of culture such as religion and social obligations. Indigenous healers are often successful because they share the medical and cultural belief systems of their patients. As David Landy states, "The curer's role is endowed with power precisely because it stands at the interstices of religion, magic, and the social system."[8] A native doctor may simultaneously take on the roles of healer, judge, priest, and even entertainer. The causes of many illnesses are attributed to broken kinship rules, shirked religious duties, or conflicts among members of the community. Treatment, too, is related to societal concerns. A folk practitioner often restores social order. Thus, an astute healer might recognize that a woman's stomach problems resulted from quarrels with her husband and so act as a marriage counselor (as well as prescribe herbs and perform certain rituals) in order to effect a cure.

In folk healing a distinction is often made between the *diagnosis* of a disease by examining its *symptoms* and the underlying *causes* of the disease. Folk healers will treat the symptoms of an illness, but, especially if this treatment fails, they will also look for causes. A cure that will last must address the ultimate cause of the illness. When it comes to causes, the element of diversity is again important. Causes may be natural or induced by God. They may arise from within the society (e.g., from breaking a rule, or a relative's curse), or they may have a supernatural origin (e.g., an ancestral spirit or a witch).

Very few folk societies have not been influenced by medical practices that are either traditional professional or biomedical. This brings us to a consideration of lay or popular health care among folk societies, incorporating both professional and nonprofessional medicine. Many researchers have noted the openness, the flexibility, the inclusiveness of popular medicine. In particular, they speak of the duality of folk practices and biomedical practices wherever the latter system has penetrated. Formally, there is usually little integration between biomedicine and folk medicine; in practice, though, people tend to be pragmatic and use both systems (see chapter 3 for more on medical pluralism). Each system, as well as the individual practitioners, will gain a reputation for effecting certain cures and will be utilized accordingly. Several scholars have found that biomedicine tends to be used for acute illnesses where quick cures are anticipated, while more chronic psysiological and psychological problems are taken to indigenous practitioners. Many people believe that biomedicine can only treat symptoms, whereas folk medicine can treat underlying causes as well. Practitioners from both systems are often visited during the same illness episode. It should be noted that use of biomedicine does not necessarily mean that people in folk societies change their beliefs about health. Western medicines and Western medical technology, rather than biomedical ideas, may be the attraction.

It is interesting to see what happens to the role of the traditional nonprofessional healer when his or her society comes into contact with biomedicine. How does the healer adapt to the new, pluralistic system? Some practitioners manage to maintain a strong position within their societies while at the same time they borrow biomedical drugs, technology, and procedures that they have found to be acceptable to their patients and effective in cures. Others fail to adapt and may begin to lose patients, who themselves have been more open to new health care ideas.

Geographic Considerations

So far, this chapter has mainly dealt with the nongeographic aspects of folk and popular approaches to health care. That is largely because very little geographic work has been done along those lines. The geography of Thai and Chinese traditional professional medicine in Bangkok, Thailand (which was discussed in terms of regions in chapter 3) is one example. In this section, in order to indicate what more might be done, I briefly discuss two studies that emphasize spatial themes.

The first study has to do with the most utilized nonbiomedical or alternative healers in the United States: chiropractors, or DCs. Despite a long history of opposition from the biomedical establishment, there are more than twenty thousand DCs, and they treat more than 7.5 million people every year. Chiropractors have been included in Medicare, Medicaid, government employee insurance, and other federal health care programs since 1974. Thus, they are an important part of what I have been calling the popular health culture.

The social science literature on chiropractic has yielded three perspectives and attendant spatial hypotheses which were tested in North Carolina.[9] One perspective, *system status*, suggested that DCs were somehow marginal to biomedical physicians (MDs), that they were outside the established health care system. System status was tested with respect to where MDs and DCs located within the urban hierarchy. Chiropractors clearly located in smaller towns and cities and were therefore marginal in that sense (table 3).

Some literature has suggested that DCs might be found among populations having certain culture traits. This *cultural*

TABLE 3.

PERCENT OF DC'S AND MD'S IN NORTH CAROLINA PRACTICING IN CITIES AND TOWNS OF DIFFERENT SIZES		
Town size (population)	% DC's	% MD's
less than 2,500	9.54	8.83
2,500 - 4,999	10.58	6.74
5,000 - 9,999	11.41	6.23
10,000 - 19,999	17.22	12.02
20,000 - 49,999	18.46	21.84
50,000 or more	32.78	44.34

SOURCE: W. Gesler, "The Place of Chiropractors in Health Care Delivery: A Case Study of North Carolina," *Social Science and Medicine* 8 (1988): 785–92. Reprinted by permission of Pergamon Press PLC.

NOTE: $p = .001$ (one-tailed K-S test).

congruence notion was tested spatially, in the eighteen multi-county planning areas of North Carolina, by correlating DC-to-population ratios with median income and proportions of populations that were white, rural, and belonged to churches that used touch in healing. It was found that chiropractic was associated (with statistical significance) with white populations and higher incomes, but not with rurality or healing religions. However, DCs were more associated than MDs with rurality and lower incomes.

National data on the characteristics of people who visited DCs provided the background for a *utilization* perspective. This perspective was tested in a manner similar to the test for cultural congruence, using data on whites, ruralness, income, and population between the ages of eighteen and sixty-four. As expected, DC-to-population ratios correlated significantly with percentages of whites and higher-income people. Contrary to expectations, ratios were not associated with ruralness or with the population age group between eighteen and sixty-four.

The second study to be considered is a comprehensive ethnographic investigation of diseases and health care among the Kamba people of Kenya.[10] The focus was on two areas where the Kamba predominate: three low-income "urban villages" in Nairobi and the Machakos District of south-central Kenya. In this study, health-seeking behavior among the Kamba was set within its cultural, social, environmental, disease, and historical context. Like most folk societies, the Kamba use traditional nonprofessional practitioners as well as biomedical personnel.

Several geographic themes emerged from the several years of fieldwork in Kenya that went into this investigation. The country was divided into regions, based on ecological, economic, social, medical (e.g., prevalent diseases and environmental sanitation), and cultural-historical conditions, and the suggestion was made that health care might be planned according to these zones. It was found that people had better access, measured by both physical and social distance, to traditional medical practitioners than to biomedical personnel. Distance decay was more a consideration with respect to the use of biomedical facilities than with respect to the use of native healers. For the latter, personal charisma was often important in attracting patients, sometimes over long distances. Work force studies in developed countries show that distributions of physicians and other biomedical practitioners can be explained partially by competition and market penetration; this was not true among the Kamba. It was found that patient mobility was a very important factor in seeking health care. Moreover, the *places* or settings where treatments were provided (e.g., in the home of a traditional medical practitioner or in a hospital) were found to be crucial to patient well-being (one of the main emphases of chapter 10 is the importance of such places).

A Wide-Open Field

I have tried to make the point in this chapter that folk and popular health care are both very significant aspects of health care delivery. Folk medicine is important because it serves the majority of the people in developing countries, many of whom have no access to biomedical care. If social scientists are really interested in the health of all the world's inhabitants, then they must study nonprofessional traditional healing. An agenda was set out for medical geographers to do this several years ago; research is trickling in, but there is not nearly enough.[11]

Popular medicine is important simply because, in folk and popular cultures alike, it represents the majority of the everyday actions that people take in trying to improve their health. Were we really to examine the popular arena, a much different perspective on health-seeking behavior would evolve. For example, suppose research efforts were directed not at home-to-doctor and home-to-hospital flows, but were concentrated instead on that complicated network of laypersons and mass media information that people actually employ when they are ill. Very different spatial patterns would emerge. Such research is much easier talked about than done, of course, a good reason that there is not much to show in this area to date.[12]

8. Language

I n introductory cultural geography texts, language is usually
given full treatment in a separate chapter.[1] Typically, language
is discussed in terms of several of the standard themes of cultural
geography. Geographers attempt to delineate language regions
(often difficult because of linguistic pluralism, which produces
overlap and fuzzy boundaries), to describe the origin and diffusion of languages and language families, to discuss how language affects people's perception of the environment, to show
how the environment affects language (the classic example is the
many Eskimo words for "snow"), and to demonstrate how languages change over time (e.g., the accumulation of high-tech
terms in English). Here I will concentrate on aspects of language
that can be usefully applied to health care delivery. I will establish links with concepts from earlier chapters but will also be
anticipating some ideas from the chapters to follow (e.g., social
interaction, cultural hegemony, the experiences of everyday life,
and interpreting landscape as a text) that are derived in large
part from the "new" cultural geography. Language will be discussed as a means of *communication;* as a *taxonomic device;* as
a medium for creating *myths, metaphors,* and *models;* and in
terms of *semantic networks.*

Communication

A sixty-year-old white Protestant woman was recovering
quite successfully from pulmonary edema secondary to athero-

sclerotic cardiovascular disease and chronic congestive heart failure in the Massachusetts General Hospital.[2] Inexplicably, she began to vomit and urinate frequently into her bed. The explanation for this strange behavior was to be found in the woman's life experiences. She had been told by the medical team working on her case that she had "water in the lungs." Her husband and father were both plumbers. Somehow she had developed the idea that her chest was connected to two pipes, one leading to the mouth and one to the urethra, and so she was trying to void the "water in her lungs" through these outlets. This, she believed, would have an effect similar to that of the "water pills" she had been taking. She could not understand why people had been angry with her. After a thorough explanation, with diagrams, of the true "plumbing" of the human body, she ceased her strange behavior.

The foregoing example is an illustration of a failure of communication between lay and medical people. In particular, the misunderstanding involved different models of the human body and different types of language used to describe those models. People use language to communicate with one another and to pass along culture traits from generation to generation. Language is a key way in which people relate to one another as they carry out their daily activities. Within any health care delivery system, of course, communication is essential if providers and patients are to understand one another. Each group needs to know both how the other group labels and classifies diseases and treatments and what explanations the other group finds personally and socially meaningful. Unfortunately, healers and those in need of healing often express themselves in different ways and thus talk at cross-purposes when they come into contact. Often, because of misunderstandings, patients do not comply with what providers have told them to do . Facilities may be underutilized because health care consumers have been deterred by a lack of communication.

It is commonly accepted that patient-provider communication has the greatest potential for success when both patient and provider participate in the same health care system. If a healer is trained in one system and the patient has been brought up to believe in another, however, difficulties inevitably arise. The classic example is the poor communication that often arises between biomedical practitioners and patients who may adhere to a variety of traditional professional and nonprofessional practices. In fact, language has been deliberately used in an effort to keep biomedical and traditional systems apart. Many Western physicians who worked in Africa during the colonial period attempted to undermine traditional medicine by labeling it "witchcraft"; they called traditional medical practitioners "witch doctors" and said that they practiced "black magic."[3]

Even in Europe and North America, where biomedicine is the dominant paradigm, biomedical personnel and the general public speak different medical languages.[4] The language of biomedicine (Lb) uses scientific terminology. It is impersonal, often a creation of new technologies, and abstract. Most nonmedical people, however, use a natural or sociophenomenological language (Lsp) when they talk about matters such as disease and health that have personal meaning for them. In other words, objective Lb collides with subjective Lsp within what should be a highly personal doctor-patient relationship.

Language can act as a link as well as a barrier when people are trying to communicate about their problems. The result, however, may not necessarily be conducive to better health. In the United States, we find that many people, particularly in the educated middle class, have picked up Lb from biomedical personnel and from advertisements that cleverly use biomedical images and phrases. These people speak very knowingly about illnesses and treatments. The danger is that they have been *medicalized*, co-opted into the professional jargon to such an extent that they can no longer express their true feelings.

Two ideas emerge from the preceding discussion: (1) more than one language is spoken in health care encounters (linguistic pluralism), and (2) medical languages change over time (linguistic evolution). Linguistic pluralism and evolution are well illustrated by an example of care-seeking behavior among rural people in central Italy.[5] In this region, people have created a "grammar" based on different fields of experience, including mythology, religion, "natural law," and modern science. Many people still believe in such old ideas as the evil eye, magical incantations, witches, and symbolic phenomena connected with Catholicism such as the stigmata (marks like those left on Christ's crucified body from the nails and spear) that some healers profess to have. Healers as well as patients, influenced by modern science and the mass media (newspapers, magazines, and films) have incorporated the terms used by biomedicine into their own popular medical language. It is not surprising in this setting to find pharmacists selling both commercial, brand-name drugs and medicines made from local herbs and plants. Olga, an indigenous practitioner, heals through the "electrical forces" in her hands, magically transforms mineral water into a healing liquid, and has cured a child at long distance by sending a packet of medicines through the mail. The symbols Olga uses are often religious, but she also uses such scientific terms as "forces," "vectors," and "gravity" in her healing language.

Taxonomy

I said earlier that language is used to label and classify things. One can tell a great deal about a culture from the names it gives to objects and ideas. Some agricultural societies, for example, have many names for different types of rain because this climatic factor is so important to them.[6] Anyone trying to practice healing within a given society must understand how diseases are named and classified in that society. Lb, Lsp, and folk-medical languages differ greatly in their classification schemes, or taxonomies. The Kamba of South-central Kenya, for example, base their disease taxonomy on four classification systems: ultimate cause, mode of treatment, disease characteristics, and attributes of those affected.[7] The International Classification of Disease codes, based on biomedical language and physiological distinctions, mean little to most people. Biomedical personnel tend to diagnose using scientific taxonomies, whereas their patients usually try to explain what is wrong with them in terms of symptoms. It is usually very difficult to translate from one medical language to another.

To cite a specific example: in Honduras, people use the word *empacho* to indicate both a symptom and an illness.[8] This word overlaps but does not coincide with the biomedical disease category of "diarrhea." It was difficult to persuade some Hondurans to use oral rehydration therapy rather than potent traditional purgatives in order to cure empacho, but these same people would use oral rehydration therapy for other diseases that were more congruent (in their taxonomy) with diarrhea.

How does one find out how people categorize diseases? Three attempts to answer this question will now be detailed. The first was a household survey of mothers and young children in southeastern Nigeria.[9] One section of the questionnaire asked about illnesses experienced over the two weeks preceding the interview. It was decided to ask mothers about symptoms (e.g., "cough," "runny nose") rather than to use diagnostic terms (e.g., "respiratory ailment") because most of the mothers were unfamiliar with biomedical language. A list of symptoms was developed based on a lecture given by the matron of a maternal and child health clinic, reports of common complaints by clinic nurses, and an open-ended question put to a small, pretest sample of mothers. This list was translated by one health worker into the local language and then, in order to check for distortions in translation, back into English by a second health worker. For purposes of analysis, the twenty-three symptoms were classified into "general," "digestive," and "respiratory" diseases (based mainly on a biomedical taxonomy).

Ethnomedical studies are also an excellent means of uncovering folk taxonomies. In rural communities of Highland Ecuador, part of the folk taxonomy places children's diarrhea into three classes according to its color, odor, and texture.[10] *Infección,* or "infection," has a natural cause: it is attributed to consuming dirt or contaminated food, putting dirty hands in the mouth, or eating foods that are difficult to digest. This belief represents a partial evolution toward biomedical thinking. Dirt and objects covered in dirt are no longer used in healing, but people still do not understand germ theory. Mothers think that this type of diarrhea can be cured by a physician. The second category includes illnesses that are caused by humoral imbalances (see chapter 2 on humoral concepts in traditional professional medical systems). Concentrations of "heat" or "cold" in the body are thought to create imbalances in the body. Children are treated for this type of diarrhea by heating their buttocks and stomach; they are not usually seen by a doctor. Finally, some diarrhea is thought to be caused by supernatural forces such as the evil eye (*el ojeado*), evil air (*mal aire*), or soul loss (*espanto* or *susto*). Treatment involves ritual cleaning and such techniques as rubbing the child's body with a hen's egg.

A statistically sophisticated method for discovering how people classify diseases compared samples, in Guatemala and the United States, of urban women with children.[11] The women were presented with either twenty-seven Spanish-language disease terms or twenty-nine English-language terms and were then asked to sort them into piles on the basis of their similarity. They were also asked to rank-order the terms according to four "dimensions": (1) most to least contagious; (2) most to least serious; (3) most common in adults to most common in children; and (4) those needing the "hottest" remedy to those needing the "coldest" (this last category was used only in Guatemala). The data were subjected to an analysis technique known as multidimensional scaling. The English speakers produced two clear and independent dimensions, severity and age, while Spanish speakers distinguished diseases along dimensions of contagion and severity. The hot/cold dimension was not thought to be a useful one because individual Guatemalan mothers varied greatly in their classification of specific diseases as either "hot" or "cold." Studies like these have policy implications. For example, it would be interesting to know whether or not Guatemalan women classify acute or chronic diarrhea as a serious disease (it should be considered serious as it often leads to fatal dehydration).

Metaphor, Myth, and Model

In recent years a few geographers have written interesting papers on the way language is used to express metaphors, myths, and models that tell us about the culture of a society.[12] A *metaphor* is formed when a word that usually means one thing is used in such a way that acquires an additional, secondary meaning. More precisely, it is "an implied analogy which imaginatively identifies one object with another and ascribes to the first one or more of the qualities of the second or invests the first with emotional or imaginative qualities associated with the second."[13] Some metaphors are quite simple; they represent a relatively direct comparison between two previously unrelated frames of reference. When one speaks of a "foothill," one carries the meaning of being-at-the-bottom from the field of human anatomy to the field of physical landscape. One is saying that a foothill, in relation to the mountain behind it, is like a human foot in relation to the rest of the body. Other metaphors evoke several different kinds of response. When one hears the phrase "concrete jungle," one thinks of hard, menacing, unrelenting, inner-city spaces where life is raw and territory is fought over tooth and nail. Metaphors like these are not literally true, but they have a strong emotional impact on people.

Metaphors can reveal what is important to a society. The Kuranko of Sierra Leone use the word "path" to indicate the movement of people, goods, and services within a community.[14] People give one another gifts "so that the path does not die." If relations between relatives or friends go sour, then "the path between them is not good." The extensive use of this metaphor is interpreted to mean that social reciprocity is very important among the Kuranko.

Societies may use extended metaphors over long periods of time to help them comprehend the world. Metaphors often reflect the demands that a society places on its environment, the ways in which it interacts with the environment (see chapter 4, on cultural ecology, for more on the relationships of humans and their environment). One geographer has found that in the Middle Ages *nature* was thought to be, like the Bible, *a sacred book* on whose pages God communicated the meaning of his universe.[15] This metaphor indicates that people were trying to make the universe *intelligible*. One doctrine that arose from this metaphor was that if an illness occurred in a place, a natural remedy would also be found to grow there (see chapter 7, concerning the herb gatherers of Appalachia). The dominant metaphor of Renaissance Europe was that of the human body as a *microcosm* of the universe; people were trying to *integrate* themselves into the cosmos. Physical features were made analogous to parts of the human body (e.g., mountains had "shoulders" and "brows"). The universe was thought to pass through the various stages of human life and even to experience human illnesses. One health-related outcome of this way of looking at the world was the discovery of the circulation of the blood. William Harvey was inspired by the prevailing idea that water circulated throughout the entire earth; that circulation, according to the thinking of the time, must have a human counterpart. Indeed, since the Renaissance, the *earth as machine* has been the predominant metaphor that shaped human attitudes toward the physical environment. This image indicates a desire to *conquer* nature—just as a machine can be tinkered with, taken apart, reassembled, and even improved upon. Likewise, the language of clocks and computers is used to understand today's world (e.g., things "run like a clock," and people "interface" with each other). This metaphor is at the root of the complaint that biomedicine is mechanical and uncaring. It helps explain the mechanical views of the above-mentioned patient who likened her body to a system of pipes.

In her book, *Illness as Metaphor,* Susan Sontag examines how people use illness as a metaphor for other features of their culture when it should not be used as a metaphor at all.[16] She goes into great detail to show how "cancer" in our society invokes horrible images ("invisible predator," "gnawing at the insides," "invasion by alien cells") that demoralize patients who have various forms of the disease. Heart disease (which kills more people than cancer in most Western countries) is viewed, in contrast, simply as a mechanical weakness. Cancerous images are often the opposite of those which tuberculosis invokes. Tuberculosis is thought to be a disease of poverty and deprivation, whereas cancer is thought to be a middle-class disease that results from affluence and excess. These images can be extended almost indefinitely; the point is that they are false and, for the good of sufferers, should be challenged and ultimately put to rest. It should be noted that some non-Western societies have not developed the same metaphors for cancer. A study in Tanzania, for example, found that people there did not equate cancer with pain, disfigurement, or death.

The concept of metaphor shifts rather easily into the idea of a *myth* because both are attempts to make the unfamiliar more familiar, to bring understanding and order out of ignorance and chaos. A myth can be defined as "anonymous stories having their roots in the primitive folk-beliefs of races or nations and presenting supernatural episodes as a means of interpreting natural events in an effort to make concrete and particular a special perception of man or a cosmic view."[17] Myths, like metaphors, help explain what particular societies think about the nature of the world and about how people should behave. In this sense, modern science is a myth: it seeks order and explanations about the world.

A dominant myth throughout the history of the United States has been that of the frontier. The historian Frederick Jackson Turner used the frontier to express ideas about the essential American character: independent, tough, restless, always seeking a better life. What are the endless cowboy stories seen in American films or on television but narratives, myths, about that kind of American? In modern times, the frontier continues to be a potent myth. John F. Kennedy used it to arouse emotion among the electorate (the New Frontier), and it has been used by the geographer David Ley to invoke such images as the "fortified stockade" and "self-sufficiency" in today's inner-city ghettos.

A recent paper on symbolic healing uses ideas about myths in an attempt to lay out a structure that can describe and explain how similar psychological processes are set in motion by such diverse healing systems as religious healing, shamanism, and Western psychotherapy.[18] That structure consists of four steps: (1) culture-specific symbols and myths are used to generalize the experiences of practitioners as well as patients; (2) a practitioner persuades a patient that his or her ailment can be defined in terms of the myth; (3) the healer extracts specific symbols from the myth and attaches the patient's emotions to them; and (4) the practitioner helps the patient to transact his or her own emotions by manipulating the symbols. It is assumed that there are processes in which symbols affect the mind and that this in turn affects the body. The practitioner joins the symbols that come from the social system to the "self system" of the patient; this in turn affects the patient's somatic system. For example, a shaman is presented with a difficult childbirth. He relates the story of some heroes known to the patient who set out on a difficult journey and then return. The places described in the narrative are analogous to places along the patient's birth canal. Symbols from the story are attached emotionally to the patient by hypnotic repetition of parts of the myth.

Lest one think that Western medicine is without myths, consider the simple example of giving a patient a placebo. Placebos often work because people believe in the myth that medicines (particularly those prescribed by a physician) will work. Perhaps there is no "story" that goes along with this particular myth, but the efficacy of biomedicine is so pervasive in Western society and we hear so many stories about medical successes that we believe strongly in the system. Indeed, the whole structure of a body of medical thought and practice such as psychotherapy is built upon a complex set of principles in which the therapist believes. The therapist's job is to indoctrinate the patient in these principles.

A *model* can be thought of as a set of systematically developed metaphors. Like metaphors and myths, models are constructed to explain reality. Theoretical models in science are based on analogies. One example is the gravity model of social interaction (i.e., groups of people will interact with one another in direct proportion to their size and in inverse proportion to the "distance" between them), which has an analogy in physics. A more complex example focuses on the myth of racial superiority, a myth that had become very important for Anglo-Saxons by the end of the nineteenth century and that was expressed in such phrases as the "white man's burden." This myth helped to rationalize a model of political control, of Western imperialism (political control or hegemony is one of the main themes of chapter 9).

The Qollahuaya Indians who live in the Bolivian Andes have developed an elaborate model of human physiology that is based on two features of the physical environment: topography and hydraulic cycles.[19] Ethnographic data were collected on a group of Qollahuaya who live in three communities located on the lower slopes, central slopes, and highlands of a certain mountain (figure 11). The people in these three places—Ninokorin, Kaata, and Apacheta—exchange produce and, since each altitude is suitable for crops that provide different carbohydrates, minerals, and proteins, all the people of the mountain enjoy a well-balanced diet. Analogously, the Qollahuaya think that the human body has a vertical axis with three levels. The upper level of the mountain corresponds to the head, eyes, and mouth; the middle level to the stomach and heart; and the lower level to legs and toenails. They see the unity of their three communities as analogous to the unity of the human body. Rivers, underground streams, and tunnels bind the three mountain communities together. In a similar fashion, the body has conduits that link its three levels together. The heart, at the center, is where food and fluids come together, separate into other fluids, and are then dispersed throughout the body. Qollahuaya rituals typically bring items from the three communities to the middle one, where they are mixed together and sent out to shrines up and down the mountainside. Health involves a process in which centrifugal and centripetal forces within the body distribute the substances (primarily air, blood, and fat) that provide thoughts, emotions, nutrients, and lubricants to various parts of the body. Herbs are prescribed in order to regulate processes of concentration, dispersal, and elimination in the body. Some illness beliefs are of special interest here. One is that illnesses such as debility and depression are attributed to the loss of blood; for this reason, it is difficult to take blood samples from the Qollahuaya. One particularly acute sickness is said to be caused by the sudden and mysterious loss of fat. Often a doctor, lawyer, or priest is thought to have secretly cut fat out of peasants during the night.

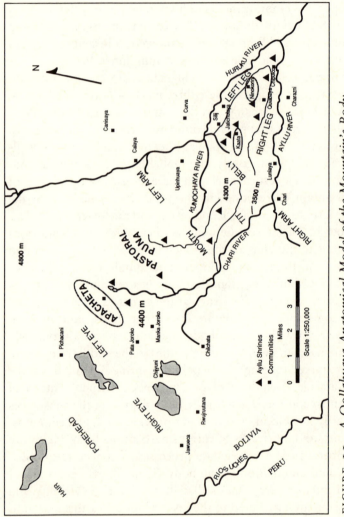

FIGURE 11. *A Qollahuaya Anatomical Model of the Mountain's Body*

SOURCE: J. W. Bastien, "Qollahuaya Body Concepts: A Topographical-Hydraulic Model of Physiology," *American Anthropologist* 87 (1985): 597. Reproduced by permission. Not for further reproduction.

Here then is a complex, ecological model that healers and healed can relate to. People who wish to introduce biomedicine to the Qollahuaya obviously should come to grips with this model. Joseph Bastien took advantage of local beliefs in order to teach people how to use oral rehydration therapy in the control of diarrhea. He writes:

> In essence, I modified an old Andean legend in which two mountains, Sajama and Sabaya, fell in love with Kariquina, a lovely maiden mountain who because of their rivalry rejected both of them. In anger, Sajama knocked the crest off Sabaya with a boulder slung from his sling. In retaliation, Sabaya sent gophers to tunnel out Sajama. The gophers dug many holes in Sajama and daily the water began to drain from this mountain. Sajama got thinnner, began drying up, and when he was almost dead, the condor (symbol of the healer) saved him by flying to Mount Illimani for a liter of *pure* water, to Mururata for two tablespoons of sugar, to Wayna Potosi for a quarter teaspoon of salt, to Condiriri for a quarter teaspoon of bicarbonate of soda, and to Illillampu for a lemon. The condor mixed these ingredients together, returned to Sajama, and gave him tablespoons of his mixture to drink every 15 minutes. After repeating this treatment for one week, Sajama was cured.[20]

Semantic Networks

Related to the preceding ideas about metaphors, myths, and models is the concept of semantic networks. This notion has been developed in an investigation of health beliefs in Iran.[21] Byron Good argues that an understanding of disease taxonomy (see above) is not sufficient if one is to understand what people really think about disease and health. A disease category is not just a set of defining symptoms, it is a syndrome of experiences, language, and feelings that are typical for a given society. This syndrome can be explored through an analysis of semantic networks. A network links together several seemingly dissimilar symbols into a single image that, like a metaphor, myth, or model, produces a core of symbolic associations in the minds of a group of people.

In the town of Maragheh in northwestern Iran, the Turkic-speaking population often complains of "heart distress." Its symptoms are described in very physical terms (the heart pounds, feels squeezed). It is associated with a variety of anxieties related to, among other things, contraception, pregnancy, old age, interpersonal problems, and money worries. But what is the connection between all of these items?

Popular medicine in this town combines elements of Galenic-Islamic (unanic) medicine, sacred medicine, and biomedicine. It has provided a language in which people can talk about their disease experiences. In one respect, it appears to be very disorganized; yet it has a coherence that is part and parcel of the social life of the society. How can a researcher discover that coherence? Returning to "heart distress," one finds that these people do not believe the principal function of the heart to be circulatory; rather, the heart provides the heat necessary for life and transforms breath into the *pneuma,* which vitalizes the body. The heart is the driving force of the body, but it is also used to express emotion. Thus, "heart distress" indicates both a physical problem (abnormal heart beat) and an emotional one (anxiety, sadness, anger).

People were asked to write down the cause of "heart distress," and they produced a wide-ranging list. Good analyzed the list in order to find semantic links between causes and then displayed the results as diagrams. Two important symbolic fields emerged: (1) female sexuality vis-à-vis potency and pollution (figure 12); and (2) the oppression of everyday life. The links between symbols could be explained using knowledge of the local culture. For example, contraceptive pills are sometimes used by women to prevent menstruation during Ramadan (the Islamic month of fasting) because menstrual blood is thought to be ritually polluting.

The implications of this kind of research are that when someone complains of something as nebulous as "heart distress" the reaction should not be simply to prescribe a medicine such as a heart stimulant. Further questioning would probably reveal, in this setting at least, that the patient was anxious about something (e.g., guilty about using the Pill) or felt closed-in (e.g.,

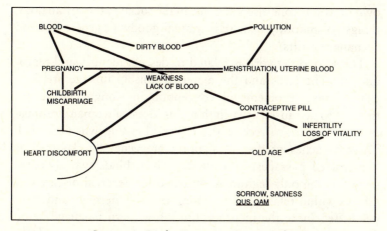

FIGURE 12. *Semantic Links Between Causes of "Heart Distress" in an Iranian Town*
SOURCE: B. J. Good, "The Heart of What's the Matter: The Semantics of Illness in Iran," *Culture, Medicine, and Psychiatry* 1 (1977): 41. Reproduced by permission.

when a woman's husband rarely allowed her to leave the confines of the house).

Another example of semantic networks comes from the Kongo people of Zaire.[22] In Kongo culture the organs and functions of the body and disease symptoms have reference to social relations, plants, and medicines. One important part of the human anatomy is the *vumu,* or abdomen. Vumu also means vulva, uterus, pregnancy, mother's breast, lactation, the family or descendants of the same mother, and food substance or "ball of meat." The unifying idea of all these semantically related items is subsistence, identity, and well-being; also, there is the connotation of social legitimacy and illegitimacy.

Two important referents or networks are related to vumu. One has to do with the first month of an infant's life. During this time, the young child should have his vumu purged three times. Behind these purges is a belief that is related to many symptoms and treatments in Kongo popular medicine: to eat well and defecate freely is a sign of good health, whereas a blockage in the bowels indicates that one is not well, whether owing to one's own or to someone else's actions. In the social realm, by analogy, things go smoothly if there is mutual goodwill, generosity, and exchange of gifts.

The second network is related to descent identity and reproduction. The fetus and the maternal kinship linkage are both called vumu. Problems of conception in Kongo culture are thought to be caused by such things as incest, a woman's promiscuity, or failure to receive the father's blessing when married. These breaches of the social norm are generally classified as "obstructed passages." Pregnancy, which binds two clans together, is the only legitimate obstruction. Venereal disease is a serious vumu-related obstruction, as are "hernie" and "appendicite" (note the incorporation of Western language here). Treatment of these diseases requires removal of the social obstruction that produced them. A dramatic example is the treatment that was used on people who were accused of being witches and of having a sack called *kundu,* which contained illegitimately obtained food (kundu also refers to a ball of strangulated food). The treatment was a very powerful purgative made from the poisonous bark of a tree. Death of the accused established guilt; life exonerated the accused. In either event, the society was cleansed or purged.

Themes and Theories

This chapter has shown several ways in which language is important in the study of health care delivery. I will summarize the role of language by looking at it in two new ways—by relating it to some of the main themes of the "old" cultural geography as well as to two of the recent theoretical approaches developed within the "new" cultural geography. Thus, this chapter on language—appropriately, given the function of language as communication—serves to bridge two perspectives within cultural geography.

Just as the principal language spoken by people varies from region to region, so the ways in which medical practitioners and their patients communicate differ from region to region (see chapter 3). Therefore, anyone practicing medicine or conducting health care research in an unfamiliar medical system (chapter 2) must become aware of how others talk about disease and its treatment. We have also seen how medical language diffuses (chapter 6) across time and space; for instance, biomedical jargon follows the diffusion of biomedical systems. Moreover, disease and health language evolves (chapter 5) as medical advances are made and as people from different medical cultures come into contact. And there is a cultural ecology (chapter 4) aspect to medical language as well. Thus, through language, many societies relate human ailments and their treatments to specific environmental features. They adapt to health problems in a manner that is similar to their overall way of adapting to their physical and built environments.

Chapter 9, on social spaces, emphasizes the importance of social relations and the underlying political and economic forces that serve to constrain health-seeking behavior.[23] In the present chapter, I have discussed the importance of language in lay-medical interaction. I have also shown how a dominant medical system (biomedicine) has used language to belittle rival systems, bolster its own image, and attain cultural and political hegemony. In chapter 10, on place and landscape, I will discuss such topics as the importance of people's everyday experiences and the meaning of therapeutic settings in the humanist tradition. The humanist perspective finds the use of language important because the words people actually use, those which are derived from everyday experience, help to explain their subjective feelings about such matters as health care delivery.[24] In a more abstract sense, the language used in medical situations helps one to interpret or "read" therapeutic landscapes. By studying disease taxonomies; metaphors, myths, and models; and semantic networks, one can gain insights into the lifeworlds of ill people who are seeking care.

9. Social Space

One of the most important emphases in the "new" cultural geography described in chapter 1 is the application of recent social theory. The perspective that many geographers and other social scientists have developed from this theory has been given different names, including *structuralist, materialist, political-economic,* and *social construction.* The basic idea behind this approach is that there are underlying institutional, economic, and political forces within society that shape human actions. These forces act both to constrain human action and to allow opportunities for action. To put it another way, human actions such as health-care-seeking behavior must be seen in their societal *context.* Knowledge of societal context enables a researcher to interpret his or her data. Thus, to understand health care delivery, one needs to know how a society is constituted and what its ideas about health and disease are. I have emphasized this idea throughout the present book—beginning in chapter 2, where medical systems were placed within their societal setting—and I shall go into detail, beginning as always with some basic concepts.

Basic Notions About Social Space

Structuralists believe that surface appearances can be explained only by hidden causal mechanisms.[1] These mechanisms produce divisions in society that are manifested in *class, ethnicity, gender, age,* and other differences or *inequalities.* A basic concept is *hegemony,* or "the power of a dominant class to persuade subordinate classes to accept its moral, political, and cultural values as the 'natural' order."[2] Hegemony may lead to a *hierarchy* of groups within society that have varying degrees of *dominance* or *power.* The dominant culture attempts to *legitimize* itself (e.g., by having laws passed that enforce their exclusionary powers); at the same time, it strives to *restrict* or *marginalize* subordinate groups. A dominant class may employ language (see chapter 8) to create favorable images of itself, to mystify, or to conceal its true purpose of domination. Although hegemony involves the attempt by one group to *control* another, that control is often *resisted* or *contested.* Competition and resistance are natural outcomes of pluralistic cultures (see chapter 3 on medical pluralism); there are always alternatives to the dominant culture, striving to legitimize themselves. Often, intergroup struggles arise over economic and political control, but they also involve spatial and *territorial conflicts.*

To illustrate the foregoing concepts, let us consider for a moment the medical example that is most familiar to most of us: biomedicine and its alternatives as they are practiced in the Western world. Among the practitioners and the users of biomedicine there are distinctions, hierarchies, and inequalities based on class, gender, ethnicity, age and other factors. Over the past century, biomedicine has fought to legitimize itself and to exclude or marginalize alternative practitioners. Physicians try to maintain political and economic control over health care delivery systems. They often brand alternative healers as "quacks." Yet, nonbiomedical practitioners such as chiropractors (see chapter 7 for more on this group) and a variety of "holistic" healers continually struggle to legitimize themselves (e.g., U.S. chiropractors can now receive Medicare payments) and to challenge biomedicine's hegemony. Within the biomedical community itself, groups such as nurses contest the power of physicians.

One example of materialist conceptualization has to do with the work patterns of "health visitors" in Great Britain.[3] Until the late 1970s, health visitors had been assigned a geographic area to serve; then they were assigned to service with a general practitioner (GP). Since the patients on GP lists were less spatially concentrated than they were in the old health visitor areas, health visitors lost some of their detailed local knowledge of patients. They also lost some degree of contact in areas where GP services were poor. Structuralist geographers would contend that the underlying problem here was the attempt on the part of the medical establishment to achieve greater cost-effectiveness by centralizing and integrating health care services. Another structural aspect was the desire of (male) physicians to maintain their dominance over the predominantly female health visitors.

The remainder of this chapter will develop social space ideas under the headings of context in cross-country comparisons, territoriality, underdevelopment, and health care privatization.

Context in Cross-Country Comparisons

There are many ways to look at similarities and differences among the health care delivery systems of the world. In this section, I will suggest only three of many possible political-economic criteria that have been found to be useful. Then the systems of a few selected countries will be briefly discussed in order to illustrate the diverse political and economic contexts that lie behind them. What can be accomplished in a health care system, we shall see, is very much influenced by local governmental and economic policies.

One very general way to classify a health care system is to place it in one of the following five categories:[4] (1) A *free-enterprise* system, characterized by competition among various medical groups to provide health services. The United States comes closest to fitting this system, although many countries around the world have some free-enterprise elements. (2) A *welfare state* system, in which national governments maintain some form of control over health care provision and attempt to distribute medical care fairly. Examples of countries with this system are Sweden, France, and the United Kingdom. (3) A *socialist state* system, in which health care is entirely controlled by the central government and in which there is also an attempt at equitable distribution of health benefits. The Soviet Union and China fit this model most closely. (4) An *underdeveloped* system, in which most people do not have access to biomedical care and in which traditional professional and nonprofessional systems are important. The least-developed countries in Africa, Asia, and Latin America fall into this category. (5) A *transitional* system, in which health care provision falls somewhere between the first three categories and the fourth one. Often an elite group receives expensive biomedical care while the bulk of the population is poorly served. Countries such as Saudi Arabia that have experienced incipient development are often transitional. Note that few, if any, countries fit exclusively into a single category. The above classifications should be viewed as representing overall tendencies.

An economic perspective on health care systems may be gained by asking how health care is funded.[5] Some countries have established a *national health insurance* scheme whereby employers and employees contribute toward the purchase of health insurance. These programs are run by or for the national government, which is responsible for paying out money for health care. Norway, the Federal Republic of Germany, and Japan have this type of program. Great Britain and the Soviet Union have *national health service* plans. These programs receive their funding from taxes collected by the central government. All citizens can use the service but, for certain treatments, may have to pay extra. A third source of funds is from private consumers who either pay for their treatment directly or buy health insurance from private companies. Again, countries do not fit neatly into these three categories. In the United States, for example, individual payment represents one of the highest proportions of total health care funding in the world, yet very important programs such as Medicare and Medicaid are funded by taxes. People in Britain may use either the National Health Service or pay privately. Canada's system is a blend between a national health service and a national health insurance program.

A third scheme for describing health care delivery systems puts an emphasis on historical evolution (see chapter 5 for more on evolution in health care systems) and decision-making processes.[6] It proceeds in three stages. First, one asks what are the structural forces that have produced the current system. Some of the issues one might address here would be the relative roles of private and public health care provision over time, the impact of various legislative acts, and how different ethnic groups and different regions of a country have fared in the past. In the second phase, one would examine how policies are made within the health care sector. Here one would be concerned with such issues as whether planning was centralized or decentralized; how professional organizations make decisions concerning training, treatment specialties, and self-regulation; the role of consumer groups; and how health care fares in relation to other services. The final phase of analysis would focus on those factors which tend to promote or inhibit change within the system. Here one would consider the policies of competing political parties or factions within parties; the extent to which innovations are borrowed from other systems; and the amount of influence various groups such as central and local governments, labor unions, lobbyists, insurance companies, pharmaceutical firms, and consumer advocate groups have on policy.

I will now provide selected details concerning the political economy of health care in countries that are probably not very familiar to most readers: namely, Australia, China, Sweden, and Ethiopia. The recent history of health care policy in Australia illustrates how different political and economic philosophies influence the way medical care is provided.[7] Prior to 1950, unsuccessful attempts were made by liberal politicians to induce the country to adopt either a compulsory health insurance scheme or a national health service. Between 1950 and 1969, conservative political leaders established a system that emphasized individual initiative and a minimal role for government in health provision. The government subsidized health care, but people received government money only if they had voluntarily purchased health insurance from private companies. The pendulum swung to the liberal side between 1970 and 1975, during which time a Labour government increased the government's health care burden substantially and tried to provide care for all in need. Funds came from collective taxation. In 1975 a more conservative government returned to power and reestablished the system of the 1950–69 period. Today, health care funds in Australia come from a mixture of private and public sources. This is typical of most developed nations.

Health care planners have taken a great interest in the struggles of the world's most populous nation, China, to provide health care for all its people through a socialist state system.[8] One interesting aspect of health care in China has been the hegemonic struggle between biomedicine and Chinese medicine since the Communist takeover in 1949. For several years after 1949, an attempt was made to introduce biomedicine on a massive scale. This did not solve China's pressing health problems, however, and so Chinese medicine was also emphasized. During the Cultural Revolution of 1966–69, the Chinese shifted to a focus on appropriate medical technology for rural areas. Public health measures such as large-scale disease eradication campaigns and the use of paramedics ("barefoot doctors" and "worker doctors") enabled the Chinese to make dramatic gains, but a whole generation of biomedically trained personnel was lost to the revolution. In recent years, China has reintroduced biomedicine. China provides the best example of an attempt to integrate traditional medicine and biomedicine.

Perhaps the best example of a welfare state system in the world today is Sweden.[9] The national government maintains a compulsory health insurance scheme, and funds come from three sources: collective taxation, fees paid by employees, and government subsidies. The geographic aspects of the Swedish system are important to note, for an attempt has been made to organize a spatial-functional system of health care facilities. The lowest level of service is provided by commune or township health centers. The next level is the district, where there are small hospitals. At the third level, the county, small hospitals also provide some specialist services. The highest level is the region; each region has a large hospital, and many specialist services are available. The Swedish system is quite expensive and relies heavily on hospitals, but it does provide at least minimal care to everyone.

The Ethiopian health care system must be viewed in the context of a Marxist form of government, a socialist economic system, and a series of destabilizing natural and man-made calamities.[10] There is very strong central control by the revolutionary government that came into power in 1974; a ten-year development plan (1984–93) has produced little economic growth to date. Along with other developing countries, Ethiopia has adopted the World Health Organization plan, which calls for "Health for All by the Year 2000." Thus, it has put more emphasis on primary health care, rural health care, and the control of common diseases. The government health care system is structured hierarchically, as in Sweden. Even though the government has nationalized most banks, businesses, and industry, it is reluctant to do away with all private health care, especially in the urban areas. Traditional medicine predominates in most rural areas, where the bulk of the population lives. Funding for health care is severely limited by the budget alloted to the Ministry of Health: each person is allocated about two dollars per year. The military, agriculture, and resettlement programs all receive more money than the health sector. The military government has some good intentions and very ambitious goals regarding health care and its equitable distribution, but it is hampered by very serious problems, including periodic invasions by Somalia, civil war, repeated famine, chronic poverty, high population growth, a history of infectious disease, and top-heavy, bureaucratic health care planning. Many physicians, if they can manage to do so, leave the country; and attrition rates among health care personnel in general are very high. In sum, the Ethiopian health care system has potential; thus far, however, it has produced little in the way of improvement.

Territoriality

Territoriality refers to the identification that humans and animals have with a particular space.[11] More formally, it may be defined as "the attempt to affect, influence, or control actions and interactions (of people, things and relationships, etc.) by asserting and attempting to enforce control over a specific geographical area."[12] The area in question ranges from a few feet around a person (*personal space*), to one's room in a house, to the boundaries of a city, and on up to the territorial limits (perhaps including the territorial waters) of a country. The idea of a *boundary*, whether definite or vague, is an important aspect of territoriality. Territories can be organized in a very complex, often *hierarchical*, manner, as when a country establishes units (nation, regions, states, counties, cities and townships) that are nested one within the other. The idea of territoriality is used by political geographers to help explain such phenomena as the formation of nation-states and the conflicts between and within countries over space. I use the notion here to shed light on territorial disputes that might arise within health care delivery systems (see chapter 3 on conflicts among health care regions).

Conflict is inherent in the notion of territoriality for several reasons. Territoriality usually implies *power relationships* or attempts by some (often of a particular class, ethnic group, or gender) within a society to impose authority or control over others. The dominant group within a society may manipulate territory to strengthen its control. People often become very emotionally involved in territorial disputes.

Territoriality can be thought of as a strategy for the control of space. As a strategy, it has at least three functions. One is to *classify* things by area. Thus, certain areas in a hospital may be accessible only to health personnel with certain qualifications, or a state may decide to divide its counties up into regional health units. A second function is *communication*, or making known to others what things are to be controlled in specific spaces. In the examples just cited, this might entail posting appropriate signs and regulations in the hospital or printing state maps. Thirdly, territoriality may serve as an efficient means of *distributing scarce resources*. In a hospital setting, resource distribution might involve space and equipment; in a state setting, it might involve human resources and facilities. It should be clear to the reader that the language used to describe territoriality (e.g., control, domination) is the *language of political economy* applied to social space. Note also that classification is related to regionalization (chapter 3), communication to language (chapter 8), and distributing scarce resources to achieving an ecological balance (chapter 4).

The following example will serve to illustrate many of the foregoing ideas.[13] The setting is the area around Rochester, in western New York State. Rochester, which has been dominated for many years by one major industry, Eastman Kodak, is well organized and provides good health care for its residents. Places outside this dominant regional center have had to compete with Rochester to establish and control health care services. Several attempts have been made over the years to regionalize health care in the Rochester area; that is to say, people have tried to classify the space around the city and to allocate resources among different spatial units. This has resulted in conflicts between rival groups. A quasi-official organization, the Rochester Regional Hospital Council (RRHC) was set up in 1951 to regionalize an eleven-county area. However, a Kodak executive, Marion Folsom, felt that the RRHC could not be counted on to carry out health care planning, so he formed a new group, the Patient Care Planning Council (PCPC), which conducted a series of hospital-utilization studies. In the mid-1960s, federal and state legislation was passed in a further attempt to regulate health care activities. One of the new laws called for the establishment of Comprehensive Health Planning (CHP) agencies. Conflict broke out between the RRHC and the PCPC over which group would be designated as a CHP agency. After a struggle that involved organizational name changes, coalitions, and other political maneuvers, the PCPC (which had evolved into the Genesee Region Health Planning Council, or GRHPC) finally won out.

At a different level, one of the communities (called "Regionville" by those who researched the situation) within the area around Rochester was carrying on its own campaign to achieve better health care. The Regionville General Hospital had been established in 1921 and was controlled by the "best families" in the town. In the mid-1960s, one of the most active physicians in the hospital became concerned about the adequacy of the hospital's facilities. In 1966, a State Department of Health team inspected the hospital and stated that if it were to be certified for further operation the hospital would have to spend a considerable amount of money on modernization. The hospital board drew up plans for an entirely new hospital, and those plans were approved by the Hospital Review and Planning Conference of the Rochester Regional Health and Hospital Council in 1968. However, in 1969 the State Hospital Review and Planning Council's Division of Review and Planning raised questions and made some suggestions that jeopardized the project. This body suggested that the new hospital be located in the faster-growing northern part of Regionville's county (Regionville was in the southern part). They also wondered whether the hospital would attract enough patients to be economically viable and whether new physicians could be recruited to replace the aging doctor population that currently served the hospital. This conflict can be seen in hierarchical terms: the state saw the county as a unit, whereas Regionville residents differentiated between northern and southern parts of the county and wanted adequate resources for their local area.

The struggle went on for several years. The GRHPC came out in opposition to some of the hospital's new plans. Regionville hired a consulting firm, made a spirited rebuttal to the arguments of the opposition, and raised 1 million dollars from the town residents. A key factor in the eventual success of Regionville was a core of "self-made men" who owned the larger businesses in the area (see chapter 10 on the role of human agency in health care). The new hospital also formed an affiliation with another hospital in the area. Further, the politically conservative hospital board formed an alliance with a socially active group that was involved in aiding migrant workers; thus, the board would be able to obtain federal funds to set up satellite clinics. The hospital marketed its services aggressively in order to build up a larger catchment area; this brought it into conflict with other hospitals.

This study illustrates several facets of territoriality. It shows that attempts to regionalize or regulate health care often lead to conflict and competition. It demonstrates struggles for hegemony or control between antagonistic groups, divided by class and other characteristics; between geographic areas; and between insiders and outsiders. It also points up the problems that occur when different levels in a territorial hierarchy disagree about their goals. Finally, it shows how a small group of prominent people can often dominate health care provision.

Underdevelopment

One of the particular concerns of structuralists or materialists is underdevelopment, or the fact that some countries or some regions within countries lag behind others in economic growth (this concern was expressed in chapter 3 as a core-periphery problem).[14] Over the past several decades, organizations such as the United Nations and national foreign aid agencies have attempted to deal with underdevelopment, with little success. Several theories have been formulated as frameworks for development projects. It is instructive to look at three of the most prominent. First is *modernization theory,* which gained prominence in the 1960s. In its simplest form, this theory states that societies develop in a linear fashion—from primitive, prerational, preindustrial, and precapitalist to modern, rational, industrial, and capitalist. Western political and cultural values, capital, and technology diffuse to less-developed areas (i.e., the West establishes cultural hegemony, which is desirable, according to this theory). Political and economic change is gradual rather than revolutionary (see chapter 5 on different types of evolutionary change). Modernization theory has been criticized for being Eurocentric, for assuming that initial conditions in developing areas were similar to those in Europe before its modernization began, for ignoring the possibility that societies can sometimes slip backward economically, for failing to see the negative effects of Western values and, finally, for not being able to reproduce substantial developmental gains in most areas. Social scientists and others have pointed to a long list of side effects that modernization produced which were detrimental to health (e.g., schistosomiasis often spread rapidly in the snail habitats created around reservoirs and irrigation canals connected with dams).[15] Critics also pointed out that groups such as the World Health Organization tried to solve health problems through technical approaches when the root causes of the problems were economic, social, and political. Some argued that developed areas provided health care to developing areas primarily in order to maintain healthy labor supplies for Western-owned industries.

Dependency theory also had its beginnings in the 1960s. It states that capitalism, instead of bringing development to countries, has actually contributed to underdevelopment. Countries that were already developed accumulated capital faster than the developing areas and maintained higher levels of capital through unequal exchanges with those areas. In this way, "core" areas were established at the expense of "peripheral" areas. Underdeveloped regions were caught in a cycle of dependency that was perpetuated by worldwide capitalism and by control of the global economy by developed nations. The result for health care was the unequal distribution of medical resources between core and peripheral areas. In the 1980s, dependency theory has also been subjected to criticism. It is said that dependency theory places unwarranted emphasis on market mechanisms and unequal economic exchanges and thus, is simply a mirror image of modernization theory. Both theories lay too much stress on narrowly economic factors. Dependency theory has also been faulted for a lack of empirical verification. Although dependency analysis does have structural elements within it, structuralists have criticized it for not paying much attention to class relations or to the role of the state at different levels.

Third is *Marxist theory*. It focuses on two basic themes: (1) capitalist versus noncapitalist modes of production; and (2) class relations. The capitalist countries or capitalist elements within countries, this theory states, have sought to expand their means of production (based on wage labor) at the expense of precapitalist countries or precapitalist regions within countries. Within developing countries, a class structure emerges that separates the ruling elites and foreign entrepreneurs who control the means of production (e.g., factory work) from the working classes. Workers are drawn into the capitalist system and are thereby removed from the control of precapitalist modes of production (e.g., traditional agriculture). In the Marxist interpretation, the health effects of underdevelopment are not (as in modernization theory) a side effect of development, but are an integral part of capitalist policies. Other, non-Marxist analyses have corroborated this conclusion. The only way out of this situation, recent structuralist theory maintains, is through a revolutionary change in the political, social, and economic structures that capitalism has fostered.

The ideas discussed in the preceding paragraph will now be developed through two examples. The first is the historical evolution of biomedical health care services in Nigeria.[16] In precolonial Nigeria (before 1861) healing was performed by full-time or part-time traditional nonprofessional practitioners; almost every extended family had at least one such person, and so medical services were well distributed. Healers knew the cultural, social, and physical environments of their patients (chapter 7 discusses these practitioners in more detail). There were special places in which particularly difficult health problems were treated (see chapter 10 for more on the importance of place). Although society was not classless and access to health services was not always equal, basic care was available to everyone. Healers often held positions of power in society, and they did restrict membership in their ranks, but few became wealthy through healing.

When the British colonized Nigeria in the latter part of the nineteenth century, they introduced Western-style health services. Christian medical missions, an important part of Western cultural hegemony, established the foundations of the modern health care system. Biomedicine was able to make dramatic advances against some diseases (e.g., smallpox) that traditional healers could not manage, but cure was given precedence over prevention, and health care facilities were located in places (mostly in cities and towns near the coast) that were not accessible to most people and that had no special meaning for them (see chapter 10 for a discussion of meaning in health care). Facilities were set up first for Europeans and then for the Africans who worked for them; healthy bodies meant higher productivity.

From the 1920s on, British hegemony in politics and economics was contested through a nationalist movement. Many Nigerian physicians joined the movement and protested against discriminatory hiring practices. Native healers and others also contested the introduction of biomedicine because they linked it to colonial oppression. On the other side, Christian missionaries called native healers idolators and devils, and the colonial government aggressively legislated against them. Nigerians trained as physicians applauded these laws, for they removed unwanted competition.

After World War II, Nigeria had the potential for rapid economic growth, and health services were expanded. A Ten-Year Health Development Plan initiated in 1946 attempted to provide biomedicine to everyone, but it focused on hospitals, dispensaries, and medical schools; rural areas were largely neglected. Regional, rural/urban, and class inequalities remain to this day. Furthermore, following independence in 1960, Nigerian physicians seized upon opportunities to become wealthy, especially in private practice. The nationalists, including physicians, became the new ruling class.

My second underdevelopment example is a case study of the nutritional status of people in eastern Kenya.[17] This study combines ideas that are drawn from both political economy and cultural ecology (see chapter 4). By way of background, it should be noted that most of sub-Saharan Africa has been enduring a food crisis for many, many years. Domestic production has stagnated and imports of food staples continue to increase. In Kenya, malnutrition has been the fourth leading cause of death in recent years. There are striking variations in food consumption, both seasonally and across regions. The researcher in this study, a materialist, states that famine conditions are largely man-made, the result of political, social, and economic conditions, although so-called natural hazards such as low rainfall do exacerbate the situation.

Like all developing countries, Kenya has a dual economy. One economy is precapitalist; it is characterized by no wage payments for labor and ownership of land by a tribe, clan, or kinship group. The tribe also controls the means of production (which is mainly subsistence agriculture), supervision of labor and technical organization, social obligations, and commodity exchange. The capitalist economy introduces wage labor and thus separates workers from the fruits of their labor (e.g., food and land). A dichotomy grows up between management and labor; supervision and technical organization are controlled by management. Areas throughout the developing world are now in transition from precapitalist to capitalist economies; this transition occurs at different rates in different places. In Kenya, the process began when the British colonists took over the best lands in the highland region and the well-watered areas of the eastern lowlands.

As subsistence production becomes peripheral to capital, the small farmer is forced to become a producer of commodities. Some labor goes into industry, some to cash cropping, and some to mining. As a result, the family or household economy begins to break down. The transition produces marginal, vulnerable people. People are assigned roles in the national economy, often under unstable conditions such as migrant labor (*economic marginality*). This leads to loss of land, loss of self-employment, population pressure on the land that is left, and deleterious practices such as overgrazing (*ecodemographic marginality*).

The Kenya study focuses on the lowland areas where native Kenyans were forced onto dryer, marginal lands. The effect of capitalist penetration here was to force people into making a new adjustment to their environment in times of drought. The precapitalist response to low-rainfall years was early planting, extra weeding, and the use of kinsmen who were obligated by ties of reciprocity to lend a hand in hard times. Some hard-hit farmers "borrowed" land with moist, black soil from kinsmen. Others sent a dependent child to live for a period of time with a relative who was better off. Common land was used for fishing, hunting, and raising crops. Such adjustments, however, were no longer possible in those areas where the capitalist mode of production became dominant. Some lands in these places were removed from peasant ownership for use as game parks or timber reserves. Grazing land was lost and overstocking resulted. Fallow periods were shortened. Vast tracts of land became eroded from improper use. Many young men left agricultural areas to search for wage labor in towns and cities, and much of the traditional agricultural labor force was thus lost. The nutritional consequences of this economic transition were often dire. Instead of producing their own food, which had provided a balanced and nutritious diet, people now tried to earn money to buy food that was often less nutritious.

It is easy to see how a structuralist analysis of underdevelopment could be applied to factors other than health service distribution and nutrition, the main emphases in the two preceding studies.[18] Furthermore, materialist analysis can be expanded to include other structural elements besides class conflicts, including gender and ethnicity.[19] There are many situations in which women and ethnic minorities receive less than their just share of health care.

Health Care Privatization

One of the greatest concerns of those who use a political-economic framework for analyzing health care delivery is the recent trend in many countries toward privatization.[20] For example, as part of a program of retrenchment, governments in the United States and the United Kingdom have been restructuring their health care systems. Many aspects of health care delivery are passing from public to private control. These changes have raised a series of questions that geographers and other social scientists are attempting to answer. What are the implications with respect to more or less equality in health care provision across space and among different groups in society? What roles do national governments, investors of capital, and health care providers play in privatization? What happens when the altruistic motives stated in public policies collide with the profit motives of private concerns? Three examples will demonstrate how privatization is being fostered and what some of its effects are on health care delivery. Concepts such as hegemony, competition, resistance, class structures, and core-periphery will, again, be in evidence.

The conservative government that has been in power in Great Britain since 1979 has passed legislation to restructure expenditures within the National Health Services (NHS).[21] Underlying this effort to restructure is a desire to reduce government expenditures; to transfer the source of funds for welfare services from the state to communities, families, and individuals; and to encourage the free market as a means of economic revival. The government has said that it is committed to maintaining the NHS; yet, it has adopted several policies that put this stated commitment in question. For example, the government has tied public expenditures on the NHS to national economic performance and has asked health authorities to deliver the same amount of services at lower costs. It has also encouraged competitive bidding for such hospital services as catering food and laundering. In some areas, there is no competition for these services, so private contractors have a monopoly. Nor do private contractors have to pay their work force the same wages that NHS staff members receive; thus, there is a built-in potential for a divided work force and a damper on union activity. In addition, general managers have been introduced into the NHS who are supposed to ensure more efficient practices. Although families and communities have been encouraged to lead healthier lifestyles, little money has been spent on eliminating the social problems that lead to ill health.

The British policy of efficiency in health care has led to the closing of many hospitals, especially small ones, and of some hospital departments such as accident and emergency services. In places such as Inner London, poorer people who must rely on public transportation are being denied access to health care. Doctors find it harder to have their patients admitted to hospitals, and waiting times for treatment have increased. Meanwhile, the government has encouraged the growth of the private health care sector. Private health care companies have been provided with tax incentives and controls on the development of private health facilities have been relaxed. Thus, the private sector has grown considerably in recent years, albeit very unevenly across space. Whereas recent government policy has been to transfer NHS funding from the Southeast to northern England and the Midlands in the name of greater equality, private facilities have concentrated in London and the Southeast. Private health care is based on profitability; hospitals and other health care facilities, therefore, tend to locate near markets that promise higher returns on investment. Obviously this creates spatial and social inequalities. Ironically, private health care has not been as profitable overall as expected, and some private concerns have asked for state intervention on their behalf. The government has also encouraged charitable and voluntary commitment to health care provision. Results have depended heavily on the purposes for which money is being raised (high-tech equipment is one favorite) and on who is leading the fund-raising drive (celebrities often do well). Clearly, there are inherent inequalities in these efforts.

In sum, recent government policy in Great Britain has acted to regulate NHS expenditures, on the one hand, and to deregulate the private sector, on the other. It has made deliberate concessions to some special groups (e.g., private hospital developers) and has weakened the position of other groups (e.g., hospital work forces).

As in Britain, the U.S. health care system in general and hospitals in paticular have undergone a radical restructuring in recent years.[22] Several hundred hospitals have been closed since 1970; others have merged or expanded their market areas; and for-profit hospital chains have grown dramatically. One key factor behind this restructuring is the increased competition among hospitals. This increase is partly explained by changes in the demand for services owing to declining populations in some areas. Also, insurance companies have placed more restrictions on hospital admissions and lengths of stay. In addition, medical technology is becoming both more available and more expensive. Hospitals respond by trying to entice patients away from other hospitals and by building up the overall quality of the affiliated physicians who refer patients to them. Thus, hospitals are trying to reduce their capacity (in order to achieve greater efficiency) at the same time that they are trying to increase personnel and equipment. Whatever hospitals do to face competition, they are becoming more and more like corporate businessess.

Meanwhile, governments at various levels have become more involved in regulating hospitals. They do this by licensing, certifying beds, enforcing building codes, limiting expansion, and adopting prospective-reimbursement programs such as diagnostic-related groups which fix payments made to hospitals for patient care (see chapter 5 on recent changes in U.S. health care). Thus, hospitals feel another type of pressure—this time from the state. The part played by the government of New York State is especially interesting. Starting in the early 1970s, New York began to encourage the closure of inefficient hospitals. At the same time, it had to deal with conflicting demands from the hospital industry, which is very important in the political and economic life of the state, to increase hospital expenditures. The solution was to close down the smaller and weaker hospitals.

A study carried out in New York City addressed the question of how hospitals that had different characteristics and that were located in areas of varying socioeconomic status had adapted to competition and regulatory pressures. All short-term general hospitals that were not municipal were included in the study, which covered the period from 1967 to 1983. Hospitals were divided into four groups based on two dichotomous categories: (1) large (270 or more beds) versus small; and (2) location in census tracts of high or low socioeconomic status (based on a principal-components analysis of several socioeconomic variables). (see figure 13.) Most of the thirty-six closures occurred among the small hospitals; more occurred in the lower-status areas (53 percent of all closures) than in the higher-status areas (47 percent). Most expansion (increases of 100 beds or more) took

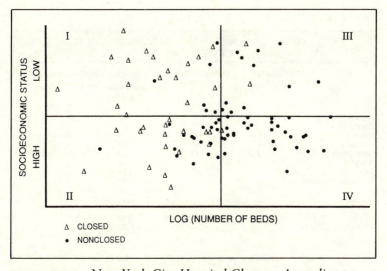

FIGURE 13. *New York City Hospital Closures According to Size and Socioeconomic Status, 1967–83*
SOURCE: S. McLafferty, "The Geographical Restructuring of Urban Hospitals: Spatial Dimensions of Corporate Strategy," *Social Science and Medicine* 10 (1986): 1083. Reprinted by permission of Pergamon Press PLC.

place in the large, high-status group because hospitals in that group had wealthier patients and were more easily able to persuade government authorities that they were financially viable. There were four mergers; all involved a larger hospital in a lower-status area and a smaller hospital in a higher-status area. Thus, overall, health practitioners and facilities abandoned smaller hospitals and poorer neighborhoods and moved to larger hospitals and richer areas. This is in line with what happens in many other industries that are in the mature stage of their life cycle. As a result, poorer people in New York City have had to travel farther than before to hospitals.

Multinational pharmaceutical companies (MPCs) are private concerns that have had a very strong influence on the privatization of health care in less-developed countries (LDCs).[23] As these firms expand their LDC markets for legal drugs (LDCs spend higher proportions of their total health care budgets on drugs than do more-developed countries, or MDCs; see table 4) and as

TABLE 4.

ESTIMATED HEALTH AND PHARMACEUTICAL EXPENDITURES BY WORLD REGIONS				
Region	GDP Used for Health (%)	Per-capita Health Expenditure (U.S. $)	Pharmaceutical Expenditures	
			Per-capita (U.S. $)	As a Percentage of Total Health Expenditure
North America	10	1160	70.5	6.1
Europe (West)	8	800	54.9	6.8
Japan	7	630	92.4	14.6
Europe (East)	7	385	25.4	6.6
South America	4	72	15.2	21.1
Africa	2	14	6.5	46.4
Asia	3	87	13.4	15.4
Southeast Asia/China	2	10	4.7	47.0

SOURCE: Joseph L. Scarpaci, ed., *Health Services Privatization in Industrial Societies* (New Brunswick: Rutgers University Press, 1989). Reprinted by permission.

they promote consumer self-care, they tend to enlarge the private health care sector in those countries. An examination of the practices of MPCs serves to point up the controversy over the advantages and disadvantages to health care consumers of privatization. On the positive side, drug companies are sound businesses that are well organized to deliver drugs efficiently to consumers. LDC governments are often inefficient and lack the infrastructure to distribute drugs effectively. Many people in LDCs turn to private drug suppliers (pharmacists, street vendors, and others) because they can not obtain medicines anywhere else. On the other hand, MPCs create many health problems. They exert a very strong control over drug markets and make it very difficult for LDC governments to have a say about what medicines are imported into their countries. Many unsafe or inappropriate drugs are dumped in LDCs. Drug firms control research and development, encourage the sale of expensive brand-name drugs over generics, promote over-the-counter rather than prescription sales, and spend very large sums on marketing and promotion. They also create social and spatial inequalities in drug provision.

Many LDC governments have tried to wrest control of drug production and distribution from the MPCs. Some have made lists of essential drugs and purchase only these. Some have established domestic industries that are state-controlled (although most succumb to the temptation of reaping profits from the establishment of MPC branch plants). International organizations within the United Nations and regional organizations have had little success in controlling the drug firms, although a handful of countries (among them Mozambique, Cuba, India, and Sri Lanka) have made some progress along these lines. Still, most LDCs have established a dominance/dependency (core-periphery) relationship with the drug companies. Politically, the MPCs are backed by the MDCs. Economically, the MPCs control the flow of capital, which goes into the production, research and development (a new drug costs 30–60 million dollars to develop), and distribution of drugs.

The record of the drug companies in LDCs makes some of the claims of the proponents of privatization questionable. Privatization is supposed to lead to competition and, thus, lower costs. Yet, the MPCs form an oligopoly (a very few firms based in a very few countries control legal drugs), and that means that drug prices tend to be higher than they would be in a "free market." Privatization, its proponents also claim, will lead to greater consumer participation in and control over health care provision. Yet, experience shows that consumers are almost powerless against the MPCs. Finally, privatization is said to lead to mutually beneficial partnerships between drug firms and LDC governments. In practice, dominance/dependency prevails.

The Political-Economic Perspective

The recent introduction of the social space concept into the study of health care delivery has brought about a change of perspective. Basically, it has heightened the importance of context that I first said was so vital (see chapter 2). In particular, geographers and other social scientists are now paying more attention to those political factors (e.g., government policies) and economic factors (e.g., methods of payment) which both constrain and provide opportunities for action related to health care. It is very important to realize that these factors vary considerably from country to country.

Political economy has made us more aware of certain aspects of health care delivery. It is often overlooked that conflict within medical systems is inevitable whenever different interests struggle for control. These conflicts may be along social class, gender, ethnic, or practitioner/patient lines as one group attempts to dominate or achieve medical hegemony over another group. My discussion of territoriality exemplifies one approach to examining the basis of conflict. The political-economic approach also emphasizes historical contingency; that is to say, underlying forces that affect health care must be traced back to their source, and their evolution needs to be described. One cannot understand the current health care system in the United States, for example, without knowing something about its European roots, about the development of health care legislation, and about how the chaotic system of funding came to be.

Two specific topics dealt with in political-economic research were discussed in this chapter. Addressing the first, underdevelopment, I traced the evolution of theoretical and empirical studies that tried to explain health care inequalities between more- and less-developed areas. The second topic was the struggle between private and public control of health care. The two sectors, it was shown, were in basic conflict over such issues as economic efficiency versus the provision of minimum health care to all who need it.

The structuralist point of view has been criticized as being too deterministic and not allowing for the role of human agency.[24] I address this criticism in the following chapter.

10. Place and Landscape

In chapter 9 I focused on one of the major concerns of the new cultural geography: social space. This chapter takes up another—one that, very broadly speaking, comes from the *humanist perspective,* although many of the ideas expressed have also been developed by those who do not consider themselves to be humanists.[1] The humanist tradition, which can be traced back to the fourteenth-century Italian Renaissance, was always an important part of cultural geography but has tended to be obscured by the positivist emphasis of the 1950s and 1960s.[2] By the late 1960s, however, there was a renewed interest in humanist perspectives. The new humanism, in fact, was in large part a reaction against the mechanical, deterministic, and overly objective aspects of positivism. Humanists, backed by *philosophies of meaning* such as idealism, existentialism, and phenomenology, searched for meaning and value in people's everyday experiences. They emphasized the *feelings,* purposes, and goals of individuals and used biographies and personal narratives to help explain human behavior. They sought *understanding* rather than explanation, using such methods as *thick description* (in-depth, layered meaning) and *participant-observation.* Special emphasis was given to how people have developed a strong *sense of place,* an identification with their immediate surroundings. The *ideologies* that people developed and used in dealing with their everyday world were also emphasized. These include ideas derived from society (e.g., belief in witchcraft or germs) that may go beyond observable phenomena. *Landscape,* which had always been an important theme in cultural geography (material landscape in particular) was revived; now, however, research was reoriented toward consideration of its *symbolic meaning*. These main ideas will now be illustrated through a series of examples.

Place and Sense of Place

"Place" has always been an important part of cultural geography.[3] The early cultural geographers described neighborhoods, towns, and regions as *unique locations* with a variety of distinguishing features. The quantitative revolution that began in the 1960s diminished the emphasis on place. Instead, abstract space and the search for spatial patterns within a number of places became the focus of attention. In recent years, though, the importance of place has been revived by geographers, including those who are developing the new regional geography (see chapter 3).

Yi-fu Tuan says that "a place is the compelling focus of a field; it is a small world, the node at which activities converge."[4] One oft-used expression in place studies is "sense of place," or the transference of moral and aesthetic judgments to particular sites. Thus, places acquire a spirit, a *personality,* that insiders and outsiders alike can sense.

Even though places inevitably change over time, they continue to make sense, largely because they have meaning for people. Meaning is the key to the importance of places, and it is the subjective experiences that people have within places that give them significance. Several geographic studies have tried to uncover the dominant meanings of places and the quality of experiences within them. The quality of experiences is reflected in people's memories and expectations and in stories that are told of events real and imagined. Some phenomenologists have developed the concept of the *lifeworld,* or the taken-for-granted world of everyday living and thinking, in order to help explain experience within places. The lifeworld involves lived experiences and shared meanings. A satisfying existence within the lifeworld depends on having firm links with the place in which a person lives.

Places have several kinds of meaning for people. They help to provide identity and satisfy a human need for roots. They are the locations of social networks; they provide settings for employment and services; and they are often sought out for their aesthetic qualities. It is worth noting that places can have negative meanings; they can also lose meaning. People, for example, complain about places that are polluted or in which the physical and human environments have been degraded in some way.

Among those geographers who have attempted to renew a professional interest in place, some have contrasted it with space. Space is an abstract notion, universal, whereas place is concrete, particular. Space is a neutral container of objects; place is an active receptacle of shapes, powers, and feelings. Place is studied with an eye to its meanings for people; space is analyzed in terms of its quantifiable attributes and patterns. Humanists stress that place is more than space, that it is space filled with people acting out their lives. They criticize positivists for focusing exclusively on the analysis of space and thereby neglecting human intentions and values.

Another dichotomy helpful for understanding the concept of place is that of place versus *placelessness*. Places are sites where people feel at home, sites that they cherish and care about. Placelessness is a feeling that a person has when he or she feels alienated from the environment, often when attempts have been made to dominate and control it. Places are, in a sense, authentic and people have sincere feelings for them. In contrast, placelessness results from a *distortion of authenticity* by arbitrary social and intellectual fashions. This distinction conjures up images of quiet, tree-lined neighborhoods, on the one hand, and garish, neon-lit strip development on the other.

It is useful to distinguish between two types of place, those which are *public symbols* and those which are *fields of care*. Public symbols appeal basically to the visual sense: their impression is immediate and direct, and they tend to inspire awe. Cathedrals, statues of military heroes, massive buildings, and striking physical features are examples of public symbols. Fields of care, in contrast, are appreciated by the nonvisual senses of hearing, touch, smell, and taste. They inspire affection rather than awe and can be known only from within over long periods of acquaintance, through networks of interpersonal concern. Examples would include close-knit neighborhoods, meeting places for support groups, and inner-city gang territories.

Ideas about place must answer the same sorts of questions that one encounters throughout the study of geography: On what scale is place encountered? What are the bounds of a place that has significance to those within it? The simple answer, but a reasonable one, is that "place" comes into being if it satisfies the criteria implicit in the definition and descriptions of place given above—in other words, when it embodies meaning, when it has intentionality, and when it is an arena for interpersonal relationships. Thus, a place can vary in size from the corner of a room to the entire earth.

One important notion that arose out of the humanist concern with place is that places are *negotiated realities*.[5] This idea traces its roots to the *symbolic interactionism* of G. H. Mead. Place is seen as an arena where people interact purposefully with one another and with their environment in the process of establishing social structures. There is a reciprocal relationship between people and place: place influences personal identity, and people give meaning to place. Furthermore, the idea of a negotiated reality suggests that a struggle or contest goes on continually within places.

Place and Health

Let us now relate these ideas to health care delivery. I will take the example of a large urban hospital, although any setting in which a health care system exists (e.g., a village in a developing country) could serve as an illustration. Our hospital is a place because it is where a wide range of people and activities converge, mostly in order to treat people's illnesses. A hospital can also be said to possess a personality—it has a local and perhaps even a national reputation, it is noted for certain specialties, and the image people have of it is influenced by what others say is good or bad about it and even by medical soap operas on television. Our hospital may be a public monument because it is an unusually imposing building and is a source of pride to the community, but it is more obviously a field of care. Most of us remember the sounds, smells, tastes, and feelings experienced during a hospital stay. There is no doubt that a hospital has a myriad of meanings, depending on one's experiences there. Some people like playing the sick role and enjoy the attentions of doctors, nurses, and technicians. Others fear the hospital; for them, it is an arena of pain and, ultimately, death. People's feelings about hospitals run the gamut from absolute loathing, after a traumatic illness, to great affection after a miraculous cure. Some complain of the impersonality, the degradation, the placelessness of a hospital while others find reassurance and identity. Hospitals generate tales, real and fictional, that people savor in dinner conversations.

Geographic studies rarely pay much attention to the meaning of places in health care delivery. It is true that some mention is made of the quality of care in places such as hospitals and that the health care setting is of great importance to traditional healing, but these qualities are difficult to measure or objectify and thus lie outside the usual positivist approach. In fact, most geographic studies of health care delivery are based on an abstract analysis of space as opposed to an analysis of place. *Where* a hospital lies within a spatial distribution of hospitals is given more importance than *what goes on* within that particular hospital. The humanist, however, would argue that it is not only spatial accessibility that is important; one should also consider such qualities in a field of care as the amount of genuine attention given to individual patients and the convenience of hours of operation.

A hospital also clearly illustrates the concepts of symbolic interactionism and negotiated reality. There are a multitude of interactions among hospital personnel that establish hospital routines and among health personnel and patients that determine provider-client relationships. Conflicts inevitably arise as doctors vie for status, nurses rebel against the authoritarianism of physicians, and patients seek to obtain a sense of belonging.

The anecdote related in chapter 8, at the beginning of the section on communication, is a good example of negotiated reality in a hospital setting.[6] In that case, the health team had to show a patient that her model of reality was incorrect.

A concrete example of basic place concepts comes from a study of the life experiences of several alcoholics.[7] The psychiatric literature has shown that attachment to place is important for a patient's self-identity. Michael Godkin's investigation demonstrates how places "became reservoirs of significant life experiences lying at the center of a person's identity and sense of psychological well-being."[8] It uses the notions of *uprootedness* and *rootedness* to show how negative self-images often accompany alcoholic behavior, whereas positive self-images often are part of the recovery process. Most alcoholics have little feeling of self-worth, partly because they feel that they belong to no place, that they are uprooted. Often they have lived in places where they felt unwanted or threatened. Certain places become symbols of failure. Loss of a sense of place contributes to psychological stress and consequent attempts to alleviate stress with drinking. On the other hand, some places may have been refuges for alcoholics; these places produce positive images, or rootedness, and help them maintain an identity. The implications of these ideas for therapy are quite clear. If patients can be made to recall places that they have associated with good, secure feelings, then they can be helped to achieve higher self-esteem. On the other hand, the recollection of threatening places has the potential to act as a cathartic agent. A rootedness strategy has been used by Godkin and others to establish a Palliative Care Unit for terminally ill cancer patients within a hospital. That field of care is designed to present patients with familiar images so that they experience a sense of continuity with the reassuring places they have lived in before.

Symbolic Landscapes

Human societies have developed a wide range of *symbols,* both concrete and abstract, to help them express meaning in their lives.[9] Think of the meanings, the emotions, attached to these symbols: a country's flag, the Christian cross, the free press, and "natural" foods. I have already discussed symbolic language in chapter 8, with respect to metaphors and myths. The symbols that we use arise from our culture and help to reproduce it. In fact, some social scientists see the study of culture as the study of symbolic systems. Symbols are crucial in the formation of social identity and everyday reality. They confirm and reify what we know and believe, and they help us to gain more knowledge. They can create emotion and impel us to action. Symbols can also be used to control information and meaning; they can be manipulated and changed to promote the ideas of the manipulators. Because symbols, by their very nature, are often ambiguous and have multiple meanings, they can be interpreted in different ways and can be used to mystify and confuse people. Thus, symbols can be used to promote the interests of dominant groups within society (see chapter 9 on dominance and control).

Consider the white coat of the biomedical physician. This symbol may represent many different things to different people: on the positive side, confidence, hope, purity, professionalism, science, and advanced technology; on the negative side, colonial oppression and the uncaring medical establishment. Incompetent physicians have hidden behind this coat; confidence men dressed in this coat have talked people out of their life's savings. I once accompanied an elderly white lady to the emergency room of a large hospital. She found it hard to believe that a very young black man dressed in a green coat was really a fully qualified physician (there were, perhaps, three negative symbols here for her).

Often dismissed as quacks by the biomedical profession, alternative healers attempt to project their own positive images. Many call themselves (w)holistic healers. What does this mean? Again, many things: being in tune with the "natural" world; treating both mind and body; caring; confidence trickery. One connotation may be that biomedical physicians are *not* holistic, but of course this is not true.

People who have grown up in societies where the Galenic tradition of medicine is still strong (see chapter 2) have internalized a symbolic system that distinguishes between "hot" and "cold" in many phases of life, including food, illness, and medicines. Thus, a person who suffers from a "cold" illness might eat "hot" foods in order to restore a humoral balance. When prescribing medicines, healers must be aware of the strength of this symbolic system.

The Ndembu of Zambia employ a set of concrete and abstract symbols whose meanings include healing.[10] There is a tree whose red, sticky gum is called *mukula*, a word that is related in meaning to "coagulated blood" and also to "maturation" (*kukula*), in particular the onset of menses in women. Young men who have been circumcised (links to bleeding, coagulation, maturity) sit on logs of mukula wood. Both coagulated blood and maturation are linked to the idea of healing and togetherness—in the personal, physical sense and in the societal sense. Thus, healing has connections with other meanings in Ndembu society; knowledge of these connections can be used to assist the healing process.

Landscape has been one of the main themes of traditional cultural geography.[11] It represents the mixture of the physical geographic features of the earth's surface with a transformation of that surface by human activities; it is the result of the evolving interaction of people with their natural and man-made environments (see chapter 4 on cultural ecology). Most cultural geographers have been concerned with the material aspects of landscapes (e.g., barn types, churches, crops, barbed wire), with discovering their origins and diffusion patterns, with mapping their locations. Over the past several years, there has been a revival of interest in landscape, but the focus has recently shifted to the meanings of, the ideas behind, the symbolic nature of, human landscapes.[12] The basic concept is that human ideas and life in society create landscapes and places and vice versa. Landscapes, therefore, are social documents, manifestations of symbolic systems. They are "ways of seeing." One can gain an understanding of cultures by *reading* or *interpreting* the landscapes they create as one would read a *text* or book. One looks for symbols and images in the landscape; one decodes landscapes to penetrate their meaning. The symbolic content of landscapes (as one would expect, given the ambiguous nature of symbols) is read differently by different people. This means that there is a *plurality* of landscapes, just as there is pluralism in medical systems (see chapter 2).

Disney Land is a landscape that represents an important aspect of American culture. Long before most children (and adults) visit Disney Land they have been exposed to hours of media hype about this land of fantasies. Most Americans and visitors from other countries expect to have a very good time there, and most of them will tell you that they indeed did have a good time. How does one read or interpret this landscape? Again, it depends on how one's images have been formed, on what kind of *ideology* has been formed in our thinking. Thus, for some it may be the ultimate experience in entertainment, the evocation of a strong sense of childhood nostalgia for cartoon characters, the fulfillment of dreams, well worth the cost; for others, it can be the epitome of a hedonistic, artificial, and shallow culture, a waste of resources, a failure to come to terms with reality.

There are many ways in which one could approach the task of illustrating symbolic landscapes in health care delivery. Three studies of therapeutic landscapes,[13] each having a different emphasis, are presented in the remainder of this chapter. The first focuses on the role of societal ideologies and the use of symbolism in creating treatment landscapes for the mentally ill; the second stresses political-economic factors in the development of therapeutic landscapes for colonial officers in West Africa; and the third combines the importance of place, symbolic landscapes, and social space with respect to the use of the "healing waters" of U.S. spas.

Treating the Mad

The history of the treatment of mentally ill people in Europe affords an excellent opportunity to illustrate the therapeutic landscapes created by societies living in different times and places. These landscapes are closely related to the ideologies that people have had concerning the nature of the world and important aspects of their culture. Note in particular the clusters of symbols used in this discussion, and also note how treatment of madness is closely associated with such political-economic themes as dominance and class structure (see chapter 9).

During the Renaissance, many insane people were driven from towns and cities and had to wander throughout the countryside.[14] Some were given over to the care of merchants and pilgrims; others were put into the hands of boatmen who moved "ships of fools" from town to town along the rivers and canals of Europe. The *Narrenschiff* (ship of fools), which carried imaginary heroes and other important figures on great symbolic voyages, was a common literary device of the time. Possibly, some of these ships of fools were on pilgrimages to religious shrines, symbolizing to the Renaissance imagination a search for reason. Two seeming opposites coincided in the treatment of the insane: they were expelled from places of habitation, but at the same time they were enclosed within a sacred circle. They were set apart from the rest of society and yet, like all humans, they awaited deliverance from their madness. *Water* and *navigation* are symbols that were connected to the exclusion/inclusion theme. Water served to carry off the mad, but it also purified. Navigation was linked to *embarkation,* setting off toward the unknown, and the soul was a boat at the mercy of the sea's madness (associated with demonic tendencies) unless saved by the anchor of faith in God.

According to Michel Foucault, Renaissance fascination with the ship of fools grew out of a great uneasiness about "a sort of unreason for which nothing, in fact, is exactly responsible, but which involves everyone in a kind of secret complicity."[15] The ambiguous figure of the madman was used to express this "great disquiet" in various ways in the painting, literature, and philosophy of the day: a figure of Death and the world's destruction; mockery of Death; the hidden bestial nature of humanity; a secret, forbidden knowledge that fools possess which would lead to

Satan's rule and the end of the world; and madness as a mirror that reveals to every person his or her own presumption. In other words, insane people came to stand for—to symbolize—people's deepest fears (a plurality of fears) about themselves and their world. The mad were forced into symbolic landscapes in an attempt to allay those fears.

In the classical period (beginning in the seventeenth century), European thinking about the insane evolved (see chapter 5 on cultural evolution). People tried to bring order to disorder by confining the mad and classifying them. *Confinement* symbolically replaced embarkation, and the great uneasiness subsided; the ship of fools was moored fast to land and became a hospital, located in the midst of society. Indeed, "the world of the early seventeenth century is strongly hospitable, in all senses, to madness."[16]

And yet, the new places of confinement had little to do with curing the insane. Rather, they reflected an attempt to control society by the authoritarian governments of the day. Starting in 1656 with the founding of the Hôpital Général in Paris, a series of European establishments began to confine the poor, the unemployed, criminals, and the insane—both those who freely presented themselves and those who were seized by royal or judicial authority. Such places were not set up to cure, but to maintain order. Places of confinement sequestered the mad and other undesirables and established "homelands" for them.

Places of confinement reflected the dominant social concerns of the classical period: a desire to aid the poor, but also a work ethic that looked unkindly on idleness; also a desire to join moral obligation to civil law. Those who were out of work were confined, and the confined were given work to do. In good economic times (full employment and high salaries) the confined provided cheap labor; in hard times, the unemployed were confined to prevent social unrest. The mad were seen as socially useless because they contributed little to productivity. Madness no longer roamed the seas; its new symbolic landscape was the place of confinement in the midst of society.

A further stage in treating the mad has been outlined from a careful reading of the first forty issues of a nineteenth-century British publication, the *Asylum Journal*.[17] When the journal began, a restructuring of the "mad-business" was being carried out in England and Wales. Attempts were being made to supplement or replace a disorganized system of private, for-profit houses, charitable institutions, local jails, houses of correction, and workhouses with a national system of county and borough asylums that would be run by people trained to take care of mental patients. Although the impetus for reform (doing away with such practices as bloodletting, emetics, chains, and whips) had come from laypeople, the restructuring can be seen as an attempt by physicians who belonged to the Association of Medical Officers of Asylums (AMOA) to carve out and maintain hegemony over the business of treating the mad. "Madness" was being medicalized into "mental illness."

Most contributors to the *Asylum Journal* (authorized by the AMOA) held the view that had been predominant in earlier times: namely, that the mad should be separated socially and spatially from the general population. This despite the fact that a few people put forward the argument that mental health could be achieved by inclusion rather than exclusion: an example was the insane colony in Gheel, Belgium, where patients lived with local families.

One of the major questions debated in the journal was the best location for asylums. The majority view may be interpreted as a reaction to the growing urban-industrial landscape, with its poor housing and dirty factories which came to be associated with an increase in insanity.[18] The mentally ill were viewed both as victims of modern civilization and as too morally weak to cope with it. Thus arose the rural asylum, located in a tranquil, "natural" setting where the mad could be set apart from that which was driving them mad. There were two main considerations in siting asylums in rural places. One was that the location should be perfectly healthy. This goal was met by looking closely at such features of the physical landscape as climate, underlying rock type, topography, elevation, vegetation cover, drainage, and water supply. The moral consideration stressed the advantage of the countryside as a place for taking refreshing walks in the pure air, as the occasion of aesthetic pleasure, and (echoing earlier sentiments about the work ethic) as a place where the mentally ill could profit by engaging in agricultural pursuits.

There were some objections to placing asylums in rural areas, however. Some said that this would hinder the training of mental health physicians in urban schools. Others said that the practice would be discriminatory because the poor could not afford to travel to rural places. Another argument was that it would be difficult to supply medical resources to and provide staff and patient recreation in remote sites. And some proponents of urban asylums said that they could be just as morally uplifting and that nature could be brought within urban walls in the form of pictures of rural scenes. Despite the objections, though, the rural view usually held sway in nineteenth-century England and Wales.

The important point here is that "the specific debates . . . were *all* connected in various ways to arguments and proposals centring on the institutional geography of the 'mad-business.' . . . These geographies were not produced by any autonomous 'logic of spatial organization,' then, but by 'creative locational acts' whose origins lay deep within a matted web of prejudices, intuitions, convictions, assumed 'facts,' hopes and fears, a few tangles of which can perhaps be discerned from a detailed scouring of contributions to the *Asylum Journal*."[19]

Protecting a Colonial Elite

At the turn of the century, the British colonial government in Sierra Leone, West Africa, attempted to create a therapeutic landscape for some of its officers in Freetown by establishing a hill station some distance from the town.[20] Freetown was begun at the end of the eighteenth century as a home for former slaves who came by various routes from the New World or who were freed from slave ships by the British. The Freetown area became the colony of Sierra Leone in 1808.

The western coast of Africa was well known to harbor a variety of often fatal diseases; in fact, it became known as the "white man's grave." Malaria, in particular, caused severe problems for the newly arriving colonials. At the end of the nineteenth century, the general belief was that people contracted malaria (literally, "bad air" in Italian) from coming into contact with the air that arose in specific environments or physical landscapes: swamps, wetlands, and newly plowed lands where damp, decaying organic material was exposed to the air. However, Ronald Ross, while an officer in the Indian Medical Service, established in 1898 that the disease was transmitted by the *Anopheles* mosquito.

While at the Liverpool School of Tropical Medicine, Ross proposed an expedition to Freetown, which was considered to be the most malarious region in the British Empire. He mapped out around one hundred mosquito breeding pools throughout the town and suggested that they be drained and swept out. The British Colonial Office was skeptical and, although they did sponsor a limited cleanup campaign, they dropped Ross's idea as too costly. The leaders of a second expedition, this one sponsored by the Colonial Office itself, suggested that the senior officers in the Sierrra Leone service be segregated from the rest of the population. The idea was that, because Africans suffered much more severely from malaria than Europeans, Europeans could not be infected by other Europeans, but only by Africans. Since it was believed that mosquitoes bit people only during the night, colonial officers could safely work among Africans during the day and seek safety in a segregated refuge after hours. Furthermore, it was thought that mosquitoes could fly only about a quarter of a mile; thus, a remove of half a mile would be sufficient. All of these assumptions we know today to be false or, at best, only partially true.

Although some colonial officials objected to the racist connotations of the segregation proposal, a community called Hill Station was established on a plateau 240 meters above Freetown and was linked to the town center by a railroad (figure 14). One of the principal reasons for this decision was that it was economically justifiable to spend money on a new community if it would prolong the lives of senior officers. Prefabricated bungalows,

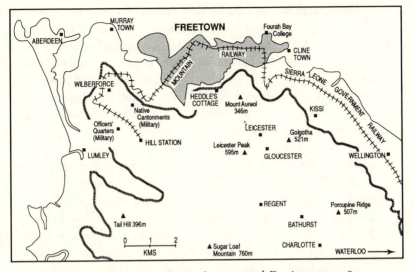

FIGURE 14. *Freetown, Sierra Leone, and Environs, 1908*
SOURCE: S. Frenkel and J. Western, "Pretext or Prophylaxis? Racial Segregation and Malarial Mosquitoes in a British Tropical Colony: Sierra Leone," *Annals of the Association of American Geographers* 78 (1988): 218. Reproduced by permission.

built for health and comfort, were sent from England. They were aligned to face the prevailing breeze and to minimize the force of the sun's rays on the front veranda or porch. Ironically, given the rationale for segregation from Africans, each household was allowed first one, then two, domestic servants, who lived behind each bungalow. It was later explained that a "sizable" African community was necessary for malaria to strike. In other words, comfort took precedence over medical theory.

It was clear that a primary motive for building Hill Station was to ensure the physical safety and well-being of the senior colonial officers (note that Ross's abandoned plans would have protected the entire Freetown community). But gains in the psychological health of the privileged few were also envisaged. One goal was to change the negative health image that western Africa had throughout the British Empire. Hill Station was therefore presented as similar to the famous hill stations of India, and proponents sang the praises of its fresh air, beautiful scenery, spacious bungalows, and gardens. Western Africa also was held in low esteem among colonial posts; indeed, the general feeling was that the Colonial Office sent its least-promising recruits there. Thus, building a hill station might attract a better class of officer. The private lives of senior officials could also now be improved: there was an officer's club (symbol of status and prestige), and the overall environment would help solve the long-standing problem of a lack of wives.

Although medical reasons were the most important public justification for segregation, it must be remembered that the construction of Hill Station took place within a colonial cultural context (see chapters 2 and 9 concerning context) which was undoubtedly racist. British policy makers considered themselves to be superior in culture to the natives in their colonies. In Freetown, poor sanitary conditions were blamed on the lazy Africans. Therefore, when different options for therapeutic landscapes were available, it is not too surprising that segregation carried the day: "Thus, the medical *language* seems often to have served as an expedient, with a *meaning* more social than scientific" (emphasis added).[21] One final irony: a 1913 Colonial Office report stated that the health of officials who lived in Freetown appeared to be no worse than that of those who resided in Hill Station.

Healing Waters and Hydropathy in the United States

Since classical Greek and Roman times, certain bodies of water such as mineral springs have been thought to possess healing powers if one either bathed in them or drank from them. Water symbolized purification and absolution and thus had extraordinary, even mystical, power (as did water in treating the mad in Renaissance Europe; see above). The idea of healing water was taken up by colonial Americans in the eighteenth century, and the tradition of establishing health spas centered around restorative springs continued into the twentieth century. Two main aspects of these resorts are of interest here: (1) their physical setting and (2) their symbolic and social meaning.[22]

The early American colonists first looked for healing waters within or near commercially important towns like Boston or Philadelphia. These places proved to be of little restorative value, however; furthermore, they often became polluted by human waste. The search for healing water turned to rural areas that satisfied two goals: pastoral cleanliness and social neutrality. In a spa such as Bristol in Bucks County, Pennsylvania, people had a sense of being in Arcadia. Bristol was also a place where the landed gentry could mingle with farmers and others from the lower social classes. By the middle of the nineteenth century, resorts built around mineral springs were a booming industry. Some places, such as Poland Spring, Maine, developed such a reputation for having unusual, mysterious healing powers that Americans traveling in Europe demanded water from this spring for drinking and bathing.

There is no doubt that early Americans sought out spas to improve their physical health. This was especially true in the south, where malaria and other diseases were endemic both in the coastal towns and in rural areas. Spas also provided for psychological and social well-being, however. Many people used resorts as an escape from the boredom and pressures of city life. Some began to frequent resorts established in higher and more airy sites in the Appalachians of western Virginia and Pennsylvania, the country around the Adirondacks, and the uplands of central New England.

By the middle of the nineteenth century, there was a change in cultural attitudes toward nature that affected the attraction spas held (see chapter 5 on cultural evolution). Earlier, nature had been viewed as brutal and frightening, a lawless wilderness that encouraged bad behavior. The Romantic movement of the early nineteenth century, however, induced a new feeling that rural landscapes should be sought out for their "picturesqueness" and "sublimity."

James Vance traces two major ideologies that the romantic idealization of nature fostered and that influenced subsequent U.S. history. One, the Hudson River school, was represented by nature painting, an emotional response to nature, and the stories of Washington Irving and James Fenimore Cooper. It looked for an unspoiled America and ultimately led to the search for ideal landscapes in California, for utopias where people could be free of industrial society and live in the once-feared wilderness. The Concord school, in contrast, was more ethical in nature and was strongly influenced by the writings of Henry David Thoreau and Ralph Waldo Emerson. Members of the Concord School maintained social ties with urban places and sought to humanize natural landscapes. The outcome of this sort of interaction with rural places was the establishment of *exurbia,* settlements at the fringes of cities which were accessible to nature. Thus, the healing powers of spas, though still important to many, began to assume less importance within the context of much more generalized feelings about the psychological and social benefits of rural landscapes. At the same time, "seeking the waters" had a lasting effect on settlement patterns in America and on the feelings that people attached to particular places.

Behind the nineteenth-century American interest in water cures was the movement called hydropathy, begun by Vincent Priessnitz, a Silesian peasant, in the 1820s. Hydropathy became an important ideology that encompassed not only healing, but also such ideals as human perfectibility, social uplift, and self-determination. For many people, "hydropathy instilled a sense of *meaning, order, power,* and *control*" (emphasis added).[23] Proponents of hydropathy resisted the attempt by the physicians of the day to dominate health care delivery. Part of its popularity, in fact, stemmed from a distrust of physicians's cures (which often were "heroic" or dramatic, leading to severe side effects). Proponents of hydropathy also promoted the idea that such events as adolescence, menstruation, and childbearing should be seen as natural physiological processes rather than as illnesses (i.e., they attempted to *demystify* these events). They encouraged more self-treatment and self-determination on the part of patients in an effort to equalize the doctor-patient relationship.

Many of the positions taken by hydropathists are clearly echoed among those who contest the dominance of biomedicine today (see chapter 5 on challenges to biomedicine). This is certainly true when it comes to gender issues in general and to the issue of the role of women in health care in particular. Hydropathy was a means of empowering women to take a much more active role in controlling what happened to their bodies. Thus, Dr. Russel Trall, who edited the *Water-Cure Journal,* fought against the idea that women could not enjoy sex and even discussed techniques for abortion. Women physicians were actively recruited into the hydropathy movement. At the same time, women were encouraged to make their way into informal political and public realms. Several prominent women reformers (including Harriet Beecher Stowe, Susan B. Anthony, and Clara Barton) were attracted to water cures, partly because spas or resorts afforded an opportunity to meet with like-minded women in relative seclusion, away from the stresses of their very active public lives.

As with spas in general, hydropathy eventually went into decline. The introduction of machines and gadgets diminished the quality of patient-healer relationships, and the rather casual training of healers came up against the growing professionalism of scientific medicine and a new emphasis on education and expertise. Sometimes, too, the biomedical profession openly attacked hydropathists. Water lost its symbolic meanings, and its mystical power was transferred to the new germ theory (see chapter 5 for a history of biomedicine). In the chaotic times of the Civil War and its aftermath, the idea of social progress through better personal health was not enough. Campaigners for women's rights began to go beyond hydropathy's emphasis on women's moral and nurturing roles to a call for justice and equal rights with men in all spheres of life. Self-denial and self-control were replaced by more hedonistic lifestyles. Even the language used by the movement changed; for example, "water cure establishment" became "resort" or "sanitarium," and the *Water-Cure Journal* was eventually simply titled *Health.*

Further Research

To date, very little research on health care delivery has taken the concepts developed in this chapter as theoretical background. Yet, as I have shown, ideas about sense of place and therapeutic landscapes can be teased out of some existing studies. This gives one hope that future studies will incorporate ideas of place and landscape more explicitly.

What guidelines can be set for future research into the importance of place? First of all, one can study a given place properly only by becoming immersed in the environment and activities of, and the interactions among, the people who live in that place. One has to see for oneself, walk the streets, perhaps even live with one's subjects. Such a method, then, includes participant-observation, or engaging in the everyday activities of one's research subjects. It may involve long interviews with people and keeping detailed diaries. It should include thick description, or the development of many overlapping layers of meaning found in a place, taken from a wide range of perspectives (e.g., political and economic structures, patterns of daily activity, attitudes and feelings). Only in this way can one understand the values, feelings, and intentions of people, and the meanings they ascribe to localities. Humanists calls this method of recovering meaning *Verstehen,* or "understanding from within." Of course, it is hard to remain detached and objective when this method is followed, for the observer becomes part of the observed; yet, philosophers of science tell us that this is so even in the work of physical science.

Further investigation into therapeutic landscapes will test our imaginations to the fullest. We will need to understand thoroughly the various facets of the concept of landscape itself. We will need to find out, through library and field research, how societies living in different places and at different times have established healing (or antihealing) settings. We will need to learn more about the various meanings of symbols that people use in thinking and talking about health care. We will need to understand how language, symbolism, ideologies, and meaning all play a role in creating specific therapeutic landscapes. We will have to learn, too, how to read or decode healing environments for their symbolic meaning. Geographers, anthropologists, sociologists, and other social scientists can all contribute to this search for knowledge.

11. Cultural Materialism

C hapters 9 and 10 dealt with two of the main concerns of recent thinking in cultural geography: (1) materialist concerns such as the role of political, economic, and social structures; and (2) humanistic concerns such as sense of place and symbolic landscapes. It is not surprising that some scholars have attempted to bring these two emphases together in a more comprehensive explanation of human behavior. That combination of emphases is the subject of this chapter. It has several names (with different meanings) that represent various attempts to link structuralist and humanist perspectives: *cultural materialism, Marxist humanism,* and *structuration* are three such labels.[1]

Putting Structure and Agency Together

The humanist and materialist perspectives have both been criticized as being unable to explain human activities. Materialist thinking, some scholars say, loses sight of the importance of everyday experiences, of the power of symbolization, of the capability of self-expressive individuals to act. Humanism, others contend, fails to consider the importance of constraints imposed by such underlying structures as modes of production, class, ethnicity, and gender. Therefore, "adequate explanation of human actions must include both the fatalism of social structures and the creative spontaneity of the lifeworld."[2] Like many dichotomies, the structuralist/humanist one has many facets and is difficult to pin down. It may also be discussed as *structure versus agency,* as *society versus individual,* as *hegemony versus self-expression,* or as *cultural norms versus individual biographies.* Our problem in this chapter is to find ways to reconcile these seeming opposites in meaningful ways.

A study of nutrition-related problems among children (malnutrition, tooth decay, and obesity) illustrates some aspects of societal structures and human agency and the possibility of investigating their interactions.[3] In this investigation, agency was looked at in terms of individual lifestyles. Many health care workers believe that the individual is basically responsible both for being at risk of illness and for reducing that risk. They emphasize the role of individual health-related actions, the role of the family, and the results of numerous knowledge, attitudinal, and practice studies. In the present example, this would include attitudes and behavior related to brushing teeth, eating sweet foods, and overeating. Educational efforts can be directed toward altering these specific behaviors. On the other side of the coin are those who feel that underlying forces within society are mainly responsible for problems such as childhood malnutrition, overnutrition, and dental caries. The main causes of illness from this point of view would include the effects of poverty brought on by the economic system, the promotion of unhealthy diets by the food industry, and the encouragement of a hedonistic lifestyle by such institutions as children's television. The main point to be made is that individual lifestyles and societywide forces are both at work and must be taken into consideration. Both continually affect and change the other as they work together to influence health behavior. The ways in which structure and agency may interact are almost unlimited. For example, children watching television may be stimulated to ask their parents to buy some candy for them, but individual parents may say no and may even campaign to restrict certain types of television advertising.

When one tries to work out how agency and structure interact in practice, one encounters many difficulties. For a start, which factors can properly be labeled "agency" and which "structure"? One usually carries out such studies at a single point in time, but interaction implies that a study over some period of time is called for. It is very hard to pin down a continually changing relationship. We know, for example, that smoking has been reduced in recent years for certain groups of people in some places (e.g., middle-aged males in the United States); this represents a significant change in behavior, including a cultural change in the attitude that smoking is a "macho" thing to do. What roles do structural forces such as government warnings about the dangers of smoking and individual changes in attitudes have to play, and how are these factors related to one another? What other individuals and institutions are involved? Admonitions from physicians, pressure from family and friends, advertising by tobacco companies, company policies about where employees can smoke, educational programs on television, and newspaper reports on deaths from lung cancer all play a role. To what extent is a factor like government warnings really "structural"? No doubt there is some political motivation behind warnings (e.g., sensing the approval of most voters), but warnings are also strongly influenced by individuals who are motivated to decrease lung cancer deaths.

Structuration

One attempt to connect structure and agency—currently the subject of extensive debate in social science—is structuration theory.[4] Anthony Giddens, a sociologist, is one of the pioneers of this rather recent body of theory; many geographers and other social scientists have also been actively engaged in developing its main ideas.

One way to explain structuration theory is through opposites. Structuration attempts to strike a middle way between an emphasis on cultural diversity versus an emphasis on cross-cultural societal structures. The structures inherent in society place constraints on human action; in this sense, they determine human behavior. Actions are not predetermined, however, because people have some freedom of movement within structures. There is a dialectical relationship between creativity and restraint. Human values are interpreted not only from the viewpoint of the actors in a situation, but also from the social relations out of which those values emerge.

One important concept in structuration theory is *duality of structure*. This means that "in the reproduction of social *life* (through systems of interaction) actors routinely draw upon interpretive schemes, resources and norms which are made available by existing structures of significance, domination and legitimation, and that in doing so they immediately and necessarily reconstitute those *structures*."[5] In other words, there is a dynamic, reciprocal relationship between structure and agency; each is continually affecting, altering the other. There are echoes here of the reciprocal relationship between place and people that is inherent in the concept of a negotiated reality (see chapter 10).

Structuration ideas can be illustrated through a reevaluation of the study of changing doctor-patient relationships in U.S. cities that was discussed in chapter 5.[6] Over the past century, there were important structural changes within American society that affected the activities of physicians and their patients. Increasing specialization and a proliferation of hospitals tended to concentrate doctors spatially. Improvements in medical technology increased the costs of health care over and above the cost of most other services. Physician status improved substantially. Class differentiation left the poor classes without recourse to even minimal health care until the advent of Medicare in the 1960s. The increasingly predominant nuclear family was less able to take care of its own health problems. Urban structure also changed; cities expanded and transportation networks made travel easier.

All these structural changes had an impact on the patient-physician relationship. Access to care required travel over longer distances, but travel was easier. Poorer people had more difficulty establishing a satisfactory relationship with a physician. Doctors assumed a more dominant role than before. More money changed hands in the relationship. But agency, or people's actions, also affected structure. Physicians, for example, have worked hard to eliminate competition, and the public in recent years has put pressure on the medical establishment to provide more physicians and greater accessibility to them.

The dialectic between agency and structure is carried out within places.[7] Since societal structures and human actions are so diverse, one can expect that each place will be unique in terms of how the agency/structure dialectic is played out. The analogy that has often been used to describe this phenomenon comes from geology—specifically, the idea of *stratigraphy,* or layers of structures and human actions that are deposited in various ways in certain places.

Although the concept of *natural nidus* has not been discussed in terms of structuration theory, it is a familiar idea taken from disease ecology and thus can serve as an illustration of the foregoing discussion.[8] The basic idea behind natural nidi (we might also call them *sick places*) is that many diseases (e.g., bubonic plague) are endemic to (i.e., they continually circulate within) certain environmental niches where the physical environment (e.g., climate and vegetation) is suitable for certain disease agents, vectors, and carriers to interact (in the case of plague, these would include plague bacteria and certain species of fleas and rats). Humans entering this environment may contract and help spread the disease. The natural environment, together with societal factors such as work routines that do or do not bring people into natural nidi, I shall call the *disease structure.* Human actions that are conducive to the spread or curtailment of disease represent *disease agency.* It is clear that structure and agency continuously affect each other within natural nidi. For example, people might be forced into an endemic plague area by high unemployment elsewhere. In turn, people within a plague nidus might eliminate the carrier rats and break the disease cycle. If constant vigilance is not maintained, however, the plague cycle could well recur at a future time.

An example of structuration in health care delivery is the attempt, beginning in the 1960s, to deinstitutionalize the mentally ill in North America and Great Britain.[9] One of the most significant outcomes of this effort was the creation of spaces within inner cities where many of the deinstitutionalized came to reside. These places have been called "service-dependent ghettoes," "landscapes of despair," and "asylums without walls." This sec-

tion describes the historical evolution of these often antithera-
peutic landscapes and the social structures and human agents that
interacted to make them what they are today. The principal social
structures involved are the welfare state and capitalist urbanization; the specific agents include professional caregivers, mental
patients, people living in the community, land-use planners, and
service operators (figure 15).

The industrial city that began to form at the end of the nineteenth century evolved into a structure whose spatial pattern
could be described, in very simple terms, as a dense commercial
core surrounded by industrial areas and segregated residential
neighborhoods. Part of the residential area at the edge of this
expanding commercial core was formed by two processes: (1)
abandonment by those who could afford to move farther out to
suburban areas; and (2) takeover by people with low incomes,
social misfits, and charitable institutions. This *zone of transition*
eventually became the locus for the service-dependent ghetto.

Meanwhile, the modern welfare state was evolving to the point
where it was deeply involved both in providing material support
to and regulating most social groups. Group interests came to be
served by specific government institutions, including lunatic asy-

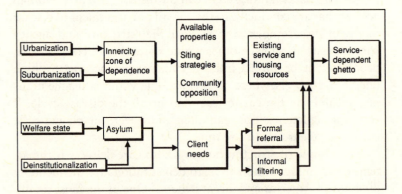

FIGURE 15. *Factors Influencing the Creation of the Service-
Dependent Ghetto*

SOURCE: M. Dear and J. Wolch, *Landscapes of Despair* (Princeton, N.J.: Princeton University Press, 1987), p. 12. Reprinted with permission of Princeton University Press and Basil Blackwell.

lums, hospitals, and almshouses. By the 1960s, large, over-crowded, largely custodial facilities had come under attack because of their extremely poor physical condition and their failure to provide adequate health care. It was discovered that for many patients, mentally ill people in particular, treatment at home was more beneficial. Also, the mentally ill were being increasingly treated with new drugs. The way was clear for an attempt to move as many patients as possible out of large facilities and into various types of smaller facilities or to negotiate residential arrangements (such as group homes) within communities.

Health care professionals played a vital role in the ghettoization process—they were "gatekeepers" in distributing health care resources, they had specialist knowledge, and they were legitimized by society. They had used their power to isolate those deemed ill, and they had employed complex tools and procedures which they described in mystical language (see chapter 8). Although they usually supported deinstitutionalization, they lost control over previously incarcerated patients. Their attempt to extend control into communities was contested by welfare agencies, clients, and individuals within those communities.

The patients or clients who left the large facilities were faced with very challenging situations. Many of them had low incomes and were separated from family and friends: their prospects for jobs and decent housing were poor. It was inevitable, then, that there was a drift toward zones of transition where housing was cheap and charitable institutions could provide some support.

The third major agent in creating the inner-city landscape of despair was the opposition of people to the potential siting of health and welfare facilities in their local communities. Among other things, these people said that these facilities would decrease property values, lead to problems of personal and property safety, and introduce "outsiders" into their neighborhoods. In other words, communities acted in a territorial manner (see chapter 9). Their reactions were symbolic in nature (e.g., the mentally ill were thought of as "a people apart'; see chapter 10), a mixture of sympathy and rejection.

Two other individual agents were involved in the formation of the service-dependent ghetto. Land-use planners helped to develop zoning laws that often protected suburban areas from such facilities as group homes for the mentally ill. Service providers tried various strategies to locate facilities. Although most providers gave in to community opposition, some attempt was made to educate the public about the mentally ill and their needs or to advocate a policy in which all communities took a *fair share* of their responsibility for mentally ill clients.

Since structuration theory emphasizes the interaction of agency and structure, it is important to reiterate some of the many possible interactions illustrated by deinstitutionalization and ghettoization of the mentally ill. The processes of urbanization provided opportunities for and set constraints on the places where deinstitutionalized patients could live. In turn, those who moved into these landscapes changed their structure and character. The state welfare system controlled much of the overall deinstitutionalization process, but health care professionals as well as clients came into conflict with this system over such matters as who should have the final say about a patient's release from an asylum or what sort of community facility a client should enter. The process of locating facilities involved a web of interactions that included community perceptions and political power, client needs, funding from welfare agencies, and the changing structure of the city (e.g., investment or disinvestment in certain areas). Yet, it is extremely difficult to pin down these interrelationships, for they are constantly evolving.

What might the future hold with respect to treatment of the mentally ill? In recent years, there has been reaction—by some health professionals, downtown real-estate interests, and neighborhood groups—against deinstitutionalization. Many communities, ill-prepared to receive the deinstitutionalized, have complained that state and federal funds were not forthcoming as had been promised. There has been much talk and some action concerning reinstitutionalization for the homeless and chronically ill; some say the pendulum is now swinging the other way.

Michael Dear and Jennifer Wolch project three possible scenarios for the future. Reinstitutionalization would lead us back to the large, isolated institutions of the nineteenth century, what (after Michel Foucault) might be called *landscapes of haunted places*. If present trends continue, inner-city ghettoes will continue to be *landscapes of despair*. Indeed, "the perfect metaphor for this terrain is provided by the homeless who nightly populate the beaches of Santa Monica and Venice, California. They sleep next to the ocean at the continent's edge, a little distance from a tide that could sweep them away."[10] The third "alternative archaeology" is the *landscape of caring*. Here the mentally ill and other service-dependent populations would be adequately cared for in and by communities. One possibility would be to develop "service hubs," neighborhood centers that already serve the community well and that could be given additional support to provide housing, employment, and other services for those in need.

Time Geography and Structuration

One of the interesting developments in geography in recent years is time-geography, which is associated with Torsten Hägerstrand and the Lund school of geographers in Sweden.[11] Time geography represents a potential way of dealing with the interaction between agency and structure. Its emphasis is on the temporal and spatial components of the practical, everyday activities of people—their *time-space routines*. Some geographers had recognized that time was very important in determining routines, and they looked for environmental and social factors or events that tended either to establish regular activity patterns (e.g., eating and sleeping, going to work) or to break up such patterns (e.g., a flood, a family problem). Time, which is a scarce resource, also has a strong influence on space; it tends to limit where activities can be carried out. Two basic concepts used in time geography are *path* and *project*. A path consists of the actions and events that make up a persons's progress through space and time (see figure 16). The path is *constrained* by social and environmental factors (displayed graphically as a prism). A project consists of the tasks necessary to fulfill certain goals or

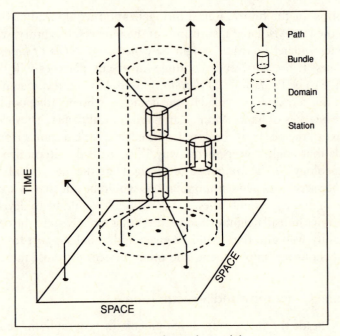

FIGURE 16. *Hägerstrand's Web Model*
SOURCE: D. Gregory, "Suspended Animation: The Stasis of Diffusion Theory," in D. Gregory and J. Urry, eds., *Social Relations and Spatial Structures* (London: Macmillan Education, 1985), p. 307. Reprinted with permission.

intentions. Projects are carried out when individual paths and tangible resources, such as food crops, machinery, and buildings, are linked together (i.e., when individual paths intersect) in space and time. Paths, projects, and constraints vary from place to place.

The relevance of time geography to health matters can be illustrated by a study that linked disease ecology and human behavior in an Ethiopian village.[12] The study's focus, which relates closely to the idea of a natural nidus (see above), was on the ways in which patterns of daily activity exposed people to different degrees of risk from a variety of diseases. Information on the following was used: disease agents present in the environment; life cycles and modes of transmission of those agents; and places where people were at different times. Moreover, six activity zones were set up to represent the interaction of people with their environment: (1) individual; (2) household; (3) compound; (4) settlement; (5) production area; and (6) further-ranging area of contact (see figure 17). These zones were related to specific behaviors (figure 18), and the activity paths of various people were diagrammed (figure 19). All this information was used to associate certain zones with specific disease hazards (e.g., at the individual level, there was a great hazard from trachoma and some hazard for tetanus; at the settlement level, there was great hazard from tuberculosis and some hazard from measles). These hazards would vary in strength for different subpopulations ac-

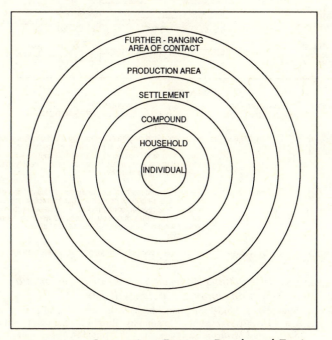

FIGURE 17. *Interactions Between People and Environment in an Ethiopian Village*
SOURCE: R. Roundy, "A Model for Combining Human Behavior and Disease Ecology to Assess Disease Hazard in a Community: Rural Ethiopia as an Example," *Social Science and Medicine* 12 (1978): 124. Reprinted by permission of Pergamon Press PLC.

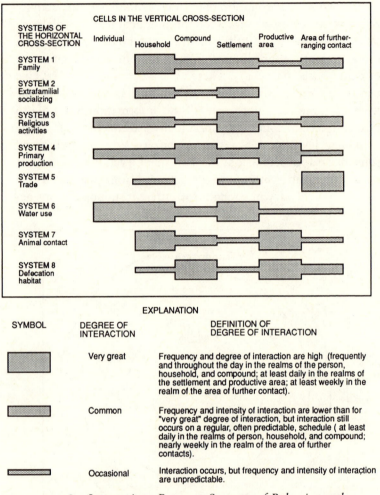

FIGURE 18. *Interactions Between Systems of Behavior and Habitat Cross-Sections in an Ethiopian Village*

SOURCE: R. Roundy, "A Model for Combining Human Behavior and Disease Ecology to Assess Disease Hazard in a Community: Rural Ethiopia as an Example," *Social Science and Medicine* 12 (1978): 125. Reprinted by permission of Pergamon Press PLC.

cording to age, sex, and so on. If one thinks of humans and disease agents as carrying out "projects" in their daily activities and life cycles, then human exposure to disease depends on the coupling or interaction of those projects over space and time.

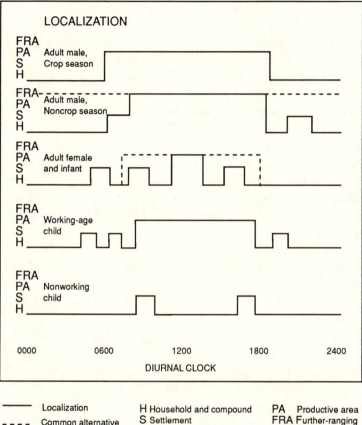

LOCALIZATION

FRA
PA   Adult male,
S   Crop season
H

FRA
PA   Adult male,
S   Noncrop season
H

FRA
PA   Adult female
S   and infant
H

FRA
PA   Working-age
S   child
H

FRA
PA   Nonworking
S   child
H

0000   0600   1200   1800   2400

DIURNAL CLOCK

——— Localization   H Household and compound   PA Productive area
- - - - Common alternative S Settlement   FRA Further-ranging
        localization   area of contact

FIGURE 19. *Activity Paths in an Ethiopian Village*
SOURCE: R. Roundy, "A Model for Combining Human Behavior and Disease
Ecology to Assess Disease Hazard in a Community: Rural Ethiopia as an Exam-
ple," *Social Science and Medicine* 12 (1978): 126. Reprinted by permission of
Pergamon Press PLC.

A very thorough study of the temporal organization of a hospital further illustrates the uses of time geography.[13] Hospital
personnel (nurses, doctors, laboratory attendants, and others)
worked on carefully planned shifts. Different people on the hospital staff worked on different time schedules (e.g., nurses
worked on a standard cycle of four-week periods). Some people
had to alternate between day shifts and night shifts. Thus, time

constraints obviously dictated to a large extent the places where workers could come into contact with one another. For example, physicians and the nurses working with them came together in certain places at certain times to discuss their patients.

Both time geography and structuration theory are concerned with interactions among people as they go about their daily routines. Structuration theorists have said that time geography has not made enough of the social context in which paths and projects are followed or carried out, and time geographers have claimed that structuration theory cannot be complete until it incorporates the idea that activities occur in specific locations in space and time. Thus, it is not surprising that attempts have been made to link the two perspectives.[14] For the purposes of the present discussion, fortunately, this has been done with respect to the concept of place. "Place," Allan Pred has said, "is . . . a process whereby the reproduction of social and cultural forms, the formation of biographies, and the transformation of nature ceaselessly become one another at the same time that time-space specific activities and power relations ceaselessly become one another."[15] For an illustration of the preceding statement, see figure 20. Paths and projects and biography formation are ideas that come mainly from time geography; power relations and social reproduction are structuralist ideas. Both sides of the diagram represent the dialectical interplay between structure and agency. The important thing to recognize is that each component of the diagram continually affects all the others. For example, power relations (e.g., within a factory or a hospital) define what projects will be carried out, who will carry them out, and when and where they will be carried out; this, in turn, affects the space-time trajectories that individual paths follow. Note, too, that the interactions among the components create a situation in which places are always *becoming*. This means that what occurs in any particular place depends on the history of component interrelations; that is to say, place is a *historically contingent* process.

The foregoing discussion can be made more concrete by reference to a study that was not carried out with the linkage of

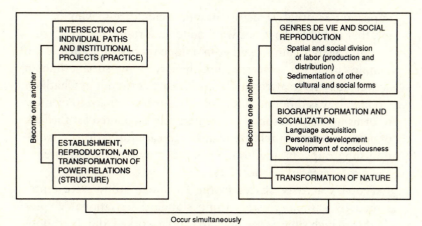

FIGURE 20. *Components of Place and Region as Historically Contingent Process*

SOURCE: A. Pred, "Place as Historically Contingent Process: Structuration and Time-Geography of Becoming Places," *Annals of the Association of American Geographers* 74 (1984): 282. Reproduced by permission.

structuration and time geography in mind.[16] This investigation examined the interactions of urban ecological structure, relative location, distance measures, demographic and socioeconomic characteristics of people (all structural elements), and people's activity spaces (time geography) as they related to health-care-seeking behavior (agency) in Chatham County, Georgia. Most of the facilities that people used as regular sources of care were near the downtown area of Savannah. Whites traveled farther than blacks to care because, on the whole, they lived farther from the city center. However, when the two races were compared by a measure of relative distance (actual distance traveled to care compared with total distance to all possible alternatives), there was no difference. Nor were there differences in relative distance traveled for four other population characteristics: sex, age, profession, and length of residence in Chatham County. On the other hand, there were substantial differences in relative distance for individuals and for twenty sample clusters throughout the city. In the light of structuration theory, one might conclude that, in the Savannah setting, demographic and socioeconomic structure was not as important as urban structure in influencing care-seeking behavior, that individual actions were quite important, and that structure and agency came together in unique ways within each of the sample clusters or places within the city. Some specific human actions may have affected the health care structure in Chatham County. It was thought that public pressure which led to medical reforms in the 1960s might have partially accounted for the lack of any difference in relative distance to care for various population subgroups. In addition, Savannah may have been more racially integrated than most U.S. cities.

People's activity spaces in the Savannah study were represented by sample clusters using standard deviational ellipses (SDEs), which summarized where people worked, did their shopping, and engaged in other activities, as well as how much time they spent there. Since these activity spaces tended to be focused downtown, they overlapped considerably with SDEs that were similarly constructed for health care visits. In time-geographic terms, then, daily activity and health-care-seeking paths and projects intersected relatively more often (i.e., more than for most of the other geographic studies that have compared daily and health care activity spaces). The study shows how structuration theory and time geography can be usefully combined. Activity spaces were clearly related to urban structure. They were also related to population structure: whites and males had significantly larger activity spaces than blacks and females. One conclusion of the study was that Savannah, a relatively small southern city, has a unique combination of human and environmental characteristics that impinge upon the behavior of people seeking health care. After almost two months of interviewing in the city, the interviewers began to gain distinct impressions and feelings about Savannah and its very varied neighborhoods.

Health in Inner London

A detailed investigation of the ideas that twenty-four people living in East London had about illness and health provides an excellent illustration of how the *everyday choices* people make interact with *societal constraints* on these choices.[17] This example recapitulates many of the themes of chapters 9, 10, and 11 (pay special attention to italicized words and phrases).

The *place* where the study was carried out was the West Bethnal Green area of the London Borough of Tower Hamlets, a deprived inner-city area. The residents live their lives on at least two levels: (1) the *material level,* where the immediate physical and social *environments* are of greatest importance; and (2) the *mythological level,* where stories are told about how ideal a *landscape* Bethnal Green is (i.e., as a cheerful, moral, cooperative community—a myth deriving from the patriotic propaganda of World War II). Romantic views of the past (perhaps softened by memory) contrast starkly with the harsh realities of today. Since the war, Bethnal Green has been radically altered by slum clearance and reconstruction. Many people have migrated out of the area. Eight of the households interviewed lived in a privately owned housing estate, and the other eight lived in council property (low-income housing).

A very important part of the Bethnal Green study was the distinction made between the "public" and "private" *language,* or discourse, that people used when talking to the investigator. "Public accounts are sets of meanings in common social currency that *reproduce* and *legitimate* the assumptions people take for granted about the nature of social reality," and "private accounts spring directly from personal experience and from the thoughts and feelings accompanying it" (emphasis added).[18] Public accounts were generally given when the interviewer was just beginning to get to know people; when she had gained their confidence, private accounts were also provided. Lay beliefs about illness and health thus represented the *interaction* between *ideologies* fostered by *dominant political, economic,* and *medical institutions* in society (which we take to be *structural* in nature) and the actual experiences and choices people made in their *everyday lives* about health matters (*human agency*).

The interplay of agency and structure for the residents of Bethnal Green is shown through their work; through their family life; and through their ideas and actions concerning illness, health, and the utilization of health services. *Gender* differences are quite evident in attitudes toward work and toward a person's position in the family and home. For women, the latter is most important; for men, the former. People felt that they were ill if their work or family obligations were disrupted. Despite poor economic conditions, recent declines in employment, and few job choices, the work ethic is still very strong; one's worth is measured by how well one fulfills one's duties. Public accounts of work stress ideological meanings such as the value of skilled labor, craftsmanship, and brotherhood (ideas expressed also in the popular press and by government ministers), whereas private accounts describe alienation and attempts to be free of work's contraints.

Gender is also very important in domestic life: women are responsible for housework and child care, whereas men help only occasionally with the children. Men control most of the economic resources of the household. Public discourse about family life produced *images* of loving relationships between spouses and between generations, but private discourse told of family stresses on individuals and of intrafamilial conflict.

The concepts of health and illness that people had were a mixture of a traditional, moral, commonsensical approach and a biomedical, scientific approach. In public accounts, respondents emphasized the importance of being seen in the right moral relationship to illness. That is to say, illness had to be seen as "real" (e.g., cancer or a cardiovascular problem); there must be no indication that one was malingering. Private accounts, on the other hand, were more concerned with everyday material concerns such as one's employment position (e.g., accepting occupational hazards as part of the job); one's position in the sexual division of labor (e.g., men could come home from work to rest from an illness, while women usually tried to "carry on"); and one's past personal experience of illness and its treatment (e.g., older people were more reluctant to use the National Health Service, which began to function in 1948, than were younger people).

When people were asked about the causes of illness, the public response, again, was couched in biomedical terms (e.g., germs, viruses, stress), whereas private responses were related to personal relationships and events (e.g., the effects of the loss of a loved one, a person's drinking habits). Public accounts of experiences with doctors were usually respectful and complimentary, but in private accounts people sometimes criticized individual doctors (hardly ever doctors in general). Views about the local health services tended to be hierarchical: hospitals received the most respect because they treated "real" illnesses; then came general practitioners, who usually treated "normal" illnesses (such as infectious childhood diseases); finally, community services (school health, maternal and child health clinics, health visiting) received the least respect. Biomedical personnel were seen as having abilities beyond the powers of ordinary people, whereas community workers were said to be doing jobs that simply required commonsense.

A Fruitful Blend

This chapter has detailed the possibilities for research on health care delivery that are inherent in a combination of humanist and structuralist thinking.[19] Drawing on recent theoretical writing by geographers and other social scientists, I have shown how understanding the interactions between structure and agency, society and the individual, and cultural norms and individual biographies can illuminate health-care-seeking behavior. A strong word of caution should be interjected here, however. Very little empirical work on health care delivery has been carried out that began with these concepts explicitly in mind. This is particularly true in regard to structuration theory. Geographers have been criticized for taking on structuration ideas without questioning their applicability in geographic studies. It is rather easy to show that structure affects agency and vice versa, but researchers have found it very difficult to provide concrete evidence of the duality between structure and agency that lies at the heart of structuration theory. The attempted linkage of time geography with structuration also requires much more empirical testing.

Despite my note of caution, the studies described in this chapter point the way to future work that should prove to be very fruitful. Many important ingredients—sense of place, underlying structure, meaning, symbols, hegemony, landscape, and others—are available to be blended into meaningful explanations of health care delivery situations.

12. Summary and Conclusions

A t the most basic level, the present book aims to convey a single message: when people seek health care, both culture and space matter. I have illustrated this message by taking a specific subject, cultural geography, in which cultural and spatial themes are conjoined, and have applied these themes to the study of various health care issues. In this final chapter, I will summarize the themes and subthemes developed in chapters 2 through 11, reiterate their importance to health care delivery, and show how they interact with one another in providing a complex spatial and cultural perspective on health issues. I will begin by reconstructing the main argument and will then show how one particular health problem, AIDS, illustrates the application of many of the concepts discussed in this book. Then the focus will shift to (1) the many links that can be found between cultural-geographic themes as they are used to gain insight into health care and (2) the interactions between spatial and cultural factors. The chapter concludes with a section on future directions in health care research.

Themes and Subthemes

Let us start with the idea that culture represents an entire way of life for a society, including the ways in which people make a living, their institutions, their arts and sciences, their beliefs and rituals. All the elements of culture are related in an infinitely complex web. If this is so, then it is impossible to separate health-care-seeking behavior from its cultural context. Medical systems are complex enough in themselves: at a minimum, they include the populations at risk and their characteristics, physical and made-made environments, resources (facilities, personnel, equipment), illnesses, and illness beliefs. These elements and their interactions and feedback mechanisms must be thoroughly examined. But one must also recognize that these systems are open; therefore, their elements form a multitude of links to other aspects of culture.

Health care systems have an important geographic or spatial dimension. This was seen first through the conceptual lens of region or areal differentiation. Dividing the health care landscape into regions based on different criteria (e.g., prevalent diseases, hospital catchment areas) helps one think both about those characteristics which make a region unique and about how one region differs from the next. Regionalization leads to the realization that boundaries are often unclear. Although this might cause some duplication of services or conflict between competing medical systems, it also means that people living in any one region usually have a plurality of medical choices. Spatial classification also helps one study inequalities in health care delivery. One finds that there are core and peripheral areas with respect to the availability and accessibility of resources.

One way to study heath care delivery systems within regions is to focus on the interplay between culture (taken here to consist of medical technology and organization, illness beliefs, and overall cultural context) and the environment (composed of physical and man-made environments, including disease environments). Throughout history, we have seen, different societies in different places have put relatively greater or lesser emphasis on either environment or culture when thinking about health care. Each situation calls for the right balance between the two emphases. The idea of balance is also the key to another aspect of cultural ecology: adaptation. Both environments and culture change, inevitably; also inevitably, each produces change in the other. It is important for societies to be prepared for change and to understand that alterations in illness loads, physical and man-made landscapes, resources, and attitudes must be continually compensated for in order to strike new equilibriums that are conducive to good health.

Closely tied to the idea of adaptation is the notion of evolutionary change. Medical systems evolve, people adapt to the changes, and those changes create further evolutionary stages in the medical systems. Thinking about cultural evolution leads one to recall the lessons of history. History tells us that some changes are gradual and others seem to happen overnight. Some changes, arising from a complex of cultural and spatial interactions, are unexpected. Because of historical inertia, moreover, many societies do not change their health care delivery systems. Experience also tells us that change is often accompanied by conflict and stress when old and new ideas collide.

The changes that occur in medical systems seldom affect an entire society or different societies in different places at the same time. Thus, it is important to track down the origins and diffusion patterns of innovations that affect health care. It has been shown that studying diffusion patterns is a very complex matter. For a start, one must describe the carriers (people, social and transporation networks, the mass media) and the barriers (physical as well as cultural). One can also distinguish the type or types of diffusion (contagious, relocational, hierarchical) that take place. The forms as well as the process of innovation diffusion must be examined. Finally, one must view diffusion within cultural contexts and look for the inevitable spatial inequalities in the availability and acceptance of innovations over time.

It is useful to discuss health care delivery as it is practiced in folk societies (defined here as traditional, nonprofessional medicine) and in popular medicine (defined as lay practices in folk as well as nonfolk societies). The study of folk medicine is important because the majority of the world's people are still strongly influenced by it. By acknowledging folk medicine one becomes aware of medical practices that are quite different in theory and practice from those of biomedicine and yet are efficacious in some respects. Biomedical and folk medicine can each learn from the other. Moreover, study of popular medicine reinforces the notion that medicine is a part of culture and, thus, part of an entire way of life. That is to say, most health-care-seeking behavior takes place in the popular arena of everyday activities, outside formal health care systems. Folk and popular medicine, we have seen, also have geographic aspects and relate to other themes discussed earlier: regions, cultural ecology, evolution, and diffusion.

One particular culture trait, language, assumes a very important role in health care delivery. I have shown how language lies at the core of patient-provider relationships, as it is a primary means of communicating ideas about health; how it determines to a large extent the ways in which one classifies such important phenomena as diseases; how language used in metaphors, myths, and models colors thought processes; and how semantic networks demonstrate that medical beliefs reach out into many areas of culture. The use of language, when it gives rise to ambiguities and conflicts or when it is used to confuse and mystify, can be a barrier to health. Or, when its resonances from other cultural components such as religion or law are usefully applied, it can enhance health.

Our understanding of spatial and cultural relations has been greatly enhanced by that recent infusion of social theory into social science which has been called political economy (or structuralism) and which has been used to inform my discussion of social space. The political-economic perspective forces one to be cognizant of underlying societal forces such as class, race, and gender that both provide opportunities and act as constraints on health-care-seeking behavior. One looks at health care delivery in a different light when one discusses it in terms of territoriality or in terms of the dominance of one group over another group that resists with an alternative system of medicine. My discussion of social space led back to other previously considered themes: cultural context, inequalities, and pluralism. It was shown how political-economic concepts could be applied to cross-country comparisons of medical systems, to health care in underdeveloped areas, and to recent moves toward health care privatization in many places.

The revival of an interest in humanist themes in cultural geography has opened up further exciting possibilities for the study of the links between space, culture, and health care. Geographers have rediscovered the importance of place; and, in this book, we have been particularly interested in places as fields of care, as therapeutic settings in which there is a true understanding about people's real feelings concerning disease and health. Going about their everyday lives within places, people negotiate health care realities and develop ideologies of illness and its treatment. Much thinking about medical matters is symbolic. This gives rise to symbolic landscapes—places that have symbolic meaning. People construct symbolic landscapes (notably, therapeutic landscapes), and those landscapes in turn affect their behavior. Discussions of how the mentally ill have been treated in Europe, of how the British protected their colonial officers in Sierra Leone, and of why early Americans sought healing waters served to illustrate the concepts of place and symbolic landscape.

Health care is influenced both by the underlying forces in society and by the actions and feelings of individuals. Indeed, society and the individual interact, continually changing each other; as a result, health-care-seeking behavior changes. I illustrated this interaction through the concept of structuration and then showed how time geography also plays a role. These ideas, I feel, difficult though they may be to operationalize, are at the cutting edge of research in the social science of health. Two of the most important examples used to demonstrate these themes were the deinstitutionalization of the mentally ill and an in-depth analysis of the everyday lives of a small group of Inner London residents.

The Example of AIDS

In this section, I will show how many of the major themes of the preceding chapters and their subthemes (italicized for emphasis) all play a role in one particular health problem of intense current interest: acquired immunodeficiency syndrome, or AIDS.[1] Much of the attention paid to AIDS has been directed toward its disease ecology and the characteristics of its victims. It has been recognized, however, that those interested in the prevention and treatment of AIDS must take into account the cultural, political, economic, and social *systems* (i.e., *context*) within which AIDS exists. Besides the characteristics of the disease itself and of the populations most at risk, one must consider human resources and facility requirements, efforts to produce effective drugs, the costs involved, cultural attitudes toward the victims, and many other factors. To cite just one example: educational efforts to prevent the further spread of AIDS may face the cultural barrier of refusal to use condoms.

Some aspects of AIDS may be better understood if one *regionalizes* them. One might map out areas of relatively high incidence in order to concentrate treatment efforts, or one might try to predict regions of future spread and target them for educational campaigns. Different groups of people are at greater or lesser risk, and attitudes toward AIDS differ from region to region. It is clear that a *plurality* of interventions will be required in order to meet a variety of needs in different cultural settings. One will undoubtedly find that there were many *inequalities* connected with treating AIDS across regions. Victims in developed countries will have far better access to expensive treatments than will most people in developing areas. Thus, whereas most AIDS patients in the United States receive at least a minimum of care, Tanzania uses a system of triage, whereby patients who are deemed hopeless are sent home to die; and "providing treatment for just ten AIDS patients comparable to that delivered in the United States exceeds the entire budget of Zaire's largest hospital."[2] Attempts to quarantine people who are known or suspected to be carriers of the AIDS virus brings us the regional concept of *boundary*. Many individuals and governments have tried to establish barriers between themselves and infected persons. Quarantine, however, would probably have little effect: AIDS has a long incubation period, and most infectious people are not even aware that they are carriers. Furthermore, quarantine is costly both in terms of money and in terms of emotional stress on those quarantined.

The AIDS problem provides an excellent example of *cultural ecology,* the interaction between culture and environment, for the environments in which the disease flourishes are largely influenced by human *organization* and *technology.* Lifestyles that include drug use, homosexuality, prostitution, or carelessness in sexual relations help to spread the disease, but such behavior can be changed. Transporation systems such as road networks and airlines, products of the society's technology, can help to transmit the disease. New drugs and contraceptive devices can prevent or treat it. We are constantly witnessing attempts to *adapt* to the AIDS menace, often with limited resources. Responses include advertising campaigns that advise people to limit the number of their sexual partners and laboratory research that aims to learn as much as possible about the AIDS virus.

Many elements of the AIDS situation are *evolving,* usually quite rapidly. Knowledge about the disease—where it can be found, how it spreads, and what might be done about it—changes week by week. Attitudes and lifestyles are also changing as people become better informed about the disease. Many people, though, especially the uneducated and those living in conditions of poverty in city slums or rural areas, *lag* behind others in their knowledge about AIDS. Furthermore, AIDS gives rise to conflict—for example, between homosexual victims and those who feel that homosexuals are being punished for their behavior; or between victims and governments that are reluctant to supply them with untested drugs.

Much of the geographic work on AIDS has attempted to model the *diffusion* patterns of the disease and thereby predict its future areas of transmission. I will focus here on the innovation and diffusion of means to prevent and treat the disease, including educational campaigns and the use of newly developed drugs. One consideration is the extent to which AIDS programs spread *hierarchically* or *contagiously.* One must study the characteristics of the people, the social networks, and the mass media that have been involved as *carriers* of information about AIDS. One must also examine such *barriers* as the common attitude that intravenous drug users are undeserving criminals or the refusal of some countries to cooperate with others on preventive programs.

Folk and *popular* culture also play a role. Here, for example, one would be interested in the opinion, expressed by many men, that AIDS is not really serious and that they would rather die than give up their promiscuous ways. The role of *traditional healers* is important; they can no more cure AIDS than a biomedical doctor can, but they may very well help victims die with dignity. In setting up AIDS programs, it will be very useful to know what people really think causes AIDS to spread and what, if anything, they think can and should be done about it. Such attitudes arise out of popular medical culture.

What people say about AIDS and its victims, the *language* they use, is often very telling. Initially, AIDS was called the "gay plague" by many people. This stigmatized homosexuals and made many people reluctant to be tested for the disease. Language can act as a barrier to effective *communication* in regard to AIDS programs, particularly programs in developing areas. For "the message of AIDS is derived from the West. It is a foreign concept in a foreign language that is dependent on the West for its *meaning* and continued development. It speaks in Western *metaphors* and with a voice that was born from that *cultural cosmology*" (emphasis added).[3]

Political and *economic* responses to the AIDS crisis fit into the overall theme of *social space*. Governments in different countries have different ways of trying to control AIDS, including mandatory testing for some high-risk groups, prevention of suspected carriers from crossing borders, and treating drug addiction as a health problem rather than as a criminal problem. Political organizations foster certain *ideologies* concerning AIDS that can either promote or deter its spread; these ideologies *compete* with one another for people's attention. The economic impact of AIDS will continue to be tremendous. Besides the costs of treating the disease, there may be legal costs (e.g., hemophiliacs may sue hospitals or physicians for having being given contaminated blood) and costs related to declining worker productivity. Developing countries face foreign-exchange losses when they purchase equipment to fight AIDS, the loss of foreign investment, and the loss of tourist dollars. There are many *inequalities* in the economic realm. In the United States, for example, much of the cost falls on public hospitals and the Medicaid program. Political and cultural *hegemony* also play a role; one suspects that Western countries may be willing to invest heavily to control a disease that affects them, paying relatively little attention to those diseases in less-advantaged social spaces which kill far more people (e.g., malaria, childhood diarrhea).

One must recognize that the impact of AIDS, attitudes toward it, and measures to control it, are very *place*-specific. Compare, for example, a homosexual community in a large U.S. city that has organized itself to educate others and to provide mutual support with a rural community that is just discovering its first AIDS victims and whose population is generally hostile to providing the victims with help. Situations in local communities can develop into climates or *landscapes* of fear and confusion when residents are prejudiced against or misinformed about AIDS victims. Attempts may be made to ghettoize AIDS victims, to put them into separate places.

As with any health problem, *individual actions* as well as *societal structures* are involved. Many people feel that the key to controlling AIDS is to change individual lifestyles. Certainly this is part of the solution; but social forces that strongly influence, say, having to make a living (e.g., as a prostitute) or taking drugs are also important. As noted in chapter 11, the individual and society continually interact with each other. For instance, an AIDS victim may have difficulty finding a job, having run up against discriminatory laws based on an *ideology* that labels certain people as dangerous and immoral. Over time, and with much give and take, individual and group protests may change such ideologies and laws. *Time geography* can also contribute to the study of AIDS—for example, by tracing the typical movements of high-risk groups, difficult as that might be.

Theme Linkages

Although each of my thematic chapters can stand alone, I have indicated throughout the text—in an effort to provide a unified spatial-cultural perspective on health care delivery—how themes discussed in one chapter are related to themes in other chapters. I showed the close connection between some chapters: chapters 2 and 3, on systems and regions; chapters 4 and 5, on ecology and evolution. Chapter 6 (on innovation and diffusion) and chapter 7 (on folk and popular culture) used many ideas from earlier chapters. Chapter 8, on language, served as a bridge between the old cultural geography of chapters 2 through 7 and the new cultural geography of chapters 9 through 11. Chapter 11 blended together concepts from chapters 9 and 10.

Some concepts made an appearance in more than one chapter. Not surprisingly, interactions played an important role in many discussions, including those on systems, ecology, folk and popular culture, language, and cultural materialism. Inequalities were found to be important in the chapters on regions, diffusion, and social space. Such ideas as the importance of place and symbolic landscape, emphasized in the new cultural and regional geographies, echo ideas inherent in the areal differentiation of the old cultural geography. The theme of conflict appeared in discussions of regions, cultural evolution, and social space. Cultural context was seen around every corner.

There were many instances when conceptual links could be related to specific examples. To cite three: language and folk culture were tied together through the medieval metaphor of nature as God's book, an image that was also expressed by Appalachian collectors of medicinal plants; medical systems and symbolic landscapes were related in a discussion of the Galenic notion of "hot" and "cold" items, including foods and medicine; social space and regionalization were connected through the idea of territoriality.

Finally, themes that were basically cultural and themes that were basically spatial were shown to interact with each other. To paraphrase Allan Pred (who used the world "social" instead of "cultural"): the cultural becomes the spatial; the spatial becomes the cultural.[4] This idea could be illustrated in many ways, but two examples will suffice. The first concerns changing patient-physician relationships in U.S. cities (chapter 5). Several decades ago, many families had a personal physician who lived nearby and who often came to the patient's home. There was a feeling among these families that the doctor, who knew a lot about his patients and their neighborhood, was almost a part of the family. Cultural changes over the past century—such as greater social stratification, enhanced professional status for physicians, and improved transportation networks—restructured spatial relationships within cities. One result was an overall increase in the distance between the patient's home and the physician's office. This spatial change had an impact on cultural attitudes that doctors and patients had toward each other. For many, the relationship became much more impersonal. Some people came to revere the more spatially and culturally distant doctor unduly, while others became unduly skeptical of his or her abilities.

The second example concerns the interaction between space and culture among those who sought healing waters in early America (see chapter 10). At first, urban dwellers sought these waters close at hand, in the cities themselves. Usually, however, contamination of the waters by human waste and other pollutants rendered these places unsuitable. This geographic factor, combined with romantic feelings about nature, changed cultural attitudes and redirected the search for healing waters to rural areas.

Future Directions

The study of health care delivery is evolving. In this concluding section, I will briefly indicate some directions in which I feel (in the overall spirit of the present book) that evolution might usefully move.

One such direction is toward a more multidisciplinary social science of health. Historical inertia tends to emphasize disciplinary boundaries and the preservation of disciplinary territoriality. The present book advocates the usefulness of an overlap between several of these territories (geographic, anthropological, sociological, and political-economic, at least). The related ideas of culture as an entire way of life, system context, open systems, and pluralism are in this spirit as well. This is not to say that scholars should not concentrate on advancing the fields in which they have been trained; some should, and are best adapted to that task. Others, with different abilities and temperaments, should explore the interstices between disciplinary fields.

A further desirable research direction would be to probe more deeply into the medical culture of a relatively small number of people, living out their daily lives in a relatively small area. This, of course, has already been done, by anthropologists in particular; what I am advocating here is that this type of study should combine cultural and spatial elements more explicitly. At this level of analysis, one can go beyond the factors immediately related to health care; probe into social, spatial, temporal, and other contexts; listen to private as well as public discourse; and find out how the constraints of society and the actions and ideologies of people influence day-to-day decisions about health care.

Still another direction is toward different theoretical frameworks. Much of the early work in medical geography, particularly in North America, was carried out in the positivist mode: it was assumed that the important facets of health care systems could be measured and tested statistically. As I noted in chapter 1, much valuable work resulted from this approach, but its limitations also became evident. More recently, different philosophies—structuralism and humanism in particular—have challenged the worth and relevance of the positivist tradition. Within cultural geography, we have seen a change from the "old" geography, with its concern for the themes of the early chapters of the present book, to the "new" geography, which emphasizes the themes of the later chapters. In the social sciences generally, there now seems to be more of a concern for examining one's philosophical roots, one's real goals in research, before embarking on a study of any sort. In short, there is a conceptual ferment that must be taken advantage of. The difficulty lies in honestly examining one's goals and in fitting theories to problems.

Along with the evolution in theory, there must be a change in research methodologies. The tendency among some social scientists is to apply ever more sophisticated statistical techniques to their data. I wonder if this strategy might not reach a point of diminishing returns. Some problems simply do not yield the type of data required by these techniques. In an attempt to solve this problem, some researchers use surrogate data that do meet the technical requirements—but that do not address the research question! The quantitative techniques that have dominated the field in recent decades will retain their usefulness, but their hegemony is being contested by qualitative and eclectic methodologies. More emphasis should be placed on fieldwork, on becoming intimately familiar with the places, the landscapes, of one's study populations. The discussion of diffusion studies in chapter 6 shows this progression in thinking. I began with a very interesting application of classical mathematical diffusion modeling, critiqued it, and slowly added on other emphases: social networks; diffusion agents and nonaccepters; process as well as form; and so on.

Notes
Index

Notes

Chapter 1. Introduction

1. See, for example, M. Harris, *Culture, People, Nature: An Introduction to General Anthropology* (New York: Harper & Row, 1988); C. R. Ember and M. Ember, *Anthropology* (Englewood Cliffs, N.J.: Prentice-Hall, 1988); and R. Williams, *Culture and Society: 1780–1950* (New York: Columbia University Press, 1983).

2. More information on the early history and themes of cultural geography can be found in P. Wagner and M. Mikesell, "The Themes of Cultural Geography," in Wagner and Mikesell, eds., *Readings in Cultural Geography* (Chicago: University of Chicago Press, 1962), pp. 1–24; M. Mikesell, "Geographic Perspectives in Anthropology," *Annals of the Association of American Geographers* 57, no. 3 (1967): 617–34; M. Mikesell, "Cultural Geography," *Progress in Human Geography* 1 (1977): 460–64; M. Mikesell, "Tradition and Innovation in Cultural Geography," *Annals of the Association of American Geographers* 68, no. 1 (1978): 1–16; W. Norton, "Humans, Land, and Landscape: A Proposal for Cultural Geography," *The Canadian Geographer* 31, no. 1 (1987): 21–30; P. Jackson, *Maps of Meaning* (London: Unwin Hyman, 1989); and R. Ellen, "Persistence and Change in the Relationship Between Anthropology and Human Geography," *Progress in Human Geography* 12, no. 2 (1988): 229–62. Some cultural geography texts were also used to develop concepts related to themes. These include W. A. D. Jackson, *The Shaping of Our World: A Human and Cultural Geography* (New York: Wiley, 1985); T. G. Jordan and L. Rowntree, *The Human Mosaic* (New York: Harper & Row, 1982); J. E. Spencer and W. L. Thomas, *Introducing Cultural Geography* (New York: Wiley, 1978); and C. E. Zimolzak and C. A. Stansfield, Jr., *The Human Landscape: Geography and Culture* (Columbus, Ohio: Charles E. Merrill, 1979).

3. See H. C. Brookfield, "Questions on the Human Frontiers of Geography," *Economic Geography* 40 (1964): 283–303; P. Wagner, "The Themes of Cultural Geography Rethought," *Association of Pacific Coast Geographers Yearbook* 37 (1975): 7–14; P. Wagner, *Environments and People* (Englewood Cliffs, N.J.: Prentice-Hall, 1972); Jackson, *Maps of Meaning;* D. Cosgrove, "Towards a Radical Cultural Geography: Problems of Theory," *Antipode* 15 (1983): 1–11; J. S. Duncan, "The Superorganic in American Cultural Geography," *Annals of the Association of American Geographers* 70, no. 2 (1980): 181–98; and L. Rowntree, "Orthodoxy

and New Directions: Cultural/Humanistic Geography," *Progress in Human Geography* 12, no. 4 (1988): 575–86.

4. See, for example, J. N. Entrekin, "Contemporary Humanism in Geography," *Annals of the Association of American Geographers* 66, no. 4 (1976): 615–32; and R. J. Johnston, *Philosophy and Human Geography* (London: Edward Arnold, 1983).

5. Material on the new cultural geography can be found in Cosgrove, "Towards a Radical Cultural Geography"; D. Cosgrove, "New Directions in Cultural Geography," *Area* 19, no. 2 (1987): 95–101; Duncan, "The Superorganic"; P. Jackson, "A Plea for Cultural Geography," *Area* 12, no. 2 (1980): 110–13; Jackson, *Maps of Meaning;* D. Ley, "Editorial," *Environment and Planning D: Society and Space* 6 (1988): 115–16; D. Ley, "Cultural/Humanistic Geography," *Progress in Human Geography* 9 (1985): 415–23; and Rowntree, "Orthodoxy and New Directions."

6. Cosgrove, "New Directions," p. 95.

7. Summaries of the geographic aspects of health care delivery appear in G. W. Shannon and G. E. A. Dever, *Health Care Delivery: Spatial Perspectives* (New York: McGraw-Hill, 1974); A. E. Joseph and D. R. Phillips, *Accessibility and Utilization: Geographical Perspectives on Health Care Delivery* (New York: Harper & Row, 1984); K. Jones and G. Moon, *Medical Geography: An Introduction* (London: Routledge & Kegan Paul, 1987); and M. Meade, J. Florin, and W. Gesler, *Medical Geography* (New York: Guilford Press, 1988).

8. This body of literature can only be commented upon selectively. Examples of work using cultural variables include S. M. Bhardwaj, "Attitude Toward Different Systems of Medicine: A Survey of Four Villages in the Punjab–India," *Social Science and Medicine* 9 (1975): 603–12; W. Gesler and G. Gage, "Health Care Delivery for Under Five Children in Rural Sierra Leone," in R. Akhtar, ed., *Health and Disease in Tropical Africa: Geographical and Medical Viewpoints* (Chur: Harwood Academic Publishers, 1987), pp. 427–68; and C. M. Good, "A Comparison of Rural and Urban Ethnomedicine Among the Kamba of Kenya," in P. R. Ulin and M. H. Segall, eds., *Traditional Health Care Delivery in Contemporary Africa,* Foreign and Comparative Studies, African Series 35 (Syracuse, N.Y.: Maxwell School of Citizenship and Public Affairs, Syracuse University, 1980), pp. 13–56. For examples of work dealing with ethnomedical systems, see C. M. Good, *Ethnomedical Systems in Africa* (New York: Guilford Press, 1987); S. M. Bhardwaj, "Medical Pluralism and Homeopathy: A Geographic Perspective," *Social Science and Medicine* 14, B (1980): 209–16; R. F. Stock, "Traditional Healers in Rural Hausaland," *Geojournal* 5 (1981): 363–68; and A. Ramesh and B. Hyma, "Traditional Indian Medicine in Practice in an Indian Metropolitan City," *Social Science and Medicine* 15, D (1981): 69–81. Work that emphasizes viewing health care in its entire societal context in-

cludes J. Eyles and K. J. Woods, *The Social Geography of Medicine and Health* (London: Croom Helm, 1983); M. Dear, S. M. Taylor, and G. B. Hall, "External Effects of Mental Health Facilities," *Annals of the Association of American Geographers* 70 (1980): 342–53; and N. R. Shrestha, "Human Relations and Primary Health Care Delivery in Rural Nepal: The Case of Deurali," *Professional Geographer* 40, (1988): 202–13. For work that incorporates the political-economic approach, see C. C. Hughes and J. M. Hunter, "Disease and Development in Africa," *Social Science and Medicine* 3 (1970): 443–93; R. F. Stock, " ' Disease and Development' or 'The Underdevelopment of Health': A Critical Review of Geographical Perspectives on African Health Problems," *Social Science and Medicine* 23 (1986): 689–700; and J. Mohan, "Location-Allocation Models, Social Science, and Health Service Planning: An Example from Northeast England," *Social Science and Medicine* 17 (1983): 493–99.

9. W. Gesler, "The Cultural Geography of Health Care Delivery," *Journal of Geography* 86 (1987): 24–29.

10. P. Jackson and S. J. Smith, *Exploring Social Geography* (London: Allen & Unwin, 1984), p. 4.

Chapter 2. Culture Systems

1. Information used to write this section has been drawn from the following: Haggett, *Geography: A Modern Synthesis* (New York: Harper & Row, 1983); D. Harvey, *Explanation in Geography* (London: Edward Arnold, 1969); T. J. Trimbur and M. J. Watts, "Are Cultural Ecologists Adapted? A Review of the Concept of Adaptation," *Proceedings of the Association of American Geographers* 8 (1976): 179–83 (on general systems theory); J. E. Spencer and W. L. Thomas, *Introducing Cultural Geography* (New York: Wiley, 1978); T. G. Jordan and L. Rowntree, *The Human Mosaic* (New York: Harper & Row, 1982); C. E. Zimolzak and C. A. Stansfield, Jr., *The Human Landscape: Geography and Culture* (Columbus, Ohio: Charles E. Merrill, 1979); M. Mikesell, "Cultural Geography," *Progress in Human Geography* 1 (1977): 460–64 (on culture systems); W. Gesler, *Health Care in Developing Countries* (Washington, D.C.: Association of American Geographers, 1984); F. L. Dunn, "Traditional Asian Medicine and Cosmopolitan Medicine as Adaptive Systems, in C. Leslie, ed., *Asian Medical Systems: A Comparative Study,* (Berkeley and Los Angeles: University of California Press, 1976), pp. 133–58 (on traditional professional and nonprofessional medical systems); E. H. Ackerknecht, *A Short History of Medicine* (New York: Ronald Press, 1955) (on biomedicine); R. Bhaskar, "On the Possibility of Social Scientific Knowledge and the Limits of Naturalism," *Journal for the Theory of Social Behavior* 8 (1978): 1–28; L. Newson, "Cultural Evolution: A Basic Concept for Human and Historical Geography," *Journal of Historical Geography* 2, no. 3 (1976): 239–55

(on open systems); and J. Eyles and K. J. Woods, *The Social Geography of Medicine and Health* (London: Croom Helm, 1983) (on system context).

2. Dunn, "Traditional Asian Medicine," p. 135.

3. Material for this section comes from A. L. Basham, "The Practice of Medicine in Ancient and Medieval India," in Leslie, ed., *Asian Medical Systems,* pp. 18–43; J. C. Burgel, "Secular and Religious Features of Medieval Arabic Medicine," in Leslie, ed., *Asian Medical Systems,* pp. 44–62; F. C. Colley, "Traditional Indian Medicine in Malaysia," *Journal of the Malaysian Branch of the Royal Asiatic Society* 51, no. 1 (1978): 77–109; Dunn, "Traditional Asian Medicine"; C. Geertz, "Curing, Sorcery, and Magic in a Javanese Town," in D. Landy, ed., *Culture, Disease, and Healing: Studies in Medical Anthropology* (New York: Macmillan, 1977), pp. 146–54; J. M. Janzen, "The Comparative Study of Medical Systems as Changing Social Systems," *Social Science and Medicine* 12 (1978): 121–29; P. S. Yoder, "Biomedical and Ethnomedical Practice in Rural Zaire," *Social Science and Medicine* 16 (1982): 1851–57; and D. L. Zeller, "Basawo Baganda: The Traditional Doctors of Buganda," in Z. Ademuwagun et al., eds., *African Therapeutic Systems* (Waltham, Mass.: Crossroads Press, 1979), pp. 1138–43.

4. Some of the ideas for this section derive from R. H. Elling, "Political Economy, Cultural Hegemony, and Mixes of Traditional and Modern Medicine," *Social Science and Medicine* 15, A (1981): 89–99; H. Mahler, "People," *Scientific American* 243 (1980): 66–77; M. Rahman, "Urban and Rural Medical Systems in Pakistan," *Social Science and Medicine* 14, D (1980): 283–89; A. Siddiqi, "Health Care Resources and Public Policy in Pakistan," *Social Science and Medicine* 14, D (1980): 291–98; M. Turshen, "The Political Ecology of Disease," *Review of Radical Political Economics* 9 (1977): 45–60; and A. Ugalde, "Health Decision Making in Developing Nations: A Comparative Analysis of Colombia and Iran," *Social Science and Medicine* 12 (1978): 1–7.

5. See I. G. Simmons and N. J. Cox, "Holistic and Reductionist Approaches to Geography," in R. J. Johnston, ed., *The Future of Geography* (London: Methuen, 1985), pp. 43–58, for a discussion of the holistic approach in systems analysis.

6. J. Gleick, "In Physics, Do Tinier Facts Add Up to the Grand Truth?" *New York Times,* January 24, 1988; G. Taylor, "A Giant LEP in the Dark in Search of the Meaning of Life," *Guardian,* July 31, 1989.

Chapter 3. Culture Regions

1. See, for example H. C. Brookfield, "Questions on the Human Frontiers of Geography," *Economic Geography* 40, no. 4 (1964): 283–303; and A. P. Vayda and R. A. Rappaport, "Ecology, Cultural and Noncultural," in J. A. Clifton, ed., *Introduction to Cultural Anthropology* (Boston: Houghton Mifflin, 1968), pp. 477–97.

2. The new regional geography is well described in two recent articles: A. Gilbert, "The New Regional Geography in English and French Speaking Countries," *Progress in Human Geography* 12 (1988): 209–28; and M. B. Pudup, "Arguments Within Regional Geography," *Progress in Human Geography* 12 (1988): 369–90. See also E. W. Soja, "Regions in Context: Spatiality, Periodicity, and the Historical Geography of the Regional Question," *Environment and Planning D: Society and Space* 3 (1985): 175–90.

3. Two cultural geography texts were drawn upon for basic ideas about regions: T. G. Jordan and L. Rowntree, *The Human Mosaic* (New York: Harper & Row, 1982); and W. A. D. Jackson, *The Shaping of Our World: A Human and Cultural Geography* (New York: Wiley, 1985). Three additional references that provided ideas for this section are P. Wagner and M. Mikesell, "The Themes of Cultural Geography," in Wagner and Mikesell, eds., *Readings in Cultural Geography* (Chicago: University of Chicago Press, 1962), pp. 1–24; A. Kleinman, "Concepts and a Model for the Comparison of Medical Systems as Cultural Systems," *Social Science and Medicine* 12 (1978): 85–93; and C. M. Leslie, "Medical Pluralism in World Perspective," *Social Science and Medicine* 14, B (1980): 191–95. Also see H. K. Heggenhougen, "Bomohs, Doctors and Sinsehs—Medical Pluralism in Malaysia," *Social Science and Medicine* 14, B (1980): 235–44; and R. M. Hessler et al., "Intraethnic Diversity: Health Care of the Chinese Americans," *Human Organization* 34, no. 3 (1975): 253–62.

4. The main source for this section is S. M. Bhardwaj, "Medical Pluralism and Homoeopathy: A Geographic Perspective," *Social Science and Medicine* 14, B (1980): 209–16. Other pertinent literature includes A. L. Basham, "The Practice of Medicine in Ancient and Medieval India," in C. Leslie, ed., *Asian Medical Systems: A Comparative Study* (Berkeley and Los Angeles: University of California Press, 1976), pp. 18–43; A. R. Beals, "Strategies of Resort to Curers in South India," in Leslie, ed., *Asian Medical Systems,* pp. 184–200; S. M. Bhardwaj, "Attitude Toward Different Systems of Medicine: A Survey of Four Villages in the Punjab–India," *Social Science and Medicine* 9 (1975): 603–12; C. M. Good, "The Interface of Dual Systems of Health Care in the Developing World: Toward Health Policy Initiatives in Africa," *Social Science and Medicine* 11 (1979): 705–13; A. Ramesh and B. Hyma, "Traditional Indian Medicine in Practice in an Indian Metropolitan City," *Social Science and Medicine* 15, D (1981): 69–81; C. E. Taylor, "The Place of Indigenous Medical Practitioners in the Modernization of Health Services," in Leslie, ed., *Asian Medical Systems,* pp. 285–99.

5. S. Rushdie, *Midnight's Children* (New York: Knopf, 1981).

6. Sources for the information in this section include A. B. Calvo and D. H. Marks, "Location of Health Care Facilities: An Analytical Approach," *Socio-economic Planning Sciences* 7 (1973): 407–22; J. W.

Florin, "Health Service Regionalization in the United States," in M. S. Meade, ed., *Conceptual and Methodological Issues in Medical Geography* (Chapel Hill: University of North Carolina, Department of Geography, 1980), pp. 282–98; "Hospital Service Areas in Ibadan City," *Social Science and Medicine* 17 (1983): 601–16; N. D. McGlashan, "The Distribution of Population and Medical Facilities in Malawi," in McGlashan, ed., *Medical Geography: Techniques and Field Studies* (London: Methuen, 1972), pp. 89–95; G. F. Pyle and B. M. Lauer, "Comparing Spatial Configurations: Hospital Service Areas and Disease Rates," *Economic Geography* 51 (1975): 50–68; G. W. Shannon and G. E. A. Dever, *Health Care Delivery: Spatial Perspectives* (New York: McGraw-Hill, 1974); W. Shonick, *Elements of Planning for Area-Wide Personal Health Services* (St. Louis: C. V. Mosby, 1974); and W. Gesler and J. Cromartie, "Patterns of Illness and Hospital Use in Central Harlem Health District," *Journal of Geography* 84 (1985): 211–16.

7. See J. Wennberg and A. Gittelsohn, "Small Area Variations in Health Care Delivery," *Science* 182 (1971): 1102–07. Other literature of interest includes J. Wennberg and A. Gittelsohn, "Variations in Medical Care Among Small Areas," *Scientific American* 245 (1982): 120–33; I. Gershenberg and M. A. Haskell, "The Distribution of Medical Services in Uganda," *Social Science and Medicine* 6 (1972): 353–72; S. Joroff and V. Novarro, "Medical Manpower: A Multivariate Analysis of the Distribution of Physicians in Urban United States," *Medical Care* 9 (1971): 428–38; D. A. Kindig et al., "Trends in Physician Availability in 10 Urban Areas from 1963 to 1980," *Inquiry* 24 (1987): 136–46; S. I. Okafor, "Inequalities in the Distribution of Health Care Facilities in Nigeria," in R. Akhtar, ed., *Health and Disease in Tropical Africa: Geographical and Medical Viewpoints* (Chur: Harwood Academic Publishers, 1987), pp. 383–401.

8. See W. Gesler and G. Gage, "Health Care Delivery for Under Five Children in Rural Sierra Leone," in Akhtar, ed., *Health and Disease in Tropical Africa*, pp. 427–68.

9. The principal source for this section is B. Techatraisak, "Traditional Medical Practitioners in Bangkok: A Geographic Analysis" (Ph.D. diss, University of North Carolina, Department of Geography, 1985). Also see B. Techatraisak and W. Gesler, "Traditional Medicine in Bangkok, Thailand," *Geographical Review* 79, no. 2 (1989): 172–82. Other pertinent literature includes A. C. Colson, "The Differential Use of Medical Resources in Developing Countries," *Journal of Health and Social Behavior* 12 (1971): 226–37; F. L. Dunn, "Traditional Asian Medicine and Cosmopolitan Medicine as Adaptive Systems," in Leslie, ed., *Asian Medical Systems,* pp. 135–55; C. M. Good and V. N. Kimani, "Urban Traditional Medicine: A Nairobi Case Study," *East African Medical Journal* 57 (1980): 301–16; and G. W. Shannon and C. W. Spurlock, "Urban Ecological Con-

tainers, Environmental Risk Cells, and the Use of Medical Services," *Economic Geography* 52 (1976): 171–80.

Chapter 4. Cultural Ecology

1. My discussion of basic concepts in this section draws from W. A. D. Jackson, *The Shaping of Our World: A Human and Cultural Geography* (New York: Wiley, 1985); T. G. Jordan and L. Rowntree, *The Human Mosaic* (New York: Harper & Row, 1982); C. E. Zimolzak and C. A. Stansfield, Jr., *The Human Landscape: Geography and Culture* (Columbus, Ohio: Charles E. Merrill, 1979); J. H. Steward, "The Concept and Method of Cultural Ecology," in P. W. English and R. C. Mayfield, eds., *Man, Space, and Environment: Concepts in Contemporary Human Geography* (New York: Oxford University Press, 1972), pp. 120–29; J. E. Spencer and W. L. Thomas, *Introducing Cultural Geography* (New York: Wiley, 1978); M. Mikesell, "Geographic Perspectives in Anthropology," *Annals of the Association of American Geographers* 57, no. 3 (1967): 617–34; L. Rowntree, "Orthodoxy and New Directions: Cultural/Humanistic Geography," *Progress in Human Geography* 12, no. 4 (1988): 575–86; A. P. Vayda and R. A. Rappaport, "Ecology, Cultural and Noncultural," in J. A. Clifton, ed., *Introduction to Cultural Anthropology* (Boston: Houghton Mifflin, 1968), pp. 477–97; L. Grossman, "Man-Environment Relationships in Anthropology and Geography," *Annals of the Association of American Geographers* 67, no. 1 (1977): 126–44; and L. Newson, "Cultural Evolution: A Basic Concept for Human and Historical Geography," *Journal of Historical Geography* 2, no. 3 (1976): 239–55.

2. Material for the health-related examples in this section comes from C. J. Glacken, *Traces on the Rhodian Shore* (Berkeley and Los Angeles: University of California Press, 1967) (on the Greeks); R. D. McConnaughey, "Medical Landscapes: Perceived Links Between Environment, Health, and Disease in Colonial and 19th Century America" (Ph.D. diss., University of North Carolina, Department of Geography, 1986) (sixteenth- to nineteenth-century medicine); and R. Dubos, *Man Adapting* (New Haven: Yale University Press, 1965) (nineteenth- and twentieth-century biomedicine).

3. The call for placing ecological studies in a wider social context is heard, for example, in H. C. Brookfield, "Intensification and Disintensification in Pacific Agriculture," *Pacific Viewpoint* 13 (1972): 30–48; Grossman, "Man-Environment Relationships"; and Vayda and Rappaport, "Ecology."

4. McConnaughey, *Medical Landscapes*.

5. See, for example, I. Illich, *Medical Nemesis: The Expropriation of Health* (New York: Pantheon Books, 1976).

6. Information for this section derives from P. W. English and R. C. Mayfield, "Ecological Perspectives," in English and Mayfield, eds., *Man, Space, and Environment: Concepts in Contemporary Human Geography*

(New York: Oxford University Press, 1972), pp. 115–20; Dubos, *Man Adapting;* Spencer and Thomas, *Introducing Cultural Geography;* B. Velimirovic, "Traditional Medicine Is Not Primary Health Care: A Polemic," *Curare* 7 (1984): 61–79, 85–93; F. L. Dunn, "Traditional Asian Medicine and Cosmopolitan Medicine as Adaptive Systems," in C. Leslie, ed., *Asian Medical Systems: A Comparative Study* (Berkeley and Los Angeles: University of California Press, 1976), pp. 133–58; Newson, "Cultural Evolution"; W. M. Denevan, "Adaptation, Variation, and Cultural Geography," *Professional Geographer* 35, no. 4 (1983): 399–406; and T. J. Trimbur and M. J. Watts, "Are Cultural Ecologists Adapted? A Review of the Concept of Adaptation," *Proceedings of the Association of American Geographers* 8 (1976): 179–83.

7. See, for example, J. Scarpaci, "DRG Calculations and Utilization Patterns: A Review of Method and Policy," *Social Science and Medicine* 26, no. 1 (1988): 111–17.

8. For a review of these types of studies, see A. E. Joseph and D. R. Phillips, *Accessibility and Utilization: Geographical Perspectives on Health Care Delivery* (New York: Harper & Row, 1984).

9. This example comes from T. G. Rundall, and J. O. McClain, "Environmental Selection and Physician Supply," *American Journal of Sociology* 87, no. 5 (1982): 1090–112. Also see D. Gifford and R. M. Mullner, "Modeling Hospital Closure Relative to Organizational Theory: The Applicability of Ecology Theory's Environmental Determinism and Adaptation Perspectives," *Social Science and Medicine* 27, no. 11 (1988): 1287–94.

10. Rundall and McClain, "Environmental Selection," p. 1098.

Chapter 5. Cultural Evolution

1. Basic concepts about cultural evolution have been derived from J. E. Spencer and W. L. Thomas, *Introducing Cultural Geography* (New York: Wiley, 1978); W. A. D. Jackson, *The Shaping of Our World: A Human and Cultural Geography* (New York: Wiley, 1985); P. Wagner and M. Mikesell, "The Themes of Cultural Geography," in Wagner and Mikesell, eds., *Readings in Cultural Geography* (Chicago: University of Chicago Press, 1962), pp. 1–24; K. V. Flannery, "The Cultural Evolution of Civilizations," *Annual Review of Ecology and Systematics* 3 (1972): 399–426; and L. Newson, "Cultural Evolution: A Concept for Human and Historical Geography," *Journal of Historical Geography* 2, no. 3 (1976): 239–55.

2. See J. L. Peacock and A. T. Kirsch, *The Human Direction: An Evolutionary Approach to Social and Cultural Anthropology* (New York: Appleton-Century-Crofts, 1970).

3. The principal source for this section is E. H. Ackerknecht, *A Short History of Medicine* (New York: Ronald Press, 1955). Other work of interest includes P. H. DeKruif, *Microbe Hunters* (New York: Harcourt,

Brace & Company, 1926); R. Dubos, *Mirage of Health: Utopias, Progress, and Biological Change* (New York: Harper & Row, 1959); B. Inglis, *A History of Medicine* (Cleveland: World Publishing Company, 1965); H. E. Sigerist, *A History of Medicine* (New York: Charles Scribner's Sons, 1951), vols. 1–2; and C. E. Singer and E. A. Underwood, *A Short History of Medicine* (New York: Oxford University Press, 1962).

4. Dubos, *Mirage of Health*.

5. The principal source for this section is P. L. Knox, J. Bohland, and N. L. Shumsky, "The Urban Transition and the Evolution of the Medical Care Delivery System in America," *Social Science and Medicine* 17 (1983): 37–43. See also P. DeVise, *Misused and Misplaced Hospitals and Doctors,* Resource Paper no. 22 (Washington, D.C.: Association of American Geographers, Commission on College Geography, 1973); P. Gober and R. J. Gordon, "Intraurban Physician Location: A Case Study of Phoenix," *Social Science and Medicine* 14, D (1980): 407–17; P. L. Knox, "The Intraurban Ecology of Primary Medical Care: Patterns of Accessibility and Their Policy Implications," *Environmental Planning* 10 (1978): 415–35; N. L. Shumsky, J. Bohland, and P. Knox, "Separating Doctors' Homes and Doctors' Offices: San Francisco, 1881–1941," *Social Science and Medicine* 23 (1986): 1051–57; and P. Starr, *The Social Transformation of American Medicine* (New York: Basic Books, 1982).

6. Knox et al., "The Urban Transition."

7. Material for this section derives from several sources: G. F. Pyle, *Applied Medical Geography* (Washington, D.C.: V. H. Winston & Sons); J. L. Scarpaci, "DRG Calculations and Utilizations Patterns: A Review of Method and Policy," *Social Science and Medicine* 26, no. 1 (1986): 111–17; D. E. Stribling, "Holistic Health: A Changing Paradigm for Cultural Geography" (Ph.D. diss., University of North Carolina, 1983); A. Wildavsky, "Doing Better and Feeling Worse: The Political Pathology of Health Policy," in J. H. Knowles, ed., *Doing Better and Feeling Worse: Health in the United States* (New York: W. W. Norton, 1977); J. D. Mayer, International Perspectives on the Health Care Crisis in the United States," *Social Science and Medicine* 23 (1986): 1059–65; S. McLafferty, "The Geographical Restructuring of Urban Hospitals: Spatial Dimensions of Corporate Strategy," *Social Science and Medicine* 23 (1986): 1079–86; and J. D. Mayer, "Patterns of Rural Hospital Closure in the United States," *Social Science and Medicine* 24 (1987): 327–34.

8. This section is based on the television film of the same name, produced by the NOVA series.

Chapter 6. Cultural Diffusion

1. The concepts developed in this section derive from T. G. Jordan and L. Rowntree, *The Human Mosaic: A Thematic Introduction to Cultural*

Geography, 4th ed., (New York: Harper & Row, 1986), pp. 13–16; W. A. D. Jackson, *The Shaping of Our World: A Human and Cultural Geography* (New York: Wiley, 1985), pp. 49–56; M. Meade, J. Florin, and W. Gesler, *Medical Geography* (New York: Guilford Press, 1988), chap. 8; and R. Abler, J. S. Adams, and P. Gould, *Spatial Organization: The Geographer's View of the World* (Englewood Cliffs, N.J.: Prentice-Hall, 1971), chap. 11. Also of interest is A. D. Kaluzny, "Innovation in Health Services: Theoretical Framework and Review of Research," *Health Services Research* 9 (1974): 101–20. J. M. Blaut, "Two Views of Diffusion," *Annals of the Association of American Geographers* 67, no. 3 (1977): 343–49, has stressed the importance of cultural context. See, too, M. A. Brown, "Behavioral Approaches to the Geographic Study of Innovation Diffusion: Problems and Prospects," in K. R. Cox and R. G. Golledge, eds., *Behavioral Problems in Geography Revisited* (New York: Methuen, 1981), pp. 123–44, who has emphasized political-economic aspects of diffusion such as structural inequalities. Also see J. D. Clarkson, "Ecology and Spatial Analysis," *Annals of the Association of American Geographers* 60, no. 4 (1970): 700–16; and W. M. Denevan, "Adaptation, Variation, and Cultural Geography," *Professional Geographer* 35, no. 4 (1983): 399–406.

2. The material in this section is based on G. W. Shannon, R. L. Bashshur, and C. A. Metzner, "The Spatial Diffusion of an Innovative Health Care Plan," *Journal of Health and Social Behavior* 12 (1971): 216–26; and Jordan and Rowntree, *The Human Mosaic*, pp. 13–16.

3. See S. R. Baker, "The Diffusion of High Technology Medical Innovation: The Computed Tomography Scanner Example," *Social Science and Medicine* 13, D (1979): 155–62. Also see A. Bonair, P. Rosenfield, and K. Tengvold, "Medical Technologies in Developing Countries: Issues of Technology Development, Transfer, Diffusion and Use," *Social Science and Medicine* 28, no. 8 (1989): 769–81.

4. See E. M. Rogers, "Network Analysis of the Diffusion of Innovations," in P. W. Holland and S. Leinhardt, eds., *Perspectives on Social Network Research* (New York: Academic Press, 1979), pp. 137–64.

5. See L. Freij et al., "Exploring Child Health and Its Ecology: The Kirkos Study in Ethiopia," *Scandanavian Journal of Social Medicine*, supp. 12 (1977); 1–99.

6. This example is based on C. Weil and J. Weil, "Differential Acceptance of Oral Rehydration Therapy in a Multi-ethnic Setting in Bolivia: A Research Strategy and Preliminary Findings," presented at the Geography Workshop, University of Chicago, May 1988 (used by permission of the authors).

7. This thinking would include L. Brown, *Innovation Diffusion: A New Perspective* (London: Methuen, 1981); Brown, "Behavioral Approaches," pp. 123–44; J. Gaspar and P. R. Gould, "The Cova da Beira:

An Applied Structural Analysis of Agriculture and Communication," in A. Pred, ed., *Space and Time in Geography: Essays Dedicated to Torsten Hägerstrand* (Lund: C. W. K. Gleerup, 1982), pp. 183–214; D. Gregory, "Suspended Animation: The Stasis of Diffusion Theory," in D. Gregory and J. Urry, eds., *Social Relations and Spatial Structures* (London: Macmillan Education, 1985), pp. 296–336; Blaut, "Two Views of Diffusion"; Clarkson, "Ecology and Spatial Analysis"; and Denevan, "Adaptation, Variation, and Cultural Geography."

Chapter 7. Folk and Popular Culture

1. On concepts of folk and popular culture, see T. G. Jordan and L. Rowntree, *The Human Mosaic* (New York: Harper & Row, 1982).

2. See A. Kleinman, "Concepts and a Model for the Comparison of Medical Systems as Cultural Systems," *Social Science and Medicine* 12 (1978): 85–93. Also see I. Press, "Urban Folk Medicine: An Overview," *American Anthropologist* 80 (1978): 71–84; A. Kleinman, "Culture, Illness, and Care: Clinical Lessons from Anthropologic and Cross-cultural Research," *Annals of Internal Medicine* 88 (1978): 251–58; and J. Eyles, "The Geography of Everyday Life," in D. Gregory and R. Walford, eds., *Horizons in Human Geography* (London: Macmillan Education, 1989), pp. 102–17.

3. This material is based primarily on I. K. Zola, "Studying the Decision to See a Doctor," *Advances in Psychosomatic Medicine* 8 (1972): 216–36. See also N. Gevitz, ed., *Other Healers: Unorthodox Medicine in America* (Baltimore: Johns Hopkins University Press, 1988).

4. This topic is discussed in E. T. Price, "Root Digging in the Appalachians: The Geography of Botanical Drugs," *Geographical Review* 50 (1960): 1–20. Note that conditions may well have changed considerably since 1960, when Price's article was written. See also E. S. Ayensu, "A Worldwide Role for the Healing Powers of Plants," *Smithsonian* 12 (1981): 86–97.

5. Price, "Root Digging," p. 4.

6. The two studies used here are J. M. Hunter, "Geophagy in Africa and the United States: A Culture-Nutrition Hypothesis," *Geographical Review* 63 (1973): 170–95; and D. E. Vermeer and D. A. Frate, "Geophagy in a Mississippi County," *Annals of the Association of American Geographers* 65 (1975): 414–24.

7. This section is based on C. M. Good et al., "The Interface of Dual Systems of Health Care in the Developing World: Toward Health Policy Initiatives in Africa," *Social Science and Medicine* 13, D (1979): 141–54; D. Landy, "Role Adaptation: Traditional Curers Under the Impact of Western Medicine," in Landy, ed., *Culture, Disease, and Healing* (New York: Macmillan, 1977); C. M. Good, "Traditional Medicine: An Agenda for Medical

Geography," *Social Science and Medicine* 11 (1977): 705–13; and S. R. Whyte, "Penicillin, Battery Acid, and Sacrifice: Cures and Causes in Nyole Medicine," *Social Science and Medicine* 16 (1982): 2055–64. Also see L. Romanucci-Ross, "Folk Medicine and Metaphor in the Context of Medicalization: Syncretics in Curing Practices," in L. Romanucci-Ross et al., eds., *The Anthropology of Medicine* (New York: Praeger, 1983), pp. 5–19.

8. Landy, "Role Adaptation," p. 480.

9. W. Gesler, "The Place of Chiropractors in Health Care Delivery: A Case Study of North Carolina," *Social Science and Medicine* 26 (1988): 785–92.

10. C. M. Good, *Ethnomedical Systems in Africa* (New York: Guilford Press, 1987).

11. Good, "Traditional Medicine."

12. One very interesting exception is J. Cornwell, *Hard-Earned Lives* (London: Tavistock Publications, 1984) (described in some detail in chapter 11).

Chapter 8. Language

1. For discussions of language in cultural geography, see P. Jackson, *Maps of Meaning: An Introduction to Cultural Geography* (London: Unwin Hyman, 1989); W. A. D. Jackson, *The Shaping of Our World: A Human and Cultural Geography* (New York: Wiley, 1985); T. G. Jordan and L. Rowntree, *The Human Mosaic*, 3rd ed. (New York: Harper & Row, 1982); and C. E. Zimolzak and C. A. Stansfield, Jr., *The Human Landscape: Geography and Culture* (Columbus, Ohio: Charles E. Merrill, 1979). See also K. J. Anderson, "The Idea of Chinatown: The Power of Place and Institutional Practice in the Making of a Racial Category," *Annals of the Association of American Geographers* 77, no. 4 (1987): 580–98 (on medical imagery among the Chinese in Vancouver); and C. Geertz, "Thick Description: Toward an Interpretive Theory of Culture," in Geertz, *The Interpretation of Cultures* (New York: Basic Books, 1973), pp. 3–30.

2. This anecdote appears in A. Kleinman, "Culture, Illness, and Care: Clinical Lessons from Anthropologic and Cross-cultural Research," *Annals of Internal Medicine* 88 (1978): 251–58.

3. This example comes from C. M. Good, *Ethnomedical Systems in Africa* (New York: Guilford Press, 1987).

4. The following discussion of Lb and Lsp is based on H. Fabrega, Jr., *Disease and Social Behavior: An Interdisciplinary Perspective* (Cambridge: MIT Press, 1974).

5. See L. Romanucci-Ross, "Creativity in Illness: Methodological Linkages to the Logic and Language of Science in Folk Pursuit of Health in Central Italy," *Social Science and Medicine* 23 (1986): 1–7.

6. A. P. Vayda and R. A. Rappaport, "Ecology, Cultural and Noncultural," in J. A. Clifton, ed., *Introduction to Cultural Anthropology* (Boston: Houghton Mifflin, 1968), pp. 477–97, discuss the use of folk taxonomies to set out rules of appropriate behavior toward the environment.

7. Good, *Ethnomedical Systems*.

8. This example comes from C. Kendall, D. Foote, and R. Martorell, "Ethnomedicine and Oral Rehydration Therapy: A Case Study of Ethnomedical Investigation and Program Planning," *Social Science and Medicine* 19 (1984): 253–60.

9. See W. M. Gesler, "Morbidity Measurement in Household Surveys in Developing Areas," *Social Science and Medicine* 13, D (1979): 223–26.

10. For this study, see L. McKee, "Ethnomedical Treatment of Children's Diarrheal Illness in the Highlands of Ecuador," *Social Science and Medicine* 25 (1987): 1147–55.

11. See S. C. Weller, "Cross-cultural Concepts of Illness: Variation and Validation," *American Anthropologist* 86 (1984): 341–50.

12. For background on metaphors, myths, and models, see D. N. Livingston and R. T. Harrison, "Meaning Through Metaphor: Analogy as Epistemology," *Annals of the Association of American Geographers* 71 (1981): 95–107; and D. N. Livingston and R. T. Harrison, "The Frontier: Metaphor, Myth, and Model," *Professional Geographer* 32 (1980): 127–31. See also G. Lakoff and M. Johnson, *Metaphors We Live By* (Chicago: University of Chicago Press, 1980), who provide numerous examples of how people use metaphors in everyday life.

13. W. F. Thrall, A. Hibbard, and C. H. Holman, *A Handbook to Literature* (New York: Odyssey Press, 1960), p. 281.

14. N. Thrift, "Flies and Germs: A Geography of Knowledge," in D. Gregory and J. Urry, eds., *Social Relations and Spatial Structures* (London: Macmillan Education, 1985), pp. 366–403.

15. See W. J. Mills, "Metaphorical Vision: Changes in Western Attitudes to the Environment," *Annals of the Association of American Geographers* 72 (1982): 237–53.

16. S. Sontag, *Illness as Metaphor* (New York: Vintage Books, 1978).

17. Thrall et al., *A Handbook to Literature*, p. 298.

18. See. J. Dow, "Universal Aspects of Symbolic Healing: A Theoretical Synthesis," *American Anthropologist* 88 (1986): 56–69. See also R. Hagey, "The Phenomenon, the Explanations and the Responses: Metaphors Surrounding Diabetes in Urban Canadian Indians," *Social Science and Medicine* 18, no. 3 (1984): 265–720.

19. I draw this example from J. W. Bastien, "Qollahuaya-Andean Body Concepts: A Topographical-Hydraulic Model of Physiology," *American Anthropologist* 87 (1985): 595–611.

20. Ibid., p. 608.

21. See B. J. Good, "The Heart of What's the Matter: The Semantics of Illness in Iran," *Culture, Medicine, and Psychiatry* 1 (1977): 25–58.

22. The discussion of vumu draws on J. M. Janzen, *The Quest for Therapy in Lower Zaire* (Berkeley and Los Angeles: University of California Press, 1978).

23. See, for example, Jackson, *Maps of Meaning* (on the social context of language, linguistic communities, language in ideology, and language used to contest space); and A. Cohen, "A Polyethnic Carnival as a Contested Cultural Performance," *Ethnic and Racial Studies* 5, no. 1 (1982): 23–41 (on the use of ambiguous symbols to mystify and control people).

24. Examples of this thinking are Geertz, "Thick Description"; D. Ley, "Cultural/Humanistic Geography," *Progress in Human Geography* 9 (1985): 415–23; and J. S. Duncan, "The Superorganic in American Cultural Geography," *Annals of the Association of American Geographers* 70, no. 2 (1980): 181–98 (on landscapes as texts).

Chapter 9. Social Space

1. This introduction to structuralist ideas is based on J. Eyles and K. J. Woods, *The Social Geography of Medicine and Health* (London: Croom Helm, 1983); K. Jones and G. Moon, *Health, Disease, and Society: An Introduction to Medical Geography* (London: Routledge & Kegan Paul, 1987); R. Stock, " 'Disease and Development' or 'The Underdevelopment of Health': A Critical Review of Geographical Perspectives on African Health Problems," *Social Science and Medicine* 23 (1986): 689–700; P. Jackson, *Maps of Meaning: An Introduction to Cultural Geography* (London: Unwin Hyman, 1989); D. Cosgrove, "New Directions in Cultural Geography," *Area* 19, no. 2 (1987): 95–101; P. Jackson and S. J. Smith, *Exploring Social Geography* (London: Allen & Unwin, 1984); and R. J. Johnston, *Philosophy and Human Geography* (London: Edward Arnold, 1986). See also M. Billinge, "Reconstructing Societies in the Past: The Collective Biography of Local Communities," in A. R. H. Baker and M. Billinge, eds., *Period and Place: Research Methods in Historical Geography* (Cambridge: Cambridge University Press, 1982), pp. 19–32; G. L. Clark and M. Dear, "State Apparatus and Everyday Life," in Clark and Dear, *State Apparatus: Structures and Languages of Legitimacy* (Boston: Allen & Unwin, 1984), pp. 60–82; M. Dear and J. R. Wolch, "The View from the Future," in M. Dear and J. R. Wolch, *Landscapes of Despair* (Princeton: Princeton University Press, 1987), pp. 247–57; D. Gregory, "Action and Structure in Historical Geography," in Baker and Billinge, eds., *Period and Place,* pp. 244–50; and M. Santos, "Society and Space: Social Formation as Theory and Methods," *Antipode* 9, no. 1 (1977): 3–13.

2. Antonio Gramsci, quoted in *Maps of Meaning,* p. 53.

3. Jones and Moon, *Health, Disease, and Society.*

4. This system of classification was used in M. I. Roemer, *Systems of Health Care* (New York: Springer, 1977).

5. This classification is based on A. E. Joseph and D. R. Phillips, *Accessibility and Utilization: Geographic Perspectives on Health Care Delivery* (New York: Harper & Row, 1984).

6. This classification scheme is adapted from T. J. Litman and L. Robins, "Comparative Analysis of Health Care Systems—A Socio-political Approach," *Social Science and Medicine* 5 (1971): 573–81.

7. The Australian example draws from Eyles and Woods, *Social Geography;* and Joseph and Phillips, *Accessibility and Utilization.*

8. On the Chinese case, see Joseph and Phillips, *Accessibility and Utilization;* and W. M. Gesler, *Health Care in Developing Countries* (Washington, D.C.: Resource Publications in Geography, Association of American Geographers, 1984).

9. For Sweden, see Gesler, *Health Care in Developing Countries.*

10. The Ethiopian case is based on R. M. Hodes and H. Kloos, "Health and Medical Care in Ethiopia," *New England Journal of Medicine* 319 (1988): 918–24.

11. Basic concepts of territoriality can be found in R. D. Sack, "Territorial Bases of Power," in A. D. Burnett and P. J. Taylor, eds., *Political Studies From Spatial Perspectives* (New York: Wiley, 1981), pp. 53–71.

12. Ibid., p. 55.

13. See S. J. Kunitz and A. A. Sorenson, "The Effects of Regional Planning on a Rural Hospital: A Case Study," *Social Science and Medicine* 13, D (1979): 1–11. Also see J. Mohan, "Location-Allocation Models, Social Science, and Health Service Planning: An Example from North East England," *Social Science and Medicine* 17 (1983): 493–99.

14. The history of underdevelopment theories and their applications to health care are related in P. J. Rimmer and D. K. Forbes, "Underdevelopment Theory: A Geographical Review," *Australian Geographer* 15 (1982): 197–211; and Stock, "Disease and Development." See also A. R. DeSouza and P. W. Porter, *The Underdevelopment and Modernization of the Third World,* Resource Paper no. 28 (Washington, D.C.: Association of American Geographers, 1974); V. Navarro, "The Underdevelopment of Health or the Health of Underdevelopment: An Analysis of the Distribution of Human Health Resources in Latin America," *International Journal of Health Services* 4 (1974): 5–27; A. G. Frank, "The Development of Underdevelopment," *Monthly Review* 18, no. 4 (1966): 17–30; and M. Turshen, "The Political Ecology of Disease," *Review of Radical Political Economics* 9 (1977): 45–60.

15. See, for example, C. C. Hughes and J. M. Hunter, "Disease and 'Development' in Africa," *Social Science and Medicine* 3 (1970): 443–93, who provide copious details on the detrimental effects of modernization in developing regions.

16. D. A. Ityavyar, "Background to the Development of Health Services in Nigeria," *Social Science and Medicine* 24, no. 6 (1987): 487–99. See also F. M. Mburu, "Implications of the Ideology and Implementation of Health Policy in a Developing Country," *Social Science and Medicine* 15, A (1981): 17–24.

17. B. Wisner, "Nutritional consequences of the Articulation of Capitalist and Non-capitalist Modes of Production in Eastern Kenya," *Rural Africana* 8–9 (1980/81): 99–132. Another study that was carried out in Nigeria and that has a similar theoretical framework is M. Watts, *Silent Violence* (Berkeley and Los Angeles: University of California Press, 1983).

18. See, for example, R. Stock, "Health Care for Some: A Nigerian Study of Who Gets What, Where, and Why," *International Journal of Health Services* 15 (1985): 469–84.

19. See, for example, C. P. McCormack, "Health and the Social Power of Women," *Social Science and Medicine* 26 (1988): 677–83.

20. A recently published book that deals with this issue is J. Scarpaci, ed., *Health Services Privatization in Industrial Societies* (New Brunswick, N.J.: Rutgers University Press, 1989).

21. See J. Mohan and K. J. Woods, "Restructuring Health Care: The Social Geography of Public and Private Health Care Under the British Conservative Government," *International Journal of Health Services* 15 (1985): 197–215.

22. This material and the accompanying example from New York City is based on S. McLafferty, "The Geographical Restructuring of Urban Hospitals: Spatial Dimensions of Corporate Strategy," *Social Science and Medicine* 10 (1986): 1079–86.

23. See W. M. Gesler, "The Role of Multinational Pharmaceutical Firms in Health Care Privatization in Developing Countries," in Scarpaci, ed., *Health Services Privatization*.

24. See, for example, J. Eyles, "Why Geography Cannot Be Marxist: Towards an Understanding of Lived Experience," *Environment and Planning A* 13 (1981): 1371–88.

Chapter 10. Place and Landscape

1. The most general discussions consulted concerning this facet of the new cultural geography were P. Jackson, *Maps of Meaning: An Introduction to Cultural Geography* (London: Unwin Hyman, 1989); D. Cosgrove, "New Directions in Cultural Geography," *Area* 19, no. 2 (1987): 95–101; D. Ley, "Cultural/Humanistic Geography," *Progress in Human Geography* 9 (1985): 415–23; D. Ley, "Editorial," *Environment & Planning D: Society and Space* 6 (1988): 115–16; W. Norton, "Humans, Land, and Landscape: A Proposal for Cultural Geography," *Canadian Geographer* 31, no. 1 (1987): 21–30; and L. Rowntree, "Orthodoxy and New Directions:

Cultural/Humanistic Geography," *Progress in Human Geography* 12, no. 4 (1988): 575–86. Specific themes will be referenced as they are discussed.

2. The following description of humanist ideas draws from D. Ley and M. S. Samuels, "Introduction: Contexts of Modern Humanism in Geography," in Ley and Samuels, eds., *Humanistic Geography* (Chicago: Maaroufa Press, 1978), pp. 1–17; Ley, "Cultural/Humanistic Geography"; S. Daniels, "Arguments for a Humanistic Geography," in R. D. Johnston, ed., *The Future of Geography* (London: Methuen, 1985), pp. 143–58; J. N. Entrikin, "Contemporary Humanism in Geography," *Annals of the Association of American Geographers* 66, no. 4 (1976): 615–32; J. Eyles, "Why Geography Cannot be Marxist: Towards an Understanding of Lived Experience," *Environment and Planning A* 13 (1981): 1371–88; and R. J. Johnston, *Philosophy and Human Geography* (London: Edward Arnold, 1986). For work dealing with the importance of meaning, see D. Ley, "Behavioral Geography and the Philosophies of Meaning," in K. R. Cox and R. C. Golledge, eds., *Behavioral Problems in Geography Revisited* (New York: Methuen, 1981), pp. 209–30; A. Kleinman et al., "Culture, Illness, and Care: Clinical Lessons from Anthropologic and Cross-sectional Research," *Annals of Internal Medicine* 88 (1978): 251–58; C. Geertz, "Thick Description: Toward an Interpretive Theory of Culture," in Geertz, ed., *The Interpretation of Cultures* (New York: Basic Books, 1973), pp. 3–30; and L. Guelke, "An Idealist Alternative in Human Geography," *Annals of the Association of American Geographers* 64, no. 2 (1974): 193–202.

3. For basic ideas about sense of place, see A. Briggs, "The Sense of Place," in *The Fitness of Man's Environment* (Washington D.C.: Smithsonian Institution Press, 1968), pp. 78–97; W. A. D. Jackson, *The Shaping of Our World: A Human and Cultural Geography* (New York: Wiley, 1985); P. Jackson and S. J. Smith, *Exploring Social Geography* (London: Allen & Unwin, 1984); Ley, "Behavioral Geography"; E. C. Relph, *Place and Placelessness* (London: Pion, 1976); D. Seamon, *A Geography of the Lifeworld* (London: Croom Helm, 1979); E. V. Walter, *Placeways: A Theory of the Human Environment* (Chapel Hill: University of North Carolina Press, 1988); Y-f. Tuan, "Space and Place: Humanistic Perspective," *Progress in Geography* 6 (1974): 211–52; Norton, "Humans, Land, and Landscape"; and D. Cosgrove, "Place, Landscape, and the Dialectics of Cultural Geography," *Canadian Geographer* 22, no. 1 (1978): 66–71.

4. Tuan, "Space and Place," p. 236.

5. For negotiated reality and related ideas, see Ley, "Behavioral Geography"; and M. Watts, "Struggles Over Land, Struggles Over Meaning: Some Thoughts on Naming, Peasant Resistance, and the Politics of Place," in R. G. Golledge, H. Couclelis, and P. Gould, eds., *A Ground for Common Search* (Goleta, Calif.: Santa Barbara Geographical Press, 1988), pp. 31–50.

6. See Kleinman et al., "Culture, Illness, and Care."

7. This example is based on M. A. Godkin, "Identity and Place: Clinical Application Based on Notions of Rootedness and Uprootedness," in A. Buttimer and D. Seamon, eds., *The Human Experience of Space and Place* (London: Croom Helm, 1980), pp. 73–85.

8. Ibid., p. 73.

9. On symbols, see V. Turner, "Symbolic Studies," *Annual Review of Anthropology* 4 (1975): 145–61; M. Sahlins, *Culture and Practical Reason* (Chicago: University of Chicago Press, 1976); L. Rowntree and M. W. Conkey, "Symbolism and the Cultural Landscape," *Annals of the Association of American Geographers* 70, no. 4 (1980); 459–74; S. Daniels and D. Cosgrove, "Introduction: Iconography and Landscape," in Daniels and Cosgrove, *The Iconography of Landscape* (Cambridge: Cambridge University Press, 1988); and A. A. Yengoyan, "Cultural Forms and A Theory of Constraints," in A. L. Becker and A. A. Yengoyan, eds., *The Imagination of Reality: Essays in Southeast Asian Coherence Systems* (Norwood, N.J.: Blex Publishing Company, 1979), pp. 325–300. See also K. J. Anderson, "The Idea of Chinatown: The Power of Place and Institutional Practice in the Making of a Racial Category," *Annals of the Association of American Geographers* 77, no. 4 (1987): 580–98; A. Cohen, "A Polyethnic Carnival as a Contested Cultural Performance," *Ethnic and Racial Studies* 5, no. 1 (1982): 23–41; D. Cosgrove, "Towards a Radical Cultural Geography: Problems of Theory," *Antipode* 15 (1983): 1–11; and C. Rose, "Human Geography as Text Interpretation," in Buttimer and Seamon, eds., *The Human Experience of Space and Place*, pp. 123–34.

10. This example is from Turner, "Symbolic Studies."

11. See, for example, P. Wagner and M. Mikesell, "The Themes of Cultural Geography," in Wagner and Mikesell, eds., *Readings in Cultural Geography* (Chicago: University of Chicago Press, 1962), pp. 1–24; and Jackson, *The Shaping of Our World*.

12. Symbolic landscapes are dealt with in detail in D. Cosgrove, "Geography Is Everywhere: Culture and Symbolism in Human Landscapes," in D. Gregory and R. Walford, eds., *Horizons in Human Geography* (London: Macmillan Education, 1989), pp. 118–35; Cosgrove, "Place, Landscape, and Dialects"; Cosgrove, "New Directions"; Daniels and Cosgrove, "Introduction"; Jackson, *Maps of Meaning;* and J. S. Duncan, "Review of Urban Imagery: Urban Semiotics," *Urban Geography* 8 (1987): 473–83; See also Anderson, "The Idea of Chinatown"; Norton, "Humans, Land, and Landscape"; and M. S. Samuels, "The Biography of Landscape: Cause and Culpability," in D. W. Meinig, ed., *The Interpretation of Ordinary Landscapes* (Oxford: Oxford University Press, 1979), pp. 51–88.

13. The phrase "therapeutic landscapes" was suggested by an anonymous reviewer of the manuscript of the present book.

14. Material on the treatment of the insane in Renaissance and classical

Europe is drawn from M. Foucault, *Madness and Civilization* (New York: Vintage Books, 1988). See also M. Dear and S. M. Taylor, "A Social History of the Asylum," in Dear and Taylor, *Not on Our Street: Community Attitudes to Mental Health Care* (London: Pion, 1982), pp. 37–52.

15. Foucault, *Madness and Civilization*, p. 13.

16. Ibid., p. 37.

17. This material comes from C. Philo, " 'Fit Localities for an Asylum': The Historical Geography of the Nineteenth-Century 'Mad-Business' in England as Viewed Through the Pages of the *Asylum Journal*," *Journal of Historical Geography* 13, no. 4 (1987): 398–415.

18. For a perspective on the perception of growing insanity in the United States during the nineteenth century, see E. Jarvis, "On the Supposed Increase of Insanity," *American Journal of Insanity* 8 (1851/52): 333–64.

19. Philo, "Fit Localities," p. 412.

20. See S. Frenkel and J. Western, "Pretext or Prophylaxis? Racial Segregation and Malarial Mosquitoes in a British Tropical Colony: Sierra Leone," *Annals of the Association of American Geographers* 78, no. 2 (1988): 211–28. See also W. Gesler and J. L. Webb, "Patterns of Mortality in Freetown, Sierra Leone," *Singapore Journal of Tropical Geography* 4 (1983): 99–118, for more on health conditions in Freetown.

21. Frenkel and Western, "Pretext or Prophylaxis?" p. 227.

22. See J. E. Vance, Jr., "California and the Search for the Ideal," *Annals of the Association of American Geographers* 62, no. 2 (1972): 185–210 (on the physical settings of spas); and S. E. Cayleff, "Gender, Ideology, and the Water-Cure Movement," in N. Gevitz, ed., *Other Healers: Unorthodox Medicine in America* (Baltimore: Johns Hopkins University Press, 1988), pp. 82–98 (on hydropathy and women's role in the movement). See, too, M. A. Kukral, "Naturopathic Medicine in Bohemia and Moravia: The Legitimization of Hydrotherapy," presented at the Annual Meetings of the Association of American Geographers, Baltimore, 1989.

23. Cayleff, "Gender, Ideology, and the Water-Cure."

Chapter 11. Cultural Materialism

1. The title of this chapter is borrowed from P. Jackson, *Maps of Meaning: An Introduction to Cultural Geography* (London: Unwin Hyman, 1989). The following are also useful sources with respect to humanist/materialist thinking: A. R. H. Baker, "On Ideology and Historical Geography," in A. R. H. Baker and M. Billinge, eds., *Period and Place: Research Methods in Historical Geography* (Cambridge: Cambridge University Press, 1982), pp. 233–43; R. Bhaskar, "On the Possibility of Social Scientific Knowledge and the Limits of Naturalism," *Journal for the Theory of Social Behavior* 8 (1978): 1–28; D. Cosgrove, "Place, Landscape, and the Dialectics of Cultural Geography," *Canadian Geographer* 22, no. 1 (1978): 66–

71; D. Cosgrove, "Towards a Radical Cultural Geography: Problems of Theory," *Antipode* 15 (1983); 1–11; D. Ley and M. S. Samuels, "Introduction: Contexts of Modern Humanism in Geography," in Ley and Samuels, eds., *Humanistic Geography* (Chicago: Maaroufa Press, 1978), pp. 1–17; D. Ley, "Behavioral Geography and the Philosophies of Meaning," in K. R. Cox and R. C. Golledge, eds., *Behavioral Problems in Geography Revisited* (New York: Methuen, 1981), pp. 209–230; W. Norton, "Humans, Land, and Landscape: A Proposal for Cultural Geography," *Canadian Geographer* 31, no. 1 (1987): 21–30; M. S. Samuels, "The Biography of Landscape: Cause and Culpability," in D. W. Meinig, ed., *The Interpretation of Ordinary Landscapes* (Oxford: Oxford University Press, 1979), pp. 51–78; L. Rowntree, "Orthodoxy and New Directions: Cultural/Humanistic Geography," *Progress in Human Geography* 12, no. 4 (1988): 575–86; and D. Gregory, "Action and Structure in Historical Geography," Baker and Billinge, eds., *Period and Place.*

2. Ley, "Behavioral Geography," p. 226.

3. R. Love and I. Kalnins, "Individualist and Structuralist Perspectives on Nutrition Education for Canadian Children," *Social Science and Medicine* 18, no. 3 (1984): 199–204.

4. For some basic notions about structuration, see A. Giddens, *New Rules of Sociological Method* (New York: Basic Books, 1976); D. Gregory, "Human Agency and Human Geography," *Transactions of the Institute of British Geographers,* n.s. 6 (1981): 1–18; R. E. Pahl, "The Restructuring of Capital, the Local Political Economy and Household Work Strategies," in D. Gregory and J. Urry, eds., *Social Relations and Spatial Structures* (London: Macmillan Education, 1985), pp. 242–64; B. Warf, "The Resurrection of Local Uniqueness," in R. G. Golledge, H. Couclelis, and P. Gould, eds., *A Ground for Common Search* (Goleta, Calif.: Santa Barbara Geographical Press, 1988), pp. 51–62; J. Johnston, *On Human Geography* (Oxford: Basil Blackwell, 1986); and G. L. Clark and M. Dear, "State Apparatus and Everyday Life," in Clark and Dear, *State Apparatus: Structures and Language of Legitimacy* (Boston: Allen & Unwin, 1984), pp. 60–82.

5. Gregory, "Human Agency," pp. 9–10.

6. See P. L. Knox, J. Bohland, and N. L. Shumsky, "The Urban Transition and the Evolution of the Medical Care Delivery System in America," *Social Science and Medicine* 17 (1983): 37–43.

7. See A. Gilbert, "The New Regional Geography in English and French-Speaking Countries," *Progress in Human Geography* 12 (1988): 209–28; for a discussion of structuration in the new regional geography.

8. See E. V. Walter, "Sick Places," in *Placeways: A Theory of the Human Environment* (Chapel Hill: University of North Carolina Press, 1988), pp. 44–67. See also M. Meade et al., *Medical Geography* (New

York: Guilford Press, 1988); and E. N. Pavlovsky, *The Natural Nidality of Transmissible Disease* (Urbana: University of Illinois Press, 1966).

9. Material for this example comes from M. Dear and J. R. Wolch, "The Social Construction of the Service-Dependent Ghetto," and "The View from the Future," in Dear and Wolch, *Landscapes of Despair: From Deinstitutionalization to Homelessness* (Princeton: Princeton University Press, 1987), pp. 8–27 and 247–57. See also Clark and Dear, "State Apparatus"; M. Dear and S. M. Taylor, *Not on Our Street* (London: Pion, 1982), C. J. Smith and R. Q. Hanham, "Any Place But Here! Mental Health Facilities as Noxious Neighbors," *Professional Geographer* 33 (1981): 326–34; and C. J. Smith and J. A. Giggs, eds., *Location and Stigma: Contemporary Perspectives on Mental Health and Mental Health Care* (Boston: Unwin Hyman, 1988).

10. Dear and Wolch, "The View from the Future," p. 254.

11. Information on time geography can be found in T. Hägerstrand, "Diorama, Path, and Project," *Tidjschrift voor Economische en Sociale Geografie* 73 (1982): 323–29; A. Giddens, "Time, Space, and Regionalisation," in Gregory and Urry, eds., *Social Relations and Spatial Structures*, pp. 265–95; and D. Parkes and N. Thrift, "Time Spacemakers and Entrainment," *Transactions of the Institute of British Geographers,* n.s. 4 (1979): 353–72. Also see G. W. Shannon, "Space, Time and Illness Behavior," *Social Science and Medicine* 11 (1977): 683–89.

12. R. W. Roundy, "A Model for Combining Human Behavior and Disease Ecology to Assess Disease Hazard in a Community: Rural Ethiopia as a Model," *Social Science and Medicine* 12 (1978): 121–30.

13. E. Zerubavel, *Patterns of Time in Hospital Life* (Chicago: University of Chicago Press, 1979).

14. On the combination of structuration and time geography, see Giddens, "Time, Space, and Regionalisation"; P, Jackson and S. J. Smith, *Exploring Social Geography* (London: Allen & Unwin, 1984); A. Pred, "Place as Historically Contingent Process: Structuration and the Time-Geography of Becoming Places," *Annals of the Association of American Geographers* 74 (1984): 279–97; A. Pred, "The Social Becomes the Spatial, the Spatial Becomes the Social: Enclosures, Social Change, and the Becoming of Place in the Swedish Province of Skane," in Gregory and Urry, eds., *Social Relations and Spatial Structures*, pp. 337–65; and A. Pred, "Structuration and Place: On the Becoming of Sense of Place and Structure of Feeling," *Journal for the Theory of Social Behavior* 13 (1983): 45–68.

15. Pred, "Place as Historically Contingent Process," p. 282.

16. See W. Gesler and M. Meade, "Locational and Population Factors in Health Care–Seeking Behavior in Savannah, Georgia," *Health Services Research* 23 (1988): 443–62. For more on activity spaces, see G. W. Shannon and C. W. Spurlock, "Urban Ecological Containers, Environmental

Risk Cells, and the Use of Medical Services," *Economic Geography* 52, no. 2 (1976): 171–80; and E. Cromley and G. W. Shannon, "Locating Ambulatory Medical Care Facilities for the Elderly," *Health Services Research* 21 (1986): 499–514.

17. This example is drawn from J. Cornwell, *Hard-Earned Lives* (London: Tavistock Publications, 1984).

18. Ibid., pp. 15–16.

19. The material in this section is based on N. Gregson, "On Duality and Dualism: The Case of Structuration and Time Geography," *Progress in Human Geography* 10 (1986): 184–205; E. Gibson, "Understanding the Subjective Meaning of Places," in Ley and Samuels, eds., *Humanistic Geography*, pp. 138–54; Ley, "Behavioral Geography"; Pred, "Place as Historically Contingent Process"; and Walter, "Sick Places."

Chapter 12. Summary and Conclusions

1. The material for this section is drawn from R. Earickson, "International Behavioral Responses to a Health Hazard: AIDS" (Ms., 1989) (used by permission of the author). See also G. W. Shannon and G. F. Pyle, "The Origin and Diffusion of AIDS: A View from Medical Geography," *Annals of the Association of American Geographers* 79, no. 1 (1989): 1–24; and W. B. Wood, "AIDS North and South: Diffusion Patterns of a Global Epidemic and a Research Agenda for Geographers," *Professional Geographer* 40 (1988): 266–79.

2. "International Behavioral Responses," p. 6.

3. Ibid., p. 21.

4. A. Pred, "The Social Becomes the Spatial, the Spatial Becomes the Social: Enclosures, Social Change, and the Becoming of Place in the Swedish Province of Skane," in D. Gregory and J. Urry, eds., *Social Relations and Spatial Structures* (London: Macmillan Education, 1985), pp. 337–65.

Index

Accessibility, in U.S. health care, 84
Activity spaces: in Ethiopian disease study, 193; in Savannah, Ga., health care study, 198
Adaptation, 64, 204–05; of traditional nonprofessional medicine, 119; to environment in Kenya nutrition study, 154–55
Agency and structure. *See* Structure and agency
AIDS, 67, 207–11
Alcoholics, and rootedness, 168
Alternative practitioners, 112; symbols connected with, 169
Areal differentiation. *See* Regionalization
Asclepius, god of cure, 80
Australia, health services in, 144–45
Ayurvedic medicine, 16, 25; in India, 40–42

Balance, in adaptation, 64–66
Bangkok, traditional medicine in, 50–54
Barriers: in diffusion studies, 92; in Detroit health study, 94; in CT scanner study, 99
Beliefs: as medical system component, 24–25, 27–30; in Inner London health study, 200–01
Biomedicine, 18; history of, 76–80; in Nigeria, 152–53
Boundaries. *See* Regional boundaries
Brissot, Pierre, and Renaissance medicine, 78

Cancer treatment: adaptation example of, 66–67; in China, 86–88
Carriers: in diffusion research, 92; in CT scanner study, 98–99; in Bolivian diffusion study, 105
Carrying capacity: in adaptation, 65–66; in physician distributions, 71
Certificate-of-need, in CT scanner study, 99–100
China, health services in, 145

Chinese medicine, 16–17, 25; in Bangkok, 51–54
Chiropractors, in North Carolina, 120–21
Classification schemes, 126–28
Communication. *See* Language
Competition: in British health services, 156; among U.S. hospitals, 157–58; in drug markets, 161
Conflict: among regions, 38; among medical systems in India, 41–42; and cultural change, 74; and territoriality, 147; in medical systems, 162
Contagious diffusion: definition of, 91; in Detroit health study, 94
Context: in systems, 20, 31–33; health care geography, 34; in diffusion, 92–93; of diffusion processes, 104–05; of folk medicine, 118; of semantic networks, 135–37; in cross-country health system comparisons, 142–46
Core and periphery: within regions, 39; in hospital regions, 45; in dependency theory, 151
Costs. *See medical costs*
Cultural accumulation, 74–75; in Chinese cancer treatment, 86–88
Cultural congruence, in chiropractor study, 120–21
Cultural ecology, 204–05; definition of, 57; of Appalachian folk drugs, 113; metaphors in, 129–30; in Andean Indian health, 133–35; and AIDS, 209
Cultural evolution, 205; stages in, 75–76; and AIDS, 209
Cultural geography, recent history of, 5–7
Cultural lag, 74
Cultural materialism, definition of, 183–84
Cultural perspective, 3–4, 8
Cultural pluralism: definition of, 38; in India, 39–40
Culture, definition of, 5
Culture and environment, interactions between, 61–62, 68, 71–72